249

W9-CUH-423

VISUAL QUICKSTART GUIDE

PALM

ORGANIZERS

THIRD EDITION

Jeff Carlson

 Peachpit Press

Visual QuickStart Guide
Palm Organizers, Third Edition
Jeff Carlson

Peachpit Press
1249 Eighth Street
Berkeley, CA 94710
(510) 524-2178
(510) 524-2221

Find us on the World Wide Web at: www.peachpit.com
To report errors, please send a note to errata@peachpit.com
Peachpit Press is a division of Pearson Education

Copyright © 2004 by Jeff Carlson

Editor: Nancy Davis
Production Coordinators: Connie Jeung-Mills, Lupe Edgar
Editorial Assistance: Agen G. N. Schmitz
Copyeditors: Brooke C. Wheeler, Liane Thomas
Composition: Jeff Carlson
Cover Design: The Visual Group
Cover Production: George Mattingly, GMD / Berkeley
Indexer: Caroline Parks, Indexcellence

Notice of rights
All rights reserved. No part of this book may be reproduced or transmitted in any form or by any means, electronic, mechanical, photocopying, recording, or otherwise, without the prior written permission of the publisher. For more information on getting permission for reprints and excerpts, please contact permissions@peachpit.com.

Notice of liability
The information in this book is distributed on an "As is" basis, without warranty. While every precaution has been taken in the preparation of this book, neither the author nor Peachpit Press shall have any liability to any person or entity with respect to any loss or damage caused or alleged to be caused directly or indirectly by the instructions contained in this book or by the computer software and hardware products described herein.

Trademarks
Visual QuickStart Guide is a registered trademark of Peachpit Press, a division of Pearson Education. Peachpit Press is not affiliated with PalmOne, Inc. Graffiti, HotSync, and Palm Computing are registered trademarks, and Palm, Palm OS, and PalmPilot are trademarks of PalmOne, Inc. or its subsidiaries. Throughout this book, trademarks are used. Rather than put a trademark symbol in every occurrence of a trademarked name, we state that we are using the names in an editorial fashion only and to the benefit of the trademark owner with no intention of infringement of the trademark.

ISBN: 0-321-18098-4

9 8 7 6 5 4 3 2 1

Printed and bound in the United States of America

Praise for *Palm Organizers Visual QuickStart Guide*

If I had to describe this book in one word, it would be "meaty." ...While each of the Palm-Pilot books to date has unique value, this book is a diamond in the rough and one of my favorites. I highly recommend it.

— Scott Sbihli, *Pen Computing Magazine*

What a great book! If you're a Palm device user, you're going to get a lot out of this book. Jeff Carlson's writing style makes everything easy to understand, yet deep, chock full of valuable information.

— David Gewirtz, Editor-in-Chief, *PalmPower Magazine* (www.palmpower.com)

One strength of the book is in Carlson's outstanding use of the Visual QuickStart Guide format, illustrating each point with plenty of screen shots and examples from the Palm, Windows, and Macintosh operating systems. I can't wait to try some of the new tips and procedures in this terrific book.

— John Nemerovski, Book Bytes Columnist and Reviewer, *My Mac Magazine* (www.mymac.com)

Carlson—clearly an avid Palmist with some accumulated wisdom on the topic—goes beyond merely rehashing the Palm's own documentation.

— David Wall, Amazon.com

Dedication

For Kimberly, who understands me more than I often realize.

Special Thanks to:

Nancy Davis, for getting this book project started in the first place, for remaining flexible and cheerful, and for simply chatting when my brain required a much-needed break.

Agen G. N. Schmitz, for deciding to quit his day job at just the right time for me to press him into service helping me update a few chapters.

Brooke C. Wheeler, for staying in touch and working against fickle technology on the other side of the globe.

Liane Thomas, for being a kindred spirit and succinctly nailing the way we both tend to work (despite our best efforts): "think, think, think, plan, plan, think, oh yeah...write!"

Jeff Tolbert, for helping to lay out the book, and for listening to me babble about handhelds.

Caroline Parks, for shouldering my work schedule in order to get the index done well and on time.

Rosie Pulido, **Samya Ghuloum**, and **Nicole Messier**, for providing me with Palm information and hardware when I needed it.

Glenn Fleishman, David Blatner, Steve Roth, Larry Chen (plus the various long-distance inhabitants) at the Greenwood compound, for their invaluable advice and experience. More important, for recognizing that look in my eye that says, "I'm totally focused now: go away," and not being offended (or at least not letting me know they were offended).

Nancy Aldrich-Ruenzel, Connie Jeung-Mills, Lupe Edgar, Gary-Paul Prince, Marjorie Baer, Kim Lombardi, Lisa Brazieal, Megan Lynch, Rebecca Ross, Mimi Heft, and **Paula Baker** at Peachpit Press. They genuinely make the book-creation process a pleasure.

Kim Carlson, for being the best study-buddy a husband could ever want.

TABLE OF CONTENTS

Introduction

I bought my first handheld, a PalmPilot Personal, in 1997 for a number of reasons. Of course, the gadget factor was pretty high. Plus, the PalmPilot was getting raves for its ability to store volumes of formerly paper-based contact and scheduling information in a device slightly larger than a deck of cards. You could download third-party software directly from the Web, then synchronize those programs and your data with your PC at the single push of a button.

However, I wasn't just looking for a new toy. (What, buy something because it's a cool gadget? Me??) A recent leap into the realm of full-time freelancing convinced me that I needed a greater measure of control over my time and my tasks. Buying a PalmPilot became more of an effort to organize myself and my data than any desire for a geeky electronic device.

This is part of the appeal of a Palm organizer. Yes, it's a cool gadget. Yes, you can accessorize it to your heart's content with styli, cases, and custom flipcovers. Yes, it piques people's curiosity and makes complete strangers walk up and ask, "What's that?" But it's also an efficient, well-thought-out organizational tool that performs its tasks exceptionally well. Instead of being a self-contained computer in a smaller container, it's an extension of the information that millions of people rely on every day.

Excerpted from an interview with Bill Gates, CEO and Chairman of Microsoft Corporation, on the television show "Charlie Rose," March 4, 1998 (used with permission).

Bill Gates: The future of the PC is to be a tablet-sized device or perhaps larger than a tablet.... But then you also have a lot of other devices, things like—I think I've got one in my pocket.

Charlie Rose: A Pilot is in his pocket.

Bill Gates: No, no, no, no. This is the competitor to the Pilot. Don't say "Pilot." Geez. This is the—

Charlie Rose: Does that look like a Pilot? I rest my case.

Palm Organizers: Visual QuickStart Guide

This book is meant to be a compact, functional extension of a Palm organizer. Not just a how-to approach to using an electronic tool, this Visual QuickStart Guide is a primer on how to effectively get control of your schedule, contacts, and all the data that used to occupy reams of papers and Post-it notes.

My aim for this book is to show you what's possible with Palm devices, from their basic features to tips and tricks for using them smarter and faster. At times I'll personally recommend a product or a technique because it's what I've found useful. As a result, and to keep this book from becoming ten times larger than the device it covers, I don't list every product on the market—I want you to have fun exploring what's available.

In fact, with millions of Palm devices in use today, it's impossible to cover every little detail. For example, the Preferences screen on a Tungsten T is different than a Tungsten C, which differs from devices that came before them—but the preferences themselves are similar.

Also in the name of generalization, you'll find that I'll often mention a shortcut Graffiti stroke (for example, ╱-B), knowing full well that some devices such as the Handspring Treo and many Sony CLIÉ variants use a thumbpad keyboard instead of Graffiti.

People who swear by their handhelds also tend to integrate them into their lives, moving beyond business meetings to birthdays, home finances, electronic books, and the occasional game of solitaire. It continues to be an invaluable part of my everyday life.

I'd love to know how your handheld helps (or hinders) your life. Feel free to email me with feedback at jeff@necoffee.com.

The Hand(held) of Progress

While I was updating this third edition, Palm, Inc. did an interesting thing: it bought its rival Handspring, Inc. More than just a corporate merger, the acquisition brought back the original inventors of the PalmPilot, who had formed their own company to create handhelds that were closer to their ideas. Although the merger wasn't complete when I finished the book, the companies did restructure and rename themselves: at press time, Palm is becoming PalmOne; the division in charge of the Palm OS is becoming PalmSource, and Handspring (my favorite name of the bunch) is going away.

Nonetheless, the Treo is currently known as the Handspring Treo, and current handhelds are referred to as Palm devices. In general, I use the more generic "Palm," even though it encompasses devices from Palm (I mean, PalmOne), Handspring, Sony, Kyocera, Samsung, etc.

And new software, too...

Also when this book was about to go to press, Palm announced new handhelds—the Tungsten T3, Tungsten E, and Zire 21. Thanks to the assistance of representatives at PalmOne and A&R Partners, I've covered the new hardware in Chapter 1.

However, this revision introduces some important changes to the core applications—not to mention name changes, such as "Date Book" to "Calendar"—but just on those devices, and models that follow. Since there wasn't time to incorporate the new information into this edition, I'll cover the changes in a new appendix, and post it as a PDF file at the companion Web site for this book: www.necoffee.com/palmvqs/.

Part 1
Using Palm
Organizers

The Handheld Portal to Your Information

You've probably read articles about them, or seen them in advertisements. More likely, you know someone who has one, and his or her enthusiasm was infectious. That's how I was introduced to Palm organizers, and now it's hard to find me without one.

Chapter 1, **Palm Basics**, introduces you to Palm OS-based organizers, discussing the different families, their hardware controls, battery usage, and available accessories.

Chapter 2, **The Palm OS**, covers the handheld's most undervalued feature: the powerful, yet minimalist, operating system. We'll explore system-wide preferences, memory management, and learn how to write Palm's celebrated—and simple—Graffiti alphabet.

Chapter 3, **HotSync**, examines the feature for synchronizing information from your handheld with the desktop software, including infrared synchronization and using other programs to tie your data into your Personal Information Manager (PIM) software.

Chapters 4–6 (**Date Book**, **Address Book**, and **To Do List, Memos, and Notes**) deal with the main built-in programs, showing you why a tiny screen can be so much better than crumpled pages of scribbled appointments and Post-it notes tucked into a bulging "personal organizer."

Chapter 7, **Calculator, Expense, and Clock**, delves into the number-crunching applications provided by Palm, plus the simple but useful Clock application.

PALM BASICS

The ancestry of today's Palm organizers can be traced to the Pilot, the original creation of inventor Jeff Hawkins. It began as a block of wood that Hawkins carried around the hallways of Palm Computing. It was the essence of the term "hardware"—no buttons, no batteries, no screen (certainly no backlight, though a fluorescent highlighter might have worked), no software.

It was also simple. The device in Hawkins's mind didn't take a modern PC and cram its guts into a smaller case, or try to woo consumers with its multimedia capabilities. Instead, the handheld machine focused on performing a handful of essential tasks well, in tandem with the computers and data that people were currently using.

As an evolutionary surprise, today's Palm devices can do much more than their founder's intent: wireless Internet access, color photos, global positioning, and more. And yet, despite the wide array of software and hardware add-ons you can get for them, today's handhelds remain true to Hawkins's original vision: simple to use and simple in scope (though not limited, as you'll discover). They also have become simply essential for millions of owners.

Palm Device Families

Like any product, the PalmPilot evolved over time; there are still thousands of people using even the earliest Pilot models. As more companies have licensed the Palm OS, multiple variations of devices have appeared, to the point where it's impractical to list them all here. Instead, let's look at the major families of devices that are shipping as of this book's publication date (Fall, 2003).

Palm Zire series

Before introducing the Zire, Palm had seen considerable success with handhelds, adding capabilities as users' needs grew. But Palm also discovered that a large number of its customers were using just the basic features: keeping track of schedules, storing addresses, making lists of to do items, and taking short text memos. Seeing an opportunity, the company created the Zire, a handheld that stuck to the basics. The first Zire included 2 MB of memory, no backlight, and the core Palm applications in an attractive white enclosure. Oh, and it cost $99. It was an unexpected hit.

The Zire 21 (**Figure 1.1**) is the next generation device, sticking to the same basics but now including 8 MB of memory and a much faster processor (but still no backlight). For synchronizing to your computer, both the original Zire and Zire 21 use a USB cable instead of a cradle, which is good for travelers but means they won't work with third-party devices, like keyboards, that require Palm's Universal Connector.

The Zire 71, by contrast, is still geared to consumers, but is much snazzier (**Figure 1.2**). It sports a gorgeous color screen, an expansion card slot, headphone jack, 16 MB of memory, 5-way navigator, Universal Connector, and a digital camera that is revealed by sliding the back panel.

Figure 1.1 The Palm Zire 21 is a bare-bones organizer, but at $99 it's all that many people need in a Palm.

Figure 1.2 The $300 Palm Zire 71 is a multimedia handheld for the masses, incorporating a color screen and a built-in digital camera.

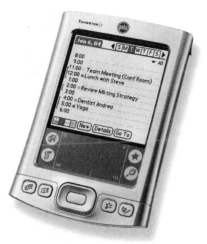

Figure 1.3 The Tungsten E is the current workhorse of the Palm line of organizers.

Figure 1.4 The bottom section of Palm's Tungsten T3 slides down to reveal more active screen area instead of a static silkscreen area.

Palm Tungsten series

Okay, so maybe these handhelds aren't actually made out of tungsten, a hard element with the highest melting point of any metal. But the Tungsten line certainly looks shiny and impressive. Featuring bright color screens, fast processors, expansion card slots, and multimedia features, the Tungsten models represent the middle and the high end of Palm's handhelds.

The compact Tungsten T2 features a sliding bottom section that reveals the silkscreen Graffiti area. The midrange Tungsten E (**Figure 1.3**) is simpler but svelte. The Tungsten T3 introduces Palm's first rectangular screen (**Figure 1.4**). Like the T2, the bottom portion of the case slides down, but in this case it reveals more active screen area—320 by 480 pixels to be specific. (When using many applications, a software silkscreen Graffiti area appears.) For applications that can take advantage of it, the T3 can be used horizontally as well—turn it sideways and read more text of an ebook, view spreadsheets, or even watch mini-movies in widescreen mode.

The Tungstens also feature examples of specialization. The Tungsten W includes a built-in cellular radio that can be used to access the Internet or double as a cellular phone from within many coverage areas (currently AT&T Wireless). The Tungsten C is equipped with Wi-Fi (802.11b) wireless networking, such as is found in an increasing number of offices, homes, coffeeshops, and airports. Not only can you access the Internet, you can do it at broadband speed.

All Tungsten models are stacked with memory, with up to 64 MB in the T3 and C, and the Tungsten T2 and T3 each include built-in Bluetooth wireless networking, an internal microphone, and a headphone port for listening to digital music or voice memos.

PALM DEVICE FAMILIES

Handspring Treo

In 1998, the creators of the original Palm-Pilot—Jeff Hawkins, Donna Dubinsky, and Ed Colligan—left Palm Computing to form Handspring, Inc. With their new startup, they licensed the Palm OS and developed a low-cost handheld called the Visor.

Although successful at first, the team saw that it would take more than offering an inexpensive device to compete with the other handheld companies. So, in 2001 Handspring shifted its focus and introduced the Treo "smartphone" that incorporated a PDA with a cellular phone. Unlike bulky phone hybrids that had come before it, the Treo is slightly smaller than most other Palm devices. It can be used against the ear like most phones, or with an included hands-free adapter (which lets you also use the Treo as an organizer as you talk).

The Treo sports a handful of combinations, depending on whether it includes a color screen (such as the Treo 270) or is sold by a particular cellular carrier (such as the Sprint Treo 300, **Figure 1.5**). The newest Treo, unfortunately not yet available at the time this book went to press, is the improved and diminutive Treo 600 (**Figure 1.6**).

In 2003, with the handheld market consolidating in a tough economy, Palm purchased Handspring and renamed the joint company PalmOne.

For more on using the Treo, see Chapter 9.

Figure 1.5 The Treo 300 is a Palm OS handheld that doubles as a cellular phone.

Figure 1.6 The Treo 600 is smaller than many cellular phones, but still packs a full Palm organizer inside.

Figure 1.7 The PEG-NZ90 comes pretty close to being a full-fledged laptop replacement.

Figure 1.8 Sony's CLIÉ devices are often packed to the gills with multimedia features, such as this organizer/ audio player/camera, the PEG-NX80V.

Sony CLIÉ

Sony has clearly decided that their Palm OS-based organizers aren't going to be "me-too" devices. The Sony CLIÉ ("clee-ay") series is geared to be the only portable multimedia device you need (`www.clieplaza.com`). One look at the PEG-NZ90 reveals a keyboard, Grafitti area, digital camera, audio inputs, and a screen that swivels 180 degrees (**Figure 1.7**).

But oh, dear Sony: why do you vex us with so many models burdened with confusing numbering schemes? PEG-NZ90, PEG-SJ330, PEG-N710C...I feel stuck in a George Lucas experimental college movie.

In addition to the standard complement of Palm features, the CLIÉ has a jog dial for navigating the interface, and an expansion slot that accepts Sony's Memory Stick modules. Several models, such as the PEG-NX80V (**Figure 1.8**) also support digital music playback (MP3 and ATRAC3-formatted files), and include headphones (see Chapter 11). Sony was also the first developer to introduce higher resolution color screens, as well as rectangular displays with the Graffiti area in software.

Kyocera Smartphone

Although Handspring has made a big splash with the Treo, that wasn't the first phone/PDA combination device to hit the market. The Qualcomm Smartphone integrated the functions in one unit; unfortunately, it was enormous and expensive. Qualcomm sold their wares to Kyocera, and now the third generation Smartphone 7135 is a much better hybrid (www.kyocera-wireless.com).

Opening the clamshell reveals a Palm organizer at the phone's heart (**Figure 1.9**). The Palm OS is actually a part of the phone's inner workings, allowing you to find someone in your Address Book and dial their number with one tap, or easily check your email and other online information.

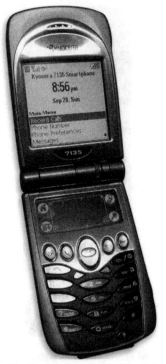

Figure 1.9 The Kyocera 7135 Smartphone integrates a Palm device and a cellular phone.

✔ Tips

- In addition to being a phone/PDA combination, the Smartphone has a few other helpful features. The Voice Dial application lets you record a spoken word or phrase and associate it with a number, so you can press a button and say a person's name to dial their number. This is a great feature if you have to make a call when driving or are otherwise occupied.
- The Call History application (**Figure 1.10**) offers a detailed breakdown of your calls, without relying on the phone company's records.
- The Smartphone can run Palm Query Applications (PQAs) to access online content (see Chapter 10).

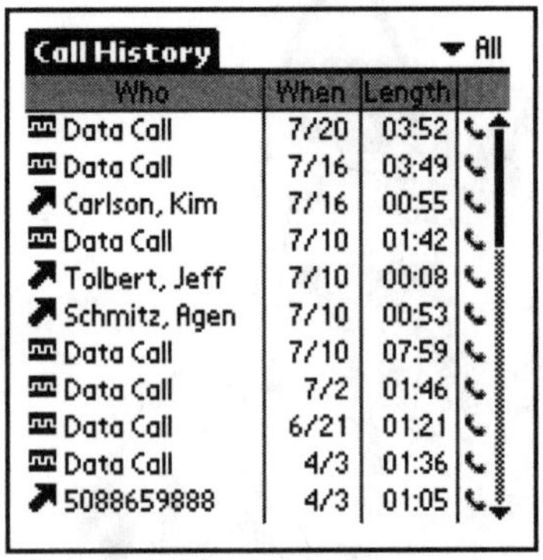
Call History ▾ All

Who	When	Length
Data Call	7/20	03:52
Data Call	7/16	03:49
Carlson, Kim	7/16	00:55
Data Call	7/10	01:42
Tolbert, Jeff	7/10	00:08
Schmitz, Agen	7/10	00:53
Data Call	7/10	07:59
Data Call	7/2	01:46
Data Call	6/21	01:21
Data Call	4/3	01:36
5088659888	4/3	01:05

Figure 1.10 Don't wait until the phone bill arrives to see your cellular usage.

Figure 1.11 The Fossil Wrist PDA is an even more portable device, packing a full Palm into a wristwatch.

Other notable Palm variants

When I say "Palm organizer," you probably think of devices like those on the preceeding pages. But the Palm OS is used for several other variations, a few of which I want to note here.

Samsung SPH-i500

Another well-regarded smartphone device is Samsung's SPH-i500, which is smaller than the Treo and Kyocera 7135 (it can be found at www.sprintpcs.com).

Fossil Wrist PDA

Who needs to carry a PDA when you can wear it instead? Fossil's Wrist PDA (www.fossil.com/tech/) puts a fully functional Palm organizer on your wrist—with style, even (**Figure 1.11**). It uses a rocker switch and three buttons to navigate, includes an infrared port for beaming data, and incorporates a small stylus as part of the watch band. It runs Palm OS 4.1, so you can use it like any other device.

Alphasmart Dana

Alphasmart's Dana (www.alphasmart.com) at first seems like a PDA on steroids because it boasts a large screen and full-size keyboard. Used primarily in education settings (though some news reporters use it in place of a laptop on assignment), the Dana is an energy efficient, ruggedized word processor that also happens to run whatever you can throw at a typical Palm OS device.

Symbol devices

Symbol Technologies (www.symbol.com) has been creating Palm devices since the early days of the PalmPilot, incorporating barcode readers and other in-the-field technologies for specialized uses.

PALM DEVICE FAMILIES

Palm Device Overview

No matter which handheld you use, they all share the following characteristics.

Screen

The average handheld's screen accounts for most of the device. Some models, such as the Zire 21, feature a liquid-crystal display (LCD) that is black and white only (or, more accurately, black on a gray-green background) and measures 160 pixels by 160 pixels.

Increasingly, organizers feature active-matrix color screens that display anywhere from 256 to 65,000 colors. Some devices, such as several Sony CLIÉ models, have higher-resolution screens of 320 by 320 pixels or vertical 320 by 480 pixels.

Most importantly, every screen is touch sensitive, which is why you can interact with it using a stylus.

Power button/backlight

Every device has a power button that turns the organizer on and off (**Figure 1.12**). The handheld will automatically power down after two minutes (you can change the time delay; see Chapter 2).

Holding the power button down for two seconds activates the screen's backlight, which illuminates the screen by lighting the active (black) pixels. In very dark situations, this tends to be more readable, though in moderate lighting it can sometimes be difficult to read the screen.

On many color devices, holding the power button activates the screen brightness control (**Figure 1.13**).

Power/ backlight button

Figure 1.12 The power button doubles as the backlight control on many devices.

Figure 1.13 You can adjust the brightness setting using the device's software controls.

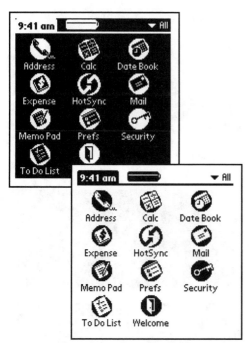

Figure 1.14 The inverted backlighting effect on recent monochrome devices (top, simulated) illuminate only the active pixels. On some models, using the "dot-8" shortcut enables you to make the backlight illuminate the background pixels instead (bottom, again simulated because batteries are not included with this book.)

Stylus

The stylus is your main method of interacting with the handheld, though just about anything that isn't sharper than a No. 2 pencil can work (that includes fingers and toes too!). In most cases, the stylus is made of a metal barrel that comes with a plastic tip and end pieces that screw at each end.

✔ Tips

■ The default brightness setting for many color devices is set at about 25-30 percent of maximum. Although you may be tempted to crank it to the highest level, you'll get more battery life out of a lower setting.

■ Newer monochrome devices employ a reverse backlighting technique: when you activate the backlight, the black pixels are illuminated instead of the "white" background pixels. However, depending on the device, you can specify that the inactive pixels, not the active pixels, are illuminated when you turn backlighting on. Go to the Memo Pad, create a new record, then write "$\mathcal{L} \cdot 8$": the shortcut stroke (like a cursive lowercase L), a period (two taps), then the number 8. You should see the words "[Inverting Backlight]" which reverses the backlighting effect (**Figure 1.14**). Repeat the steps to return to the default backlighting style.

■ Unscrew the top or bottom section of the stylus to find a surprise: a pin that pushes the handheld's reset button.

■ To take care of your screen, just wipe it with a clean cloth occasionally. Since the Graffiti area tends to get the most use, one low-tech solution to protecting it is to put strips of tape (Scotch 811, in the blue box, is the preferred variety). Other people have used Post-it notes, tape flags, and transparency film.

Silkscreen Graffiti area

This is where you input text using Graffiti, the Palm method of handwriting (see Chapter 2). It's usually referred to as the "silkscreened" area, because the Graffiti input area and the buttons on either side of it are printed on a layer of glass by a silkscreening process. The Applications (also known as Home) and Calculator buttons are located here, as well as the triggers for accessing menus and using the Palm OS's Find feature (**Figure 1.15**).

A few devices, such as the Tungsten T3 and select Sony CLIÉs, incorporate the silkscreen area in software, making the space available to other applications (**Figure 1.16**).

Application buttons

The plastic buttons on the case activate a pre-assigned application. On most devices these are Date Book, Address Book, To Do List, and Note Pad (**Figure 1.17**). Wireless devices tend to substitute an Email button for To Do List and a Web button for Note Pad. I rarely launch the main programs any other way.

Scroll buttons/Navigator

These up and down buttons are a handy way to scroll through text and other information.

Some newer devices use what Palm calls the Navigator, a five-way controller that is quite useful (in addition to the four compass points, the fifth direction is a middle button used as a selector in some applications). It's great for looking up addresses, for example (see Chapter 5).

Contrast/brightness control

Adjust the screen's contrast or brightness using the button in the silkscreened area (**Figure 1.18**).

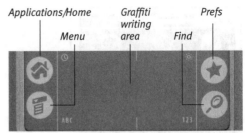

Figure 1.15 Use the silkscreened area to input text using Graffiti, plus launch certain functions.

Figure 1.16 Devices such as the CLIÉ PEG-NX90 with vertical displays feature a "silkscreened" area in software (top), which can be moved out of the way if necessary (bottom).

Figure 1.17 The plastic application buttons take you directly to the built-in programs. The scroll buttons or Navigator (shown here) are often a better substitute for tapping the scroll arrows in many applications.

Contrast/brightness button

Figure 1.18 Many devices place the contrast/brightness control in the silkscreened area.

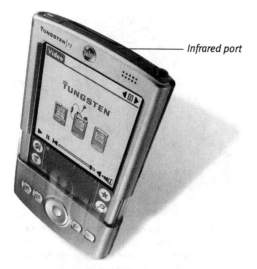

Infrared port

Figure 1.19 The infrared port can be used to beam information between Palm organizers, and for synchronizing with an infrared-equipped PC.

Infrared port

Every handheld includes an infrared port that enables you to "beam" information from one device to another (**Figure 1.19**). See Chapter 2 for more information about beaming applications, and program-specific chapters (such as Chapter 4) for more on beaming individual records and categories.

Reset button

There will probably come a time when something has happened that renders your handheld unusable (it will stop responding to your input). To get back to business, locate the tiny reset hole in the back of the unit. Use the reset pin located in the stylus, or straighten part of a paperclip, and insert it into the hole to reset the Palm OS (known as a *soft reset*—it won't erase your data).

✔ Tips

- Pressing one of the application buttons when your handheld is powered down will turn it on and launch that program.

- You can launch any program—not just the built-in ones—by pressing one of the application buttons. To remap their functions, go to the Buttons section of the Preferences application (see Chapter 2).

- On handhelds equipped with the Navigator controller, press the center button when the power is off to display the current date and time briefly. Press and hold it in any program to go to the Applications list.

- As neat as it is to find the secret reset pin in a stylus, device makers are finally getting wise and making the slots for accessing the reset button big enough to accommodate the stylus tip itself (such as on the Tungsten T models).

PALM DEVICE OVERVIEW

HotSync cradle

The ability to synchronize information between the handheld and a desktop computer is one of the reasons for Palm's success. All Palm devices include synchronization software for your PC, and most come with an angled HotSync cradle (**Figure 1.20**). Place the device into the cradle so that the connector at its base slides into the cradle's serial port. To begin synchronizing, press the HotSync button on the front of the cradle.

Today's cradles are USB-based. A few devices, such as the Tungsten E and Zire 21, use direct USB cables instead of cradles.

If you use a computer that doesn't have USB, you'll need to purchase the PalmConnect USB Kit. See Palm's online store (`store.palm.com`) for more information.

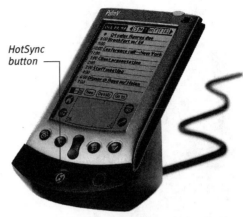

HotSync button

Figure 1.20 To transfer data between the handheld and your PC, use the accompanying HotSync cradle: Slide the organizer into place and press the HotSync button in front to synchronize the information.

✔ Tip

■ The cradle is also where devices with internal lithium ion batteries are recharged. The same is true of devices with just USB cables, since USB cables carry power from the computer they're attached to.

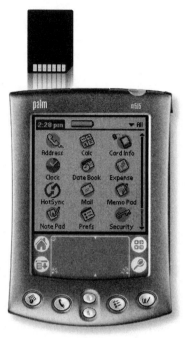

Figure 1.21 Many current handhelds accept postage-stamp–sized Secure Digital/MultiMediaCard expansion cards.

Expansion Cards

The latest Palm organizers have begun offering slots for expansion ports, enabling you to add removable memory or peripherals without occupying a device's serial port. For information on transferring data to and from cards, see Chapter 2.

Secure Digital/MultiMediaCard

The most common expansion cards on handhelds are Secure Digital or MultiMediaCard expansion cards (www.palm.com/products/accessories/expansioncards/). The formats use the same physical specification, which is only about the size of a postage stamp (**Figure 1.21**). Cards add more memory or include reference materials like electronic books or other data, but the format also supports devices such as digital cameras, GPS receivers, and wireless modems.

CompactFlash

CompactFlash is a card standard used in several types of devices, especially digital cameras, and therefore offers a wide variety of uses. The Sony PEG-NZ90, for example, can accept a CompactFlash-based Wi-Fi wireless networking card.

Sony Memory Stick

Sony's expansion card offering is the Memory Stick, a card that's literally about the shape and size of a stick of gum. Memory Sticks offer more memory, and can be swapped between multiple devices (from Sony Vaio computers to the AIBO electronic pet). Sony has several types of Memory Sticks: the MagicGate variety supports encrypted data.

Battery Use

Most Palm organizers run either on a built-in
rechargeable lithium ion battery or on two
AAA batteries, and last anywhere between
four and six weeks (except for color models,
which average two weeks). Feel free to read
that sentence again, especially if you're a
laptop computer (or Windows CE device)
owner who's used to measuring battery life
in *hours*. The battery use is minimal (the
CPU is asleep most of the time, even when
powered on), so even if you use it often, you
can still expect about three weeks of life
from one set.

Rechargeable lithium ion battery

Most devices today include built-in lithium
ion batteries that recharge whenever they're
in their HotSync cradles; a light on the cradle
or the handheld indicates that the battery is
charging.

AAA batteries

For handhelds that use replaceable batteries,
a new set of two store-bought AAA batteries
gives you 3 volts of power. When their
capacity approaches 2 volts, the device will
begin to warn you that it's time to install a
fresh pair. Although some people go ahead
and swap out the old batteries after the first
warning, you can probably get several more
days of moderate use before switching. Since
I hate being nagged about such things, I usually go ahead and replace the batteries after
the first or second warning.

Battery level indicator

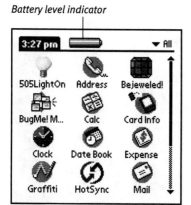

Figure 1.22 The battery level is shown at the top of the Applications screen.

✔ Tips

- It only takes a few minutes each day to refill a rechargeable battery. Under normal use, the charge applied during a HotSync should be sufficient to top off the gauge (**Figure 1.22**). The fact that the batteries won't fall out or get knocked loose accidentally makes these devices the most solid handhelds I've used.

- If you've just opened your brand new device with a rechargeable battery, stop! Be sure you charge the unit for three or four hours before first use to ensure that the battery is fully charged. Not following this simple step can cause the battery to hold less of a charge over the long run.

- It's almost inevitable that at some point you'll find yourself without power. If you have a rechargeable device, you can purchase USB power cables that siphon power from your computer. I find this essential when I'm on the road, because it means I can leave my bulky cradle and even more bulky power brick at home in favor of a lightweight USB cable. For example, Keyspan offers a Sync + Charge cable for Palm that retracts into a compact hub (www.keyspan.com).

BATTERY USE

Recommended battery types

Palm recommends using Alkaline batteries, which have a steady rate of discharge (as opposed to nickel-cadmium, or NiCad, batteries, which drop off suddenly when they're spent; you may not have enough juice to HotSync your data before installing new batteries). Many users also report longer battery life using the newer Duracell Ultras and Energizer Advanced Formula batteries.

If you want to use rechargeable batteries, go with rechargeable alkalines like Rayovac Renewal. Just be sure to recharge them at around 50 percent capacity—don't wait until they're dead—to get the best use out of them.

To change batteries:

1. HotSync your data. There are provisions built into Palm devices to prevent data loss during a battery swap, but the best is to have a backup of your data. For more on synchronizing data, see Chapter 3.

2. Shut off your handheld, turn it over, and remove the battery door (**Figure 1.23**).

3. Pull out the old batteries and replace with the new ones. Palm recommends swapping them one at a time (i.e., bad battery out, good battery in, repeat). You have about 60 seconds from the point when you remove the batteries to when you install fresh ones to avoid data loss.

4. Replace the battery door, and turn the device back on.

✔ Tip

■ If you're using different battery types (Alkaline/NiCad/Rechargeable Alkaline/NiMH), write the following in a text field (such as the Memo Pad) to toggle between more accurate battery gauges: "ℓ · ┐" (shortcut, period, 7).

Remove the battery door, then replace the batteries, first one, then the other.

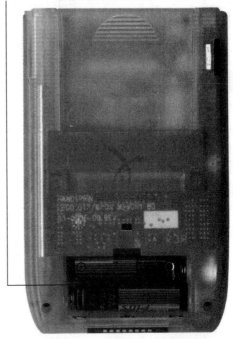

Figure 1.23 Batteries are included with new Palm devices that use them (versus built-in rechargeable batteries). When it's time to replace the AAA batteries, you have about 60 seconds after removing them to swap them out before your data is lost.

Figure 1.24 Replacement styli range from simple substitutes to pen/stylus combinations to traditional pens with PDA nibs. The LandWare Floating•Point stylus is shown here.

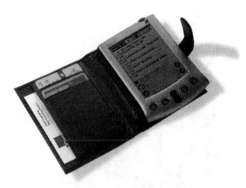

Figure 1.25 Handheld case manufacturers have taken advantage of this niche market—you can buy a style of case customized for your needs.

Accessorizing

A characteristic of a successful product is how well you can accessorize it, so it's not surprising to find a cottage industry that caters to handheld accessories. These range from stylish styli to screen protectors to clothing specially designed with PDA-ready pockets.

Styli

As you might expect, you can buy replacement styli, ranging from brass styli that fit into the stylus slots to hybrid pens such as the Cross DigitalWriter (www.cross.com). The LandWare Floating•Point stylus, for example, has a special nib that replicates the feel of writing on paper (www.landware.com) (**Figure 1.24**). For more variations, see PDA Panache (www.pdapanache.com).

Cases

There are numerous case variations on the market, ranging from Palm's Slim Leather Case (**Figure 1.25**) to RhinoSkin's Cockpit (www.saunders-usa.com/rhinoskin/), a titanium hard case with a melting point of 1,666 degrees Celsius! There are also varieties of belt-loop cases, zippered pouches, carriers with shoulder-straps. For a few good resources on cases, check out Fredlet's Pilot Page (www.fredlet.com/palm/) or the Gadgeteer (www.the-gadgeteer.com).

Other accessories

Depending on your needs, a variety of other helpful goodies can be ordered. Examples include extra HotSync cradles, travel kits and chargers, and extra HotSync cables.

Keyboards

The Palm's pen has proved mightier than the chiclet keyboards on many other PDAs, but there are times when a real physical keyboard can come in handy. Anyone who has tried to work on a regular-sized laptop computer in an airplane's coach seat knows that space is at a premium.

Although perhaps overkill for everyday handheld usage, they're great for typing long memos, emails, and especially for taking notes during a meeting.

Of all the handheld peripherals I've carried around lately, the Palm Ultra-Thin Keyboard is the one that knocks people out. Designed by Think Outside (www.thinkoutside.com) and sold by Palm (store.palm.com), the Palm Ultra-Thin is a full-size keyboard that folds into a compact rectangle not much larger than a Palm device (**Figure 1.26**). In addition to being small and light, it has special keys that launch applications and access Palm OS features such as command shortcuts.

Palm has also introduced a wireless keyboard that interfaces with any handheld via infrared. A swiveling arm ensures that the IR port is lined up properly, and lets you use devices horizontally, as well (**Figure 1.27**).

Figure 1.26 The Palm Ultra-Thin Keyboard is a full-size keyboard that folds up to a size slightly larger (and much slimmer) than a Palm device.

Figure 1.27 Palm's new wireless keyboard variation uses infrared to work with any Palm device, no matter what type of connector it uses.

Figure 1.28 Palm Desktop for Windows replicates most of the Palm OS's functionality, but puts most of the information on the same screen.

Palm Desktop

Most of this book concerns the Palm OS and the handhelds that use it, but there's also another very important component to the organizer: the desktop software. A Palm OS handheld is primarily intended to be an extension of your personal data, so the desktop software acts as the core.

You also have the option of using other PIM programs like Microsoft Outlook or Lotus Notes. But Palm Desktop is the one that most closely resembles what you find on the palmtop.

Palm Desktop makes it easy to access your data when you're working on your computer, printing information, installing software on the handheld, or just need to enter a lot of data without cramping your fingers writing Graffiti. At the very least, Palm Desktop provides the framework for keeping backup copies of the data on your handheld.

Throughout the book, I'll cover specific features of each module in its respective chapters (such as Chapter 4, *Date Book*).

Palm Desktop for Windows

Most of the functionality found on the Palm translates directly to the Windows version of Palm Desktop (**Figure 1.28**). On the desktop, however, you get the advantage of a computer's larger screen size, so you can see more information at a glance than on a handheld.

Palm Desktop is also the place to access archived data (which you've deleted from the handheld but want to store on the PC).

Palm Desktop for Macintosh

The first incarnation of the Macintosh Palm Desktop only synchronized the built-in applications, with no way for developers to write additional conduits (software bridges between the Palm OS and the desktop). For a few years, Pilot Desktop 1.0 remained the only choice for Palm-owning Macintosh users. Eager to reestablish contact with its Mac user base, Palm made an interesting choice when updating the desktop software: it bought Claris Organizer from Apple. Rather than build something new from scratch, they built upon Organizer.

The result is a vastly different desktop PIM from both Pilot Desktop 1.0 and the Windows counterpart (**Figure 1.29**). Although it shares basic functionality with Palm Desktop for Windows, there are notable differences: some features, such as support for a second address field (so you can store home and work addresses, for example), exist only on the desktop, not under the Palm OS (**Figure 1.30**); you can assign sub-categories to records; and, of course, the interface is quite a bit different.

✔ Tip

■ The latest version of Palm Desktop for Macintosh is 4.1 as of this writing, and it's available for both Mac OS 9 and Mac OS X. However, Palm notes that you shouldn't synchronize a device under both versions on the same machine (for example, if you have to switch between the two environments)—your data could get damaged, lost, or otherwise annoyingly screwed up.

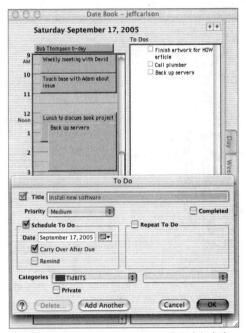

Figure 1.29 The Palm Desktop for Macintosh includes the features of the late Claris Organizer, upon which it was based.

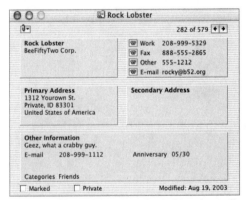

Figure 1.30 You can store more data, although not all of it will transfer to the handheld.

The Palm OS

Much is said and written about the portability of Palm organizers and the ease of synchronizing data with a desktop PC. When the attention is turned to the software running inside it, though, the focus usually shifts to how many events can be stored, or how quickly one can look up an address.

I would argue that the Palm Operating System (Palm OS) is actually the strongest, and most overlooked, of the Palm device features. Like a well-scored movie soundtrack, which adds to the atmosphere of a film without drawing attention to itself, the Palm OS provides a lot of power while remaining essentially invisible to most owners. If you're used to the shaded buttons and colors of Windows, the Palm OS probably looks sparse and boring (and if you're a Macintosh user, you may think you've returned to the early days of System 6!). As a result, using a Palm device for the first time is surprisingly easy.

Yet it isn't just ease of use that makes the Palm OS notable. Beneath the uncluttered interface lies an operating system that's been designed with an emphasis on efficiency and usability. After using the Palm OS for only a few hours, you'll realize that your stylus is only tapping its surface.

Navigating the Palm OS

There are four basic methods of interacting within the Palm OS, three of which depend on the stylus. The fourth, on some models, is a scroll or "jog" wheel. Since the screen is touch-sensitive, there's no need for a proxy device such as a mouse.

Tap

Tapping a record with the stylus selects it by either opening up a new window or placing a cursor within the text. You also use taps to manipulate the following interface elements (**Figure 2.1**):

- **Icons.** In the Applications screen, tapping a program's icon or name launches it. Smaller custom icons, such as the alarm clock and note, are also used.

- **Buttons.** Similar to the buttons found under Windows and the Mac OS, these rounded-corner boxes are used to activate commands or confirm actions.

- **Menus.** When you tap a title bar or the silkscreened Menu icon, drop-down menus become visible at the top of the screen. Tap to select menu items.

- **Scroll arrows.** When data spills beyond the size of the screen, tap the up/down scroll arrows to move the active information up and down. You'll also encounter left/right scroll arrows, like the Date Book arrows that move between weeks (see Chapter 4).

- **Popup menus.** Whenever you see a small triangle pointing down next to a word, it indicates that more options are available via a popup menu.

- **Checkboxes.** Tap on a checkbox to mark or unmark it, toggling the action that is assigned to it (such as the Private indicator in most records' detail screens).

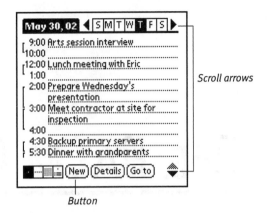

Scroll arrows

Button

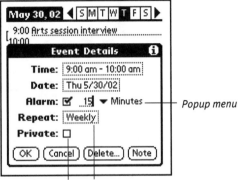

Popup menu

Checkbox   Dotted-rectangle field

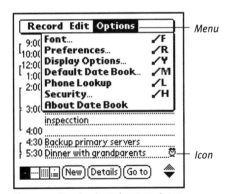

Menu

Icon

Figure 2.1 Tapping just about any interface element in the Palm OS evokes a response.

NAVIGATING THE PALM OS

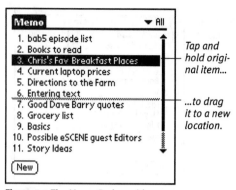

Figure 2.2 The Memo Pad provides one example of dragging a list item to a new location.

Figure 2.3 Tap to set your cursor, then drag through letters to highlight them.

♦ **Dotted-rectangle fields.** These fields display the information that has been selected for them, but also indicate that tapping the field allows you to change it.

Drag

In a few cases, you will want to drag an item using the stylus. The most common examples include (but are not limited to):

♦ **Scroll bars.** If you have more than 11 memos displayed in the Memo Pad, a vertical scroll bar appears at the right side of the screen. Tap and hold on the solid scroll bar area, then drag it vertically.

♦ **Custom ordered memos.** In the Memo Pad and some applications, you can "grab" an item and drag it to a new position within a list (**Figure 2.2**). A thick dotted line indicates where the item will be placed when it is "dropped" (i.e., when you lift the stylus from the screen).

♦ **Highlighting text.** To select a series of letters or words, tap to place your cursor, then drag to select the text (**Figure 2.3**).

♦ **Weekly Date Book entries.** In the Date Book's week view, you can select events and reschedule them by dragging to a new date and time. (See Chapter 4.)

Write

Using the silkscreened Graffiti area, you can use the stylus as a pen and write letters that appear within text fields.

Scroll

Some models include a scroll wheel or a multi-directional controller to navigate data. Pressing the wheel can also act as a tap, depending on the application.

✔ Tip

■ Under Palm OS 3.5 and later, double-tap to select a word; triple-tap to select a line.

NAVIGATING THE PALM OS

Accessing Menus

Although hidden to conserve valuable screen space, drop-down menus similar to those found in Windows and the Mac OS are available for most applications. Access menus to take advantage of commands not displayed on the current screen, and to edit text using Cut, Copy, Paste, and Undo commands.

To access menus in applications:

◆ Tap the program's title bar to make the menus appear.

or

1. Tap the Menu icon located in the lower-left corner of the silkscreened area of the screen. You'll see a row of words appear at the top of the screen such as Record, Edit, or Options.

2. Tap a word to see a drop-down menu of related commands (**Figure 2.4**). You don't have to maintain contact with the stylus; these menus are "sticky" and will stay visible until you tap the stylus on a command or elsewhere on the screen.

3. Tap the desired menu item to perform its action.

✔ Tips

■ You can't tap the title bar to access menus on devices using Palm OS versions earlier than 3.5.

■ If you're not running Palm OS 3.5, you can get the same functionality by installing the HackMaster extension MenuHack (www.daggerware.com/mischack.htm).

To make menus visible...

...tap this icon first.

Figure 2.4 It may not make much sense to jump from bottom to top to access menus, but it's nice that menus are normally hidden to save space.

Figure 2.5 Tap the "circle-i" icon in the upper-right corner of dialog boxes to access help and other information.

Figure 2.6 It's worth checking out a new program's Tips screens—often you'll find real tips, not just online help.

Onscreen Help and Tips

Nestled within the tight memory confines of the Palm OS exists a handy location for accessing onscreen help and application tips. Most dialog boxes (windows that are identified by a thick outside line and a black title bar at the top) include a "circle-i" information icon in the upper-right corner (**Figure 2.5**). Tapping this small icon displays a screen titled Tips, which often provides instruction or pointers for using an application's features (**Figure 2.6**). It's often worth poking around the dialog boxes of a new program to see if any "hidden" features may be revealed on the Tips screen.

Using the Onscreen Keyboard

The Palm OS includes two methods for entering information: Graffiti, the style of lettering you use to write individual letters (see the next section), and a virtual keyboard for tapping letters on the screen. The keyboard can be accessed only when your cursor is in a text field. Activating it brings up a new window containing the text field (or as much as can be displayed in the smaller space), with the keyboard located below (**Figure 2.7**).

Three separate keyboards are available: the abc keyboard, which is laid out in Qwerty format (like most computer and typewriter keyboards); the 123 keyboard, which gives you access to numbers and common symbol characters; and the Int'l ("international") keyboard, which creates common letters with diacritical marks (such as é) as well as characters like ß, ¿, and æ. Switch between layouts by tapping the corresponding button beneath the keyboard.

To activate the keyboard:

There are three ways of accessing the keyboard: tap either the abc or 123 sections in the lower corners of the Graffiti area; select Keyboard from the Edit menu (when available); or write ╱-K in the Graffiti area. Tap Done when finished.

✔ Tips

- If you like the onscreen keyboard but find the Qwerty layout difficult, install Fitaly (www.fitaly.com), which arranges letters based on frequent usage.

- If you don't mind Qwerty, but don't like tapping the small letter squares, install DotNote (or ".Note") (www.utilware.com) to display larger keys.

Figure 2.7 If you'd prefer to tap on letters instead of write them, bring up one of the onscreen Keyboard layouts. This is often the best way to access symbol and international characters.

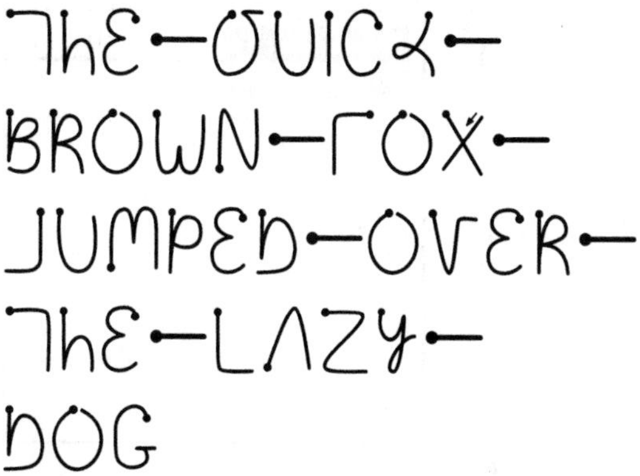

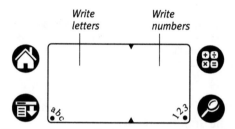

Figure 2.8 At first glance, Graffiti looks like an alien scrawl, but pretty soon you'll find yourself writing like this on everything—not just your handheld.

Write letters   Write numbers

Figure 2.9 Create Graffiti letters on the left side of the Graffiti area; write numbers on the right.

Graffiti

One of the few things that makes potential Palm organizer buyers hesitate before purchasing is the prospect of hand-writing letters on the screen. Some are concerned that they'll have to learn a new "language." Others are gun-shy after hearing about the difficulties with handwriting recognition that plagued other handhelds (notably Apple's discontinued Newton MessagePad). In the Palm OS, you use the stylus to write the Graffiti alphabet, which translates those written gestures into proper text characters (**Figure 2.8**).

Call me a Graffiti evangelist, but I'm here to reassure you that: (a) Graffiti is simpler than you think (you'll pick up the basics in the first few hours, I promise); and (b) because it doesn't technically do any handwriting recognition, your chances of writing something like "The quack bruin fax junked over the hazy fog" are fairly minimal (unless that's what you meant in the first place).

The Graffiti area

One of the key differences between traditional handwriting recognition and Graffiti is that you don't write directly on the active portion of the screen using Graffiti. Instead, you form letters in the silkscreened Graffiti area, where they are interpreted and displayed wherever your cursor happens to be.

The Graffiti area is split into two sections: write letters on the left side, numbers on the right (**Figure 2.9**). This is an important distinction, because some characters, such as B and 3, can be written using identical strokes.

✔ Tip

- Some recent devices let you write Graffiti anywhere on the screen. See the Prefs application to enable this feature.

GRAFFITI

Writing Graffiti

Here's the big secret about Graffiti: nearly every character can be written with only one stroke of the stylus. (The exception is X, which requires two strokes—but you can also use an alternate version of X that's still just one stroke.) The identity of the character is determined both by the shape of the stroke, and by the combination of the stroke's origin point and direction. As an example, let's write the word "Tack" (**Figure 2.10**).

To write basic Graffiti characters:

1. First, you need to be in an application where you can write text. Press the Memo Pad button on the front of the handheld, then tap New to create a new memo. Place the tip of the stylus at the left side of the Graffiti area.

2. Write the Graffiti stroke for T (⌐), starting at the dot. Make sure you write the complete stroke without lifting the stylus until the end (**Table 2.1**). You should see a capital T in the memo above.

3. Using the same side of the Graffiti area, write the stroke for A (∧), again starting at the dot. Repeat the process for C (C), and—my favorite letter to write—K (⋠).

4. Admire your (sharp) handiwork.

Writing numbers is exactly the same, only you write strokes in the right side of the Graffiti area (**Table 2.2**).

✔ Tip

■ You probably noticed that the first letter was automatically capitalized, and subsequent letters were in lowercase. When you begin a new field, or write an end-of-sentence punctuation such as a period or exclamation point, the Palm OS assumes that you want a capital letter.

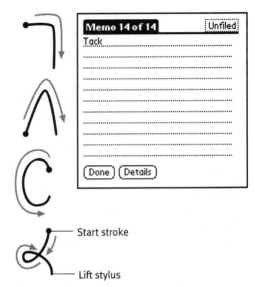

Figure 2.10 Each character can be written using one stroke of the stylus in the Graffiti area. Start at the dot (but don't try to draw the dot), and lift the stylus at the end of the stroke.

Table 2.1

The Graffiti Alphabet			
LETTER	**GRAFFITI**	**LETTER**	**GRAFFITI**
A	∧	N	N
B	ß	O	O
C	C	P	p
D	D	Q	Ơ
E	Ɛ	R	ß
F	⌐	S	S
G	G	T	⌐
H	h	U	U
I	I	V	V
J	J	W	W
K	⋠	X	X
L	L	Y	y
M	⋔	Z	Z

WRITING GRAFFITI

Table 2.2

Graffiti Numbers and Special Strokes

Symbol	Graffiti	Symbol	Graffiti
1	I	8	8 8
2	2	9	9
3	3	0	O O
4	L	backspace	→
5	5 b	return	/
6	6	shift	|
7	7	space	← —

Table 2.3

Graffiti Punctuation (with Alternates)

Symbol	Graffiti	Symbol	Graffiti
.	· ·	+	· ∝
,	· /	=	· Z
'	· ↑	|	· ⅃
?	· ? ⅂	⟨	· ⊂
!	· ↓	⟩	· ⊃
-	· —	\	· \
(	· C	{	· ε
)	· ⊃	}	· 3
/	· /	[	· ε
$	· S	]	· 3
@	· O	~	· N ~
#	· ⋃ h	`	· \
%	· ⋈	;	· /
^	· ∧	:	· ↓
&	· 8	"	· N
*	· ⋈	tab	· Γ
—	· —		

In Graffiti, there are no separate strokes for upper- and lowercase letters. Instead, as when typing on a computer keyboard, you need to specify when to enable Caps Shift.

To write uppercase letters:

1. Write the Caps Shift stroke (I) in either side of the Graffiti area. An up arrow symbol (⬆) will appear in the lower-right corner of the screen to indicate that Caps Shift is enabled.

2. Write a normal Graffiti letter. You'll see the uppercase version appear in the text field. The up arrow will disappear.

3. If you're going to write a series of upper-case letters, you can enable Caps Lock by writing two Caps Shift strokes. The up arrow is replaced by an underlined up arrow (⬆).

To write punctuation:

1. Tap once on either side of the Graffiti area to enable Punctuation Shift. You'll see a large dot in the lower-right corner.

2. Write the stroke for the punctuation mark you want (**Table 2.3**).

✔ Tip

- If you change your mind and want to switch back to normal writing before committing to a capital letter or punctuation character, write a Back Space stroke (→), which effectively "deletes" the Caps Shift or Punctuation Shift stroke you just made.

WRITING GRAFFITI

To write symbols and extended characters:

1. Enable the Symbol Shift mode by drawing a diagonal line in either side of the Graffiti area, starting at the top-left corner and finishing at the lower right. You'll see a similar line (\) in the lower-right corner of the screen.

2. Write the stroke for the symbol you want (**Table 2.4**).

To write accented characters:

1. It takes two strokes to create accented characters. First, draw the letter you want to apply the accent to, such as E ($\mathcal{E}$).

2. Write the corresponding accent stroke. The character changes to the new accented letter (**Table 2.5**).

Navigating using Graffiti

You can move your cursor within a field or to an adjacent field without erasing the letters you've already written using Graffiti navigation strokes (**Table 2.6**).

Command strokes

There's a better way than menu items to access commands. Rather than use three taps to access a menu item (tap the Menu icon, tap the menu name, tap the menu item), it's much easier and faster to write a command stroke. Draw a diagonal line from the bottom-left to the upper-right of either side of the Graffiti area (∕). You'll see the word Command, or the command bar (see next section), appear at the bottom of the screen. Write the stroke that activates the menu item you want (such as ∕-C for Copy).

Table 2.4

Graffiti Symbols/Extended Characters

SYMBOL	GRAFFITI	SYMBOL	GRAFFITI
●	\ ·	X	\ /
TM	\ ⋒	÷	\ ⋙
®	\ ℝ	=	\ Z
©	\ C	¢	\ C
'	\ Γ	¥	\ ४
,	\ ⅂	£	\ L
"	\ N	¿	\ L
"	\ И	i	\ ↓
§	\ S	ß	\ B
·	\ Ω	μ	\ ⋒
+	\ ∝	f	\ S
−	\ ─	Ø	\ Ω

Table 2.5

Graffiti Accent Characters

SYMBOL	GRAFFITI	SYMBOL	GRAFFITI
à	∧─\	è	$\mathcal{E}$─\
á	∧─∕	é	$\mathcal{E}$─∕
â	∧─∧	ê	$\mathcal{E}$─∧
ä	∧─⋙	ü	U─⋙
å	∧─Ω	ç	C
ñ	N─N	æ	$\mathcal{E}$

Table 2.6

Graffiti Navigation Strokes

COMMAND	GRAFFITI	COMMAND	GRAFFITI
cursor right	─	next field	↓
cursor left	─	shortcut	⅄
previous field	↑	command	∕

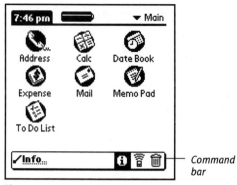

Command
bar

Figure 2.11 In Applications, the command bar provides access to common features, like the Info or Delete screens.

Figure 2.12 With nothing selected, the command bar offers few choices.

Figure 2.13 With a record selected, the command bar displays icons for commands which work in that context.

The Command Bar

Palm OS 3.5 and higher takes the concept of command strokes one step further with the command bar (**Figure 2.11**). When you write a command stroke, the command bar displays icons for actions that are usable depending on the current context.

For example, with no records selected in the To Do List, the only icon to appear is the Security icon (**Figure 2.12**). However, with a task selected, the Beam Item, Paste, and Delete Item options appear (**Figure 2.13**).

If you don't act within three seconds, the command bar disappears until invoked again.

To access the command bar:

1. Draw a diagonal line from the bottom-left to the top-right corner of either Graffiti area (╱).

2. Tap an icon on the command bar to perform an action. You can tap and hold on an icon to see its description; when you lift the stylus, the action is executed.

✔ Tips

■ The command bar is an addition to the Palm OS's command-stroke function; if a command isn't represented by an icon, you can still invoke it by writing the command shortcut letters found in the application's menus.

■ If you've tapped an icon but decide not to invoke its action, drag the stylus away from the icon before lifting it from the screen's surface.

THE COMMAND BAR

Graffiti Improvement Tips

Simple tips for improving Graffiti recognition

- **Write large.** Feel free to use the full Graffiti area to write your letters—that way, more touch-sensitive sensors are registering your strokes.

- **Write at a natural speed.** If you write too slowly, you can confuse the sensors and generate errors.

- **Don't write on a slant.** Try to keep vertical strokes vertical, and horizontal strokes horizontal.

Alternate characters

If you're finding that the downstroke on the B is creating a D and vice-versa, or if you just want to write faster, there are a number of built-in alternate strokes that work just as well (or sometimes better) than the standard Graffiti set (**Table 2.7**).

TealEcho

Install TealEcho (www.tealpoint.com) to see Graffiti characters as you write them. Having that visual feedback helps improve Graffiti skills by showing you exactly why your scribbles may be incomprehensible.

TealScript

If you'd rather go in and tinker with each individual Graffiti character, install Teal-Script (www.tealpoint.com). By marking the Enable Globally checkbox on the main screen, you can replace Palm's Graffiti alphabet (though you're not deleting the original) with the infinitely configurable TealScript. You're still using Graffiti, but you can set up a TealScript profile that reacts better to the way you write (**Figure 2.14**).

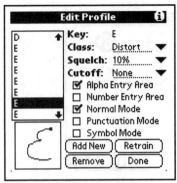

Figure 2.14 TealScript builds profiles based on your Graffiti usage.

Table 2.7

Normal and Alternate Characters			
LETTER	GRAFFITI	LETTER	GRAFFITI
A	∧	T	⌐
B	ß B 3	U	U
C	C <	V	V V
D	Ɗ Ɋ ℓ	W	ⱳ
E	Ɛ ≤ ℮	X	X ℀
F	Γ ⌐	Y	ỿ ℽ ℾ
G	G 6	Z	Z
H	h	1	I
I	I	2	2 ₂
J	J J	3	3
K	≺	4	∟ C <
L	L ∠	5	5 Ƅ S
M	m m	6	6
N	N ∕∖ ∼	7	⌐ ⊃
O	O O	8	8 8 ⁄ ℽ
P	P P Ƿ	9	9
Q	℧ Ʊ	0	O O
R	R R ℞	æ	Ɛ
S	S ⌇ Ƅ		

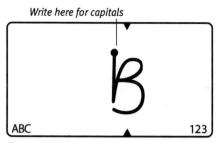

Write here for capitals

ABC   123

Figure 2.15 Graffiti 2 capitals are written in the space dividing the letter and number sections.

Table 2.8

Graffiti 2 Letters and Numbers

LETTER	GRAFFITI	LETTER	GRAFFITI
A	∧	N	N
B	ß	O	O
C	C	P	p
D	Ɗ	Q	q
E	Ɛ	R	R
F	Γ	S	S
G	G	T	⊬
H	h	U	U
I	i	V	V
J	J	W	W
K	K	X	X
L	L	Y	y
M	M	Z	Z
1	I	8	8
2	2	9	9
3	3	0	O
4	⊬	backspace	⟶
5	5	return	/
6	6	shift	I
7	7	space	⎯

Graffiti 2

In 2003, Palm switched to using Graffiti 2 instead of Graffiti due to a lawsuit by Xerox, who claims Graffiti was misappropriated. A version of Graffiti 2 was previously available as a third-party utility called Jot, which Palm purchased. The good news is that Graffiti 2 retains the spirit of Graffiti, with many pen strokes remaining the same. However, some are different, requiring two strokes to complete a letter (**Table 2.8**).

Some rules have changed, too. You don't have to write a Caps Shift stroke to make capitals, for example, and some characters are made by writing one stroke on the left side and one on the right.

To write uppercase letters:

◆ Write the letter in the middle of the Graffiti area, overlapping both the letter side and the number side (**Figure 2.15**).

To write special characters (such as $, #, %):

1. Write a Punctuation Shift upstroke (|); the symbol appears in the lower-right corner of the screen.

2. Write the character on either side of the Graffiti area.

3. Write another Punctuation Shift upstroke to finish the character.

✔ Tip

■ For more Graffiti 2 characters, see the decals that came with your organizer, or choose Graffiti 2 Help from the Edit menu in any application where you can enter text.

GRAFFITI 2

Setting General Preferences

The Prefs application looks mundane at first, but closer inspection reveals that the rest of the OS hinges upon the settings you choose here. To access the preferences, tap the popup menu in the upper-right corner (**Figure 2.16**).

To set General preferences:

1. Choose General from the Preferences popup menu (**Figure 2.17**).

2. As a battery-saving feature, a device will shut itself off after a period of inactivity. Tap the Auto-off After popup menu to choose a delay of 30-seconds, one minute, two minutes, or three minutes.

3. If you own a device with a rechargeable battery, check the Stay on in Cradle box to prevent the device from powering off when it's docked in the HotSync cradle. This is a good way to use your organizer as an expensive desk clock.

4. Specify the volume settings for the System, Alarm, and Game default sound levels as High, Medium, Low, or None.

5. Use the Alarm Vibrate and Alarm LED controls to enable or disable those features on supported devices.

6. Specify whether people can beam to you using the Beam Receive popup menu.

✔ Tip

- Leaving the Beam Receive option on can drain your battery at a higher rate. However, returning to Prefs each time you wish to receive something can be a pain. Instead, write the ShortCut ℓ .I (shortcut stroke, period, I) in any text field, which turns on Beam Receive for a single instance.

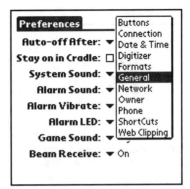

Figure 2.16 All of the Preferences settings can be accessed via the popup menu in the upper-right corner.

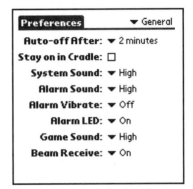

Figure 2.17 Set several volume levels, as well as choose if you want to receive beamed materials. Devices that use rechargeable batteries can be left on while in their recharging cradles.

Do Your Prefs Look Different?

Palm has modified the Preferences screens several times during the progression of the Palm OS. If you don't see something where I'm describing it, check another screen. Also, the Preferences screen of some Palm OS 5 devices looks completely different (**Figure 2.18**), but the settings are similar to other devices. As long as it works, I'm sure that consistency isn't important.

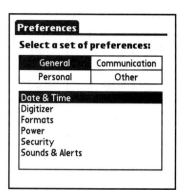

Figure 2.18 The Preferences screen can vary between device models (Palm OS 5.0 on a Tungsten T shown here).

Figure 2.19 Time keeps on slippin', slippin', slippin'...sorry, having a Steve Miller Band moment.

Figure 2.20 Tapping the targets ensures that your touch-sensitive screen is accurately registering the tap locations.

Setting the Date and Time

An organizer without the correct time can't do a good job of organizing. Get started by setting your temporal status (**Figure 2.19**).

To set the Date and Time:

1. Tap the Set Date field to select today's date from a calendar.

2. Tap the Set Time field to configure the hour and minute values.

3. From the Location popup menu, choose a city located closest to your own.

✔ Tip

■ Be careful about changing the time to reflect new time zones on your handheld and laptop when traveling. Since the time and date stamps are referred to when you perform a HotSync, having your organizer and your PC living in separate zones can cause data to be overwritten incorrectly.

Setting the Digitizer

Due to temperature variations, repeated use, and the general passing of time, the digitizer can gradually slide off track. If your pen taps don't seem to be working the way they used to, run the Digitizer.

To calibrate the Digitizer:

1. Choose Digitizer from the Preferences popup menu.

2. Tap the center points of the X shapes that appear (**Figure 2.20**). This process ensures that the pixels you tap on the screen correspond with the pixels that the Palm OS thinks you're tapping.

Customizing Buttons

Although the plastic application buttons on the case and the silkscreened icons near the Graffiti area are handy for directly launching the built-in applications, there are times when you might want to specify different programs, such as Super Names (www.standalone.com) instead of the Address Book application (**Figure 2.21**).

To customize buttons:

1. Choose the Buttons preferences option.

2. Select the button you wish to replace, and tap the popup menu to the right of its icon.

3. Choose an application from the popup list. To return to the Palm OS factory settings, tap the Default button.

✔ Tip

■ You can configure not only the plastic buttons and the silkscreened icons, but also the one-stroke pen drag. In the Buttons screen, tap More, then tap the popup menu in the center (**Figure 2.22**). You can choose to turn on the backlight, activate the onscreen keyboard (this is the default), display Graffiti help, turn off and lock the device, or (using Palm devices with infrared capability) beam data. Setting this feature to turn on the backlight is better than pressing the power button for two seconds.

Figure 2.21 Launch other programs from the physical application buttons.

Figure 2.22 Specify an action for the bottom-to-top screen stroke shortcut.

CUSTOMIZING BUTTONS

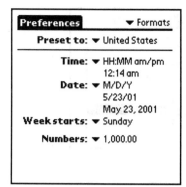

Figure 2.23 The Formats screen offers preconfigured settings for 24 countries.

Preferences ▼ Owner

This handheld computer is owned by:

Patrick O'Hanrahan
University of Chicago
www.necoffee.com/matthias/|

Figure 2.24 The Owner screen can be filled with whatever text you like, though most people enter contact information.

Changing Formats

If you dream of traveling abroad, select Formats from the Preferences popup menu and tap the Preset to popup menu to select the country in which you'd like to reside. Otherwise, it's probably a better idea to choose your current location.

To change time, date, week, and number formats:

1. The formats have already been configured for each country, but you can adjust them individually by tapping each setting's popup menu (**Figure 2.23**).

2. Switch to another application or Preferences menu item to apply the settings.

Editing the Owner Screen

Since you'll likely become attached to your handheld, you should go ahead and put your name in it (thereby resolving any potential playground ownership disputes by asserting that yes, your name *is* on it!).

To set up the Owner screen:

1. Select Owner from the Preferences popup menu.

2. Write your contact information (or other text) on the lines provided. If you should misplace your Palm device someday, the honorable person finding it can learn where to ship it back (**Figure 2.24**).

✔ Tip

■ After configuring your preferences, return to the Owner screen before switching to another program. This should speed up access the next time you open the Preferences application, as some sections—especially ShortCuts—take longer to load.

Using ShortCuts

Graffiti is an efficient way to input data, but you'll soon get tired of entering commonly used words and phrases letter by letter. Instead, set up ShortCuts that substitute full texts when you enter an abbreviation.

To create and edit ShortCuts:

1. Select ShortCuts from the Preferences popup menu (**Figure 2.25**).

2. Tap New to create a ShortCut, or Edit to change an existing one. The Palm OS includes seven built-in ShortCuts.

3. In the ShortCut Entry window, write the abbreviation under ShortCut Name. The shorter the abbreviation, the fewer letters you'll have to write to activate it, but you're not limited to just two or three (**Figure 2.26**).

4. Write the full text that will replace the abbreviation when you activate the ShortCut. Tap OK when you're done.

To use a ShortCut:

1. In any text field, write the ShortCut Graffiti character (ℒ); you will see it appear in your text.

2. Write the abbreviation for the word or phrase you're going to use. The abbreviation and ShortCut character will be erased and replaced by the full text.

Figure 2.25 All but one of the predefined ShortCuts are named with two-letter abbreviations, but you're not bound to that limit.

Figure 2.26 ShortCuts make entering frequently used texts much easier.

Figure 2.27 Preconfigure a variety of methods of moving data to and from your handheld.

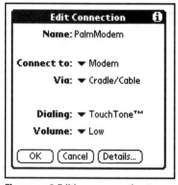

Figure 2.28 Editing a connection type controls how the OS interacts with devices such as modems.

Figure 2.29 Changing the speed or editing the initialization screen can sometimes improve a poor connection.

Setting Connection Preferences

If Palm OS devices are truly "connected organizers," as Palm says, then they need to connect with a variety of devices. Under Palm OS 3.3 and later, the Connection preferences handle peripherals like modems as well as serial and infrared connections.

To create or edit a configuration:

1. Select Connection from the Preferences popup menu (**Figure 2.27**).

2. Tap the New button, or tap a configuration to highlight it, then tap Edit.

3. From the Connect to popup menu, choose the type of connection that fits your purpose: PC, Modem, or Local Network (**Figure 2.28**).

4. Next, use the Via menu to choose the route the connection will take: Cradle/ Cable or Infrared.

5. If connecting to a modem, choose Touch-Tone™ or Rotary from the Dialing popup menu, and specify the loudness from the Volume popup menu. These aren't available if connecting to a PC or network.

6. Tap the Details button (**Figure 2.29**).

7. Select a data speed from the Speed popup menu. If you're running into HotSync problems under a serial connection, reducing the data speed may help.

8. If you're using a modem, the Country and Init String options will be available. Choose your country and enter a modem initialization string if you need one.

9. Set the flow control on the Flow Ctl popup menu. Flow control regulates the rate of incoming information. Leaving this set to Automatic should be fine in most cases.

SETTING CONNECTION PREFERENCES

Setting Network Preferences

Attaching a modem to your handheld enables you to connect directly to an Internet Service Provider (ISP) (**Figure 2.30**).

To set up Network preferences:

1. Select Network from the Preferences popup menu.

2. Choose the name of your ISP under the Service popup menu. If yours is not listed, select New from the Service menu, or write /-N.

3. Write the name you use to connect in the User Name field.

4. Tap the dotted box next to Password to write your login password. If you leave this blank, you will be prompted for your password each time you connect.

5. Choose a connection mode from the Connection popup menu (this setting comes from the Connection screen; see the previous page).

✔ Tip

■ The Palm OS keeps a log of network connections; select View Log from the Options menu (**Figure 2.31**).

Figure 2.30 The Network preferences screen allows you to connect directly to an Internet Service Provider.

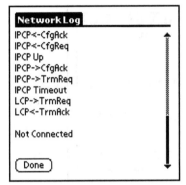

Figure 2.31 Secret code? Not if you know how to read modem commands. Use the Network Log to troubleshoot your connections.

SETTING NETWORK PREFERENCES

Figure 2.32 Tapping the Phone field in the Network preferences screen displays several dialing options.

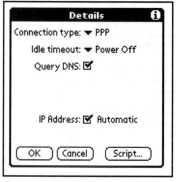

Figure 2.33 Choose the type of Internet connection, along with the action to take if the connection is idle.

To configure Network phone settings:

1. Tap the dotted box next to Phone to configure dialing options (**Figure 2.32**). In addition to the phone number required to dial, you can specify that a calling card be used, that a prefix be dialed (for example, dialing 9 to reach an outside line), or that call-waiting be disabled (if your phone package includes this; the signal tone generated by call-waiting services often breaks existing Net connections). Tap OK.

2. Tap the Details button to continue with the setup (**Figure 2.33**). Depending on the service you use to connect to the Internet, choose PPP, SLIP, or CSLIP from the Connection type popup menu.

3. Use Idle timeout to specify when the network connection should be terminated if there is no activity. The default Power Off setting ensures that an active connection continues until the unit shuts off—even if you switch between applications.

4. Use Query DNS (Domain Name System), to instruct your Internet application (such as an email client or Web browser) to ask your ISP's server to resolve domain names (addresses) on the Internet. If you uncheck this box, you will need to enter your primary and secondary DNS server addresses.

5. Check IP Address: Automatic to grab a random IP (Internet Protocol) address from your ISP, which identifies your machine on the Internet. If you have a fixed IP address, uncheck the box and enter it into the blanks that appear.

6. Finally, tap the Script button to create a customized login script to facilitate connecting to your ISP's server. If you don't require one, leave the first line so that it reads "End."

SETTING NETWORK PREFERENCES

Setting Phone Preferences

Palm OS 4.0 and later include built-in support for using a mobile phone to connect to the Internet.

To set Phone preferences:

1. Choose Phone from the Preferences popup menu.

2. Select a connection from the Connection popup menu (**Figure 2.34**). If your phone doesn't appear in the list, you can choose Edit Connections to set up a profile.

3. Tap the Test button to make sure the handheld and phone are communicating (**Figure 2.35**).

Setting Web Clipping Preferences

Palm's Mobile Internet Kit gives any Palm device the capability to use the Web Clipping technology introduced with the Palm VII (see Chapter 10).

To set Web Clipping preferences:

1. Choose Web Clipping from the Preferences popup menu (**Figure 2.36**).

2. If you have a Palm.Net account set up (see my.palm.com) and you've used your device to get online, your user name appears in the User ID field.

3. Tap the Server field to manually change the proxy server information.

4. A Palm.Net device's communication with nearby radio towers can identify its location. If you're uncomfortable with this, mark the checkbox for Warn when sending personal information.

Figure 2.34 You can connect to a cellular phone by selecting a profile on the Phone screen.

Figure 2.35 Use the Test feature to make sure your handheld and phone are communicating clearly.

Figure 2.36 Web Clipping allows you to access Web information quickly and easily.

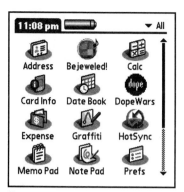

Figure 2.37 Each program has its own icon, listed alphabetically on the Applications screen.

Figure 2.38 Sony's Applications screen takes advantage of devices with longer screens. Click a blank area to the left to specify a frequently-used application.

Launching Applications

Finally, it's time to start using applications. (You've probably been using applications from the beginning, but I felt it was important to cover some preferences early.)

Unlike nearly all personal computers, a Palm device has no hard drive or floppy disk to store its data—everything is held in RAM (random access memory), including third-party applications and their data (the built-in applications and the core Palm OS files are stored in separate read-only memory, or ROM). As a result, you never have to open or quit programs, technically. All the applications are running concurrently, paused at the state where you last left them. Although I may refer to "launching" or "opening" applications throughout this book, Palm OS is actually only switching between them. (But "launching" sounds more exciting.)

To open an application:

1. Bring up the Applications screen by tapping the silkscreened Applications icon.

2. Tap a program's name or icon to launch it (**Figure 2.37**).

✔ Tips

■ If you have more programs than will fit onto a single screen, write the first letter of the program you want in the Graffiti area to make it visible.

■ Repeatedly tapping Applications switches between application categories (see "Categorizing Applications" later in this chapter).

■ Sony developed its own application launcher for the CLIÉ (**Figure 2.38**). Applications are grouped at the upper left; turn the Jog Wheel to shuttle through the programs, and press it to launch one without the stylus.

Installing Applications

Many handheld owners get by just fine using the built-in applications. However, thousands of third-party programs and utilities are available to install. In most cases, you can download the software from the Web on your desktop computer, then install it onto your Palm organizer.

To install applications using Quick Install (Windows):

1. Launch the Palm Quick Install either from the Windows Start menu, or by clicking the Quick Install button from within Palm Desktop.

2. Click Add to select the programs to install. Palm OS applications end with the extension .prc (whether you use a PC or a Mac). You can also drag the program files from the Windows desktop to the Palm Quick Install window to add them to the list (**Figure 2.39**).

3. When you've added the programs you want to install, click Done.

4. Perform a HotSync to transfer the programs into the handheld's memory.

To install applications using the HotSync Manager (Macintosh):

1. Launch HotSync Manager or Palm Desktop.

2. From the HotSync menu, choose Install Handheld Files (or press Command-I in HotSync Manager).

3. Click the Add To List button to locate the .prc file you want to add. You can also drag the files to the installation window from the Finder (**Figure 2.40**), or even just drag them to the Finder's HotSync Manager icon.

4. Perform a HotSync operation.

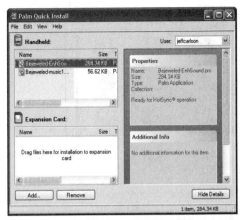

Figure 2.39 Under Windows, click the Add button to prepare programs to be installed. Alternately, you can drag the files to the Palm Quick Install window.

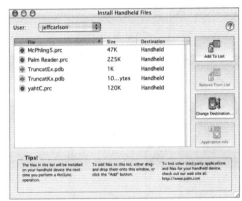

Figure 2.40 The Macintosh installer looks different than its Windows cousin, but works much the same. Clicking the Application Info button displays attributes of the selected file, such as creation date and version number.

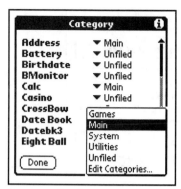

Figure 2.41 Tap the popup menus at right to specify a program's category. New applications are set to Unfiled.

Figure 2.42 Viewing applications by category lets you organize them according to your preference. Tapping Remember Last Category prevents all applications from being viewed the next time you tap the Applications icon.

Categorizing Applications

Grouping all of your applications onto the same screen isn't always helpful. That's why the Palm OS lets you set up categories to help organize your programs.

To switch between views:

1. In Applications, choose Preferences from the Options menu, or write /-R.

2. Choose either Icon or List from the View By popup menu.

To categorize applications:

1. In Applications, choose Category from the App menu, or write /-Y.

2. You'll see a list of all installed applications. Tap a category name from the popup menu to the right of a program.

3. If you don't see the category you want, select Edit Categories from the popup list to create a new category or edit an existing one (**Figure 2.41**).

To remember the last category:

1. All categories are shown if you switch to the Applications screen from another program. To keep the same category visible, choose Preferences from the Options menu, or write /-R (**Figure 2.42**).

2. Mark the Remember Last Category box.

✔ Tip

■ Tapping the Applications button repeatedly scrolls through the categories, but you won't see everything: Unfiled programs don't appear. So, to take advantage of this switching view, be sure to file your unfiled programs.

Memory Management

Palm data is teeny compared to data on a typical PC, but you can still get carried away and load your memory to maximum capacity.

To view the amount of free memory:

1. From the Applications screen, choose Info from the App menu, or write ╱-I. Under Palm OS 3.5 and later, you can tap the Info icon (**ⓘ**) on the command bar.

2. The Size button displays memory usage in kilobytes (**Figure 2.43**); tap the Records button to view how many records are stored in each application; tap the Version button to see each program's version number (**Figure 2.44**).

3. Tap Done when finished.

Deleting Applications

At some point a program will no longer hold your attention, or maybe it's time to free up some memory to add more applications. Deleting the ones you don't want is painless.

To delete applications:

1. From within Applications, choose Delete from the App menu, or write ╱-D. Under Palm OS 3.5 and later, you can also tap the Delete icon (🗑) on the command bar.

2. Choose the application you wish to remove, then tap the Delete button and confirm your choice.

✔ Tips

- You cannot delete the Palm OS's built-in applications; they are stored in ROM.

- When you delete an application, any data files associated with it are deleted as well.

- To quickly jump down to the program you want to delete, write the first letter of its name in the Graffiti area.

Figure 2.43 View your memory usage from within Applications by choosing Info from the App menu.

Figure 2.44 The Info dialog box is also where you can see the version numbers of the Palm OS and installed software.

Replacing the Applications Application

The Applications screen does its job moderately well, but people with more than a handful of programs soon grow weary of scrolling. It wasn't long before an enterprising programmer built a way out of the old Applications box.

The result was Eric Kenslow's LaunchPad, one of those programs that makes you want to say, "Why didn't they think of that sooner?" Currently, a few variations of LaunchPad have appeared, but the current favorite seems to be Launcher X (www.launcherx.com).

Instead of one long scrolling field, Launcher X provides a configurable tabbed interface, visual and numeric battery level display, and time and date display (**Figure 2.45**). It also hooks into many features of the Palm OS such as Show/Hide Records, backlighting, Lock & Turn Off, and dragging programs to a trash icon to delete them.

Perhaps the best improvement is the ability to categorize applications simply by dragging their icons to a tab. Forget the endless popup menus in Applications' Category screen.

✔ Tips

- Launcher X makes it easy to work with files stored on an expansion card. Tap the Card Tools icon (it looks like a SD card) to move, copy, and delete files between your Palm's built-in memory and the card.

- Launch 'Em includes an extra feature that allows you to hide individual tabs, so you can keep some programs and their data under at least one level of security (**Figure 2.46**).

Figure 2.45 A familiar tabbed interface greets users of Launcher X, a replacement application launcher based on Eric Kenslow's LaunchPad utility.

Figure 2.46 Launcher X provides many more options for working with, and viewing, your applications.

Security Settings

You're probably carrying around your most important information in a device no bigger than your hand. Although you're no doubt careful with your organizer, there's a half-decent chance that it may get swiped, or even left on top of your car as you're rushing off to work. The Palm OS's built-in security features provide a first line of defense in case your Palm is picked up by the wrong person.

The Security preferences (which in earlier versions of the Palm OS exist as a separate application) control whether or not records marked private—no matter which program they reside in—are shown or hidden (**Figure 2.47**). Palm OS 3.5 enhanced Security by adding a third option that masks private records (**Figure 2.48**). It also provided a means for changing the global security setting within individual programs, saving a trip to the Security application itself.

To set up a password:

1. Tap the dotted Password box, which should read Unassigned if this is your first time using Security.

2. Enter a password and a hint, then tap OK.

3. Re-enter your password to verify it.

To change or delete a password:

1. Tap the dotted Password box, which should read Assigned.

2. Enter your current password.

3. Write a new password to change it; tap the Delete button if you want to not have an assigned password at all.

4. If you changed your password, re-enter it to verify it.

Figure 2.47 Security controls whether records marked as Private throughout the Palm OS are shown or hidden.

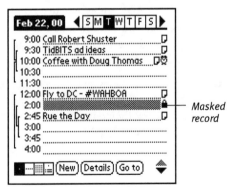

Masked record

Figure 2.48 Palm OS 3.5 added the capability to mask private records instead of just hiding them.

Figure 2.49 If you want to see your data again, write your password in the blank provided.

Figure 2.50 If you've forgotten your password, your private records will be deleted until the next HotSync.

Figure 2.51 To be diligent about securing your data, enable the Auto Lock Handheld feature.

To use the Lock & Turn Off feature:

1. In the Security application, tap the Lock & Turn Off button. You will be prompted to verify your choice.

2. The next time you turn on your handheld, enter your password to access your data (**Figure 2.49**).

To access a forgotten password:

1. If you've forgotten your password, you can remove it, but at a price. Tap the Password field, then tap the Lost Password button in the Password screen.

2. If you wish to proceed, tap Yes (**Figure 2.50**). The state of the Password field will revert to Unassigned.

To automatically lock your handheld:

1. Tap the Auto Lock Handheld field.

2. Select a time period to have Security automatically lock your device. The default is Never, but you can choose to engage the feature whenever the handheld is turned off, at a specific time of the day, or after a delay of several minutes or hours (**Figure 2.51**). Tap OK.

✔ Tips

- You don't have to set up a password if you don't want to. Setting Security to hide or mask records without specifying a password still makes private records unreadable. You won't be asked to provide a password if you switch to Show Records.

- Don't use easy passwords: birthdates, addresses, family members' names, and especially pet names. The best passwords are a combination of letters, numbers, and symbols.

- Unlike earlier releases, Palm OS 4.0 and higher recognize upper- and lowercase letters.

SECURITY SETTINGS

Beaming Applications

All but the first Palm devices possess the ability to send data between similar devices equipped with infrared hardware. In addition to sending records (such as addresses), you can transfer full applications.

To beam applications:

1. From the Applications screen, choose Beam from the App menu, or write ╱-B. Under Palm OS 3.5 and later, you can also tap the Beam icon (📡) from the command bar.

2. Select an application from the list that appears (**Figure 2.52**). Programs marked with a padlock symbol beside them cannot be beamed.

3. Aim your infrared port at the recipient's handheld and tap the Beam button.

To receive beamed applications:

1. Go to the Preferences application and make sure that Beam Receive is set to On in the General preferences screen.

2. Aim your infrared port at the sender's handheld and wait for her to initiate the transfer.

3. When the application has been beamed, choose to accept or deny the program (**Figure 2.53**).

✔ Tips

- Palm asserts that infrared transfers can be achieved from a maximum distance of one meter (39.37 inches).

- Write the ShortCut ℓ .| (shortcut stroke, period, I) in any text field, which activates Beam Receive in the General preferences for a single instance.

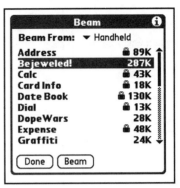

Figure 2.52 Beam programs from the Applications screen.

Figure 2.53 Choose whether or not to accept a beamed application.

Beaming under Tight Memory

If you don't have much free memory on your organizer, you may have trouble beaming applications or records to another handheld: the Palm OS needs enough free memory to store a temporary copy of what you're beaming. So if you're trying to beam a large app and getting an out of memory error, you need to delete some files first. The good news is that if the recipient's handheld has plenty of free space on it, you can temporarily beam smaller files to her, delete them from your device, then get them back after you've transferred the larger file.

BEAMING APPLICATIONS

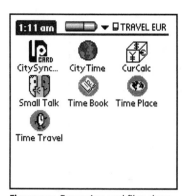

Figure 2.54 Expansion card files show up in the Applications screen as if they belong to another category.

Figure 2.55 You don't need a special application to transfer data files under Palm OS 4.0 and higher.

Figure 2.56 Sony Memory Sticks are formatted hierarchically like Windows disks.

Using Expansion Cards

Expansion cards provide extra memory to store more data: but how do you access the data and copy it to and from the cards? Palm OS 4.0 and higher supports data transfers from the Applications screen; the Sony CLIÉ models use different (but similar in functionality) programs for transfers.

To access files:

Insert an expansion card into the slot on the Palm device. The Applications screen will display a new category containing the programs stored on the card. The category name includes an icon indicating that you're looking at the card's contents (**Figure 2.54**).

To transfer files:

1. Go to the Applications screen.

2. Choose Copy from the App menu, or write ✏-C. The Copy dialog box appears.

3. Set the Copy To popup menu to the file's destination (**Figure 2.55**). The Copy From popup menu changes automatically.

4. Highlight a file and tap the Copy button.

5. Tap Done.

To transfer files on the Sony CLIÉ:

1. Launch the CLIE Files program.

2. From the popup menu in the upper-right corner, select either MS (Memory Stick) or Internal to choose files to copy.

3. Locate and tap the checkbox of the file you want to transfer. Data on Memory Sticks are stored hierarchically with a Windows-like interface. Tapping folders opens them; tapping the up arrow exits a folder (**Figure 2.56**).

4. Tap the Copy or Move buttons to transfer the file, or Delete to get rid of it.

Bluetooth Networking

If you've spent years fighting cords and cables, as I have, you'll love Bluetooth. This wireless networking technology is built into some Palm OS handhelds as well as an increasing number of computers and cellular phones. It works within a relatively short range, which makes it ideal for communicating between, say, two handhelds or a handheld and a cellular phone.

Bluetooth works by setting up pairs of trusted devices—just as you wouldn't (or shouldn't) start screaming at lots of people in a crowded room, you need to set up a one-on-one relationship with another Bluetooth device. Once you've established a pair, you can send messages or files, browse directories, or use one device to act as a gateway for another (such as getting online).

To set up your device for Bluetooth:

1. Go to the Bluetooth preferences in the Prefs application (**Figure 2.57**).

2. Select On from the Bluetooth popup menu.

3. Optionally, configure these other settings:

   ▲ **Device Name:** Your HotSync user name appears here by default. If you want a different name, tap the field and enter a new name.

   ▲ **Discoverable:** This lets other Bluetooth devices locate your handheld.

   ▲ **Allow Wakeup (or "Connectable" on some devices):** When the handheld turns off, it is no longer discoverable. To let trusted devices connect while your device is off, set this popup menu to Yes. You can also set a time frame for this feature by choosing Scheduled and tapping the time field that appears (**Figure 2.58**).

4. Tap Done to exit Preferences.

Figure 2.57 Set up Bluetooth network connections in Bluetooth preferences.

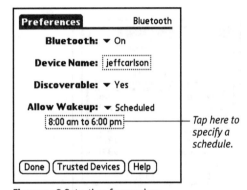

Tap here to specify a schedule.

Figure 2.58 Set a time frame when other devices can connect to your Palm, even if it's powered off.

Figure 2.59 The Discovery Results screen shows you which Bluetooth devices are nearby.

Figure 2.60 Passkeys ensure that no one can connect to your device clandestinely.

Figure 2.61 Transfer applications using Bluetooth networking.

To pair with a trusted device:

1. In the Bluetooth preferences screen, tap the Trusted Devices button.

2. Tap the Add Device button to begin searching for other signals within range. The Discovery Results screen displays which devices responded (**Figure 2.59**).

   If you don't see the one you expected, tap the Find More button to initiate another search. Make sure the other device has Bluetooth active and is discoverable.

3. Select a device by tapping its name, then tap OK.

4. When prompted, enter a passkey for that device. This is a password or series of numbers that you and the other device's owner have agreed to use (**Figure 2.60**). Tap OK.

   The other person then needs to enter the same passkey. They also have the option to add your device to their trusted list.

5. Tap Done to exit the Trusted Devices screen, or Add Device if you want to pair with another one.

To transfer files via Bluetooth:

1. Once a Bluetooth pair is made, switch to the Applications screen.

2. Choose Send from the App menu.

3. Select the file you wish to send and tap the Send button.

4. In the Send With dialog box, select Bluetooth and tap OK (**Figure 2.61**). The Palm then searches for other devices.

5. Tap the name of a trusted device and tap OK.

To connect to a Bluetooth-enabled cellular phone:

1. Go to the Connection preferences and click New to create a new connection.

2. Select Phone from the popup menu marked Connect to.

3. From the Via popup menu, select Bluetooth (**Figure 2.62**).

4. Tap the field next to Device to locate the Bluetooth phone.

5. Choose a phone model from the Model popup menu.

6. Tap OK to exit the Connection preferences screen.

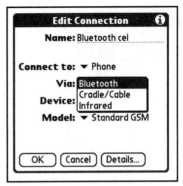

Figure 2.62 Connect to a Bluetooth-enabled cellular phone.

✔ Tips

- Once connected to a phone, you can get onto the Internet. See Chapters 9 and 10.

- I use a USB Bluetooth adapter with a couple of different computers, and have found that sometimes I need to re-establish a trusted pair between my Palm and the computer if I'm having trouble connecting.

- If you use a Bluetooth-capable Macintosh along with a Bluetooth Palm, I highly recommend installing Salling Clicker (www.salling.com). With it you can control your Mac from the Palm to do numerous things: control PowerPoint or Keynote presentations remotely; play music using iTunes; search for and display digital photos using iPhoto; and just about anything else that can be scripted on the Mac using AppleScript. Clicker also has a proximity sensor, so you can set up actions that trigger when you enter the room, such as playing your favorite song or even firing up a Web browser and loading your favorite sites.

BLUETOOTH NETWORKING

Figure 2.63 Opening the Wi-Fi preferences initiates a network scan.

Figure 2.64 Encrypted networks require a WEP key to access.

A Head Start on Wi-Fi Handhelds

As of this writing, the Palm Tungsten C and Sony CLIÉ PEG-UX50 are the only Palm OS devices with built-in Wi-Fi support, but the CLIÉ PEG-NZ90 can also get connected using a Wi-Fi Compact Flash card. Look for more devices with integrated Wi-Fi to appear soon as the technology becomes widely adopted.

Wi-Fi Networking

A friend of mine recently moved into a new house where the previous owner had spent a great deal of time wiring every room with Ethernet for easy networking. A great idea, to be sure, but it might be a couple of years too late. Wi-Fi networking (also known by its technical moniker, 802.11b networking) enables you to connect multiple computers in your house or office without running a meter of wire, as well as go to several coffeeshops with a Wi-Fi enabled laptop—or, recently, Palm OS handheld.

The easiest method for connecting to a Wi-Fi network is to use Palm's Wi-Fi Setup application, if present on your device. However, I'm going to cover the settings found in the Preferences application, so you can tweak them later if necessary.

To connect to a Wi-Fi network:

1. Open the Wi-Fi preferences and select On from the Wi-Fi popup menu. The device will start scanning for a nearby Wi-Fi network (**Figure 2.63**).

2. Tap the Network popup menu to view a list of networks, then choose the one you wish to use.

3. Some Wi-Fi networks require a WEP (Wireless Equivalent Password) key to access them. If this is the case, enter the WEP key in the dialog that appears; you need to get this information from the network's administrator (**Figure 2.64**).

4. Once you're connected, tap Done to exit the Wi-Fi preferences.

WI-FI NETWORKING

To connect to a closed Wi-Fi network:

1. If you do not see the network you're expecting in the Wi-Fi preferences' Network popup menu, it could be closed, accessible only to those who know of its existence. In this case, choose Edit Networks from the same popup menu.

2. Tap the Add button.

3. Enter the name of the network in the Network Name (SSID) field (**Figure 2.65**). If access is password-protected, mark the WEP Encryption checkbox and enter the WEP key (as before, you need to get this information from the network's administrator).

4. Tap OK if you're finished connecting to the network.

To manually assign IP numbers:

1. Many Wi-Fi networks assign an IP (Internet Protocol) address to computers when they connect; this information routes Internet traffic to your device. By default, this automatic setting is in place. But if you need to manually specify an IP address, tap the Details button instead of OK at step number 4, above.

2. Tap the Advanced button (**Figure 2.66**).

3. Change the IP Address popup menu to Manual. You can then enter the appropriate information.

4. If necessary, enter addresses for DNS (Domain Name Service) servers, which translate understandable Web addresses, such as www.jeffcarlson.com, into the correct IP address numbers.

✔ Tip

■ For much more about Wi-Fi networking, go get the *Wireless Networking Starter Kit*, by Glenn Fleishman and Adam Engst.

Figure 2.65 You need to supply the name and password to connect to a closed network.

Figure 2.66 If the Wi-Fi network isn't doling out IP addresses, you need to manually specify here.

WI-FI NETWORKING

3

HOTSYNC

The underlying approach to functionality in the Palm OS is almost more philosophical than practical: the handheld is not a computer in itself, but an extension of one's computing environment. It recognizes that people aren't going to abandon PCs in favor of PDAs, but rather use both tools to accomplish the greater task of organizing and managing one's information. For it is this goal, grasshopper, that leads to greater productivity, plus the justification to purchase yet another cool electronic gadget.

The key that unlocks this data convergence is the HotSync feature, the ability to synchronize data between the handheld and the PC—not just copy it from one box to the other. This is an important distinction, because it means both platforms will always have the most current information at your disposal.

HotSync Overview

Performing a HotSync operation is essentially a one-step procedure: push a button and it happens. You can do this when connected directly to your PC, or over a modem or network. However, knowing about what's going on in the background will help you deal with potential problems in the future.

How HotSync works

In normal copy operations, such as when you copy a file from a CD-ROM to your hard drive, the PC's operating system checks to see if a similarly named file exists in the location you're copying to. If a match is found, it checks the modification dates of each file to determine which is newer, then throws up a dialog box requesting confirmation to continue (under some operating systems, this feature can be disabled). If the user clicks OK, the old file is overwritten. The problem here exists when both files have been separately modified; if so, the older data is wiped out (**Figure 3.1**).

In contrast, the Palm OS (by way of the Hot-Sync Manager on the PC) compares every record within a file like the Address Book database. If you make a change to different records on the handheld and the desktop, the changes appear on both platforms following a HotSync. If you make separate changes to the same record on each platform, both versions are retained, and you are notified of the duplication (**Figure 3.2**).

Standard file date comparison

Entire file copied   *New records deleted*

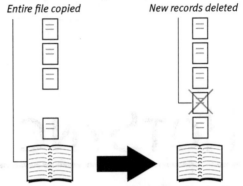

Figure 3.1 Most files on your PC are "synchronized" by comparing their modification dates and overwriting the older file—big trouble if both files have changed.

HotSync synchronization

New records added   *Each record compared*

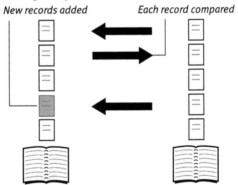

Figure 3.2 HotSync synchronization compares each record within Palm database files, ensuring that you have up-to-date information on your handheld and on your PC.

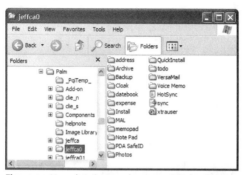

Figure 3.3 Your data is stored on your PC's hard drive, in the user folder matching your Palm user name.

Table 3.1

User Folder Contents (Windows)

FOLDER	CONTENTS
address	Address Book data
Backup	Nearly everything except data for the built-in applications. This includes program files, related database files, Doc text files, some preferences files, etc.
datebook	Date Book data
Install	Program files to be installed at the next HotSync. See the Tip on this page for important information about this folder.
memopad	Memo Pad data
Note Pad	Note Pad data
QuickInstall	Files to be installed on the handheld or on expansion media
todo	To Do List data

Table 3.2

User Folder Contents (Macintosh)

FOLDER	CONTENTS
user name	No funky truncation of the user name on the Mac—in my case, the folder is titled "Jeff Carlson." The file within, User Data, contains all of the built-in databases' data.
Conduit Settings	Preferences for each conduit
Archived Files	Records deleted from the device, but stored on the desktop computer
Files to Install	Files to be transferred at the next HotSync
Backups	Everything else

Where HotSync stores your data

A HotSync operation copies data from the handheld to the PC and vice-versa, which means that information has to live on your hard drive—but where?

When you install the Palm Desktop software, enter your name (or whatever name you wish to use) at the Create User Account screen. This name becomes the name of the device.

You'll find a new folder on your hard drive named "Palm" (unless you specified a different location and folder name during setup). Within that folder is a folder that closely matches your User Name; on my PC, for example, the files are located in the folder "CarlsoJ" (**Figure 3.3**), though on my Mac it comes up as "Jeff Carlson." The information in **Table 3.1** and **Table 3.2** details the folder structure on each platform.

✔ Tips

- When you run the Palm Quick Install utility, the programs you choose are stored in the Install folder within your user folder. However, under Windows you can't just toss .prc files there and expect them to be transferred at the next HotSync. The HotSync Manager needs to be told that the Install folder is "active" before it will copy the files located within. Running the Install program once toggles this setting—so, after you install one program using the Palm Install Tool, switch to the Windows desktop to copy new program files to the folder in bulk.

- The Backup(s) folder stores all programs you've installed on your handheld—even ones you've deleted from the handheld. So, if the folder size seems impossibly large, don't be alarmed.

- It's a good—no, great—idea to regularly make backups of your user folder.

HOTSYNC OVERVIEW

Configuring HotSync Manager

The HotSync Manager isn't often seen, but it does quite a bit of work behind the scenes to ensure that your data is transferring properly. Its primary task is to monitor the port reserved for the HotSync cradle so it can act when the handheld signals a sync operation.

To access the HotSync Manager under Windows:

From within Palm Desktop, choose Setup from the HotSync menu. You can also click the HotSync icon on the Taskbar, then select Setup from the popup menu (**Figure 3.4**).

To access the HotSync Manager under Mac OS:

Launch HotSync Manager from the Palm folder on your hard disk, or choose Setup from the HotSync (*active user name*) submenu of the Instant Palm Desktop menu (from the Dock in Mac OS X, or next to the Applications menu in Mac OS 9; **Figure 3.5**).

To enable HotSync port monitoring:

Make sure the cable attached to your HotSync cradle is connected to one of your PC's USB or serial ports.

Access the HotSync Manager as described above and go to the Setup screen. Under Windows, you have three options for enabling port monitoring (**Figure 3.6**):

◆ **Always available.** Activates HotSync Manager when you start your computer.

◆ **Available only when Palm Desktop is running.** Enables and disables port monitoring when you use Palm Desktop.

◆ **Manual.** Starts port monitoring at your discretion, freeing up the port for other uses when you're not using HotSync.

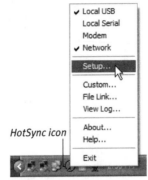

HotSync icon

Figure 3.4 The HotSync icon on the Windows Taskbar offers a quick way to configure HotSync settings.

Figure 3.5 The Mac Palm Desktop software includes the Instant Palm Desktop menu, where you can access HotSync Manager commands.

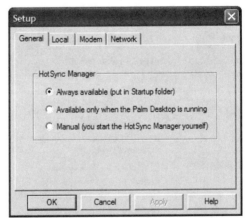

Figure 3.6 Choose when HotSync Manager will be active to avoid port conflicts with other devices.

CONFIGURING HOTSYNC MANAGER

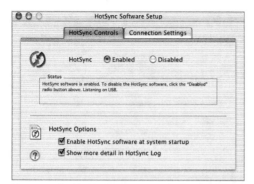

Figure 3.7 Enable HotSync port monitoring from the HotSync Controls tab on the Macintosh.

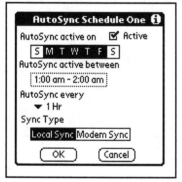

Figure 3.8 Schedule your HotSync operations at a more convenient hour with AutoSync.

Under the Mac OS, you can leave HotSync running all the time by selecting Enable HotSync software at system startup under HotSync Options, or you can choose the Enabled or Disabled radio buttons at the top of the screen (**Figure 3.7**).

✔ Tips

■ Do you find yourself forgetting to Hot-Sync during the course of your busy day? Let the handheld do the work for you: AutoSync (`www.rgps.com/Auto-Sync.html`) can automatically HotSync your handheld according to one or two schedules. Be sure to have your computer running and the handheld in its cradle, then let it go to work (**Figure 3.8**).

■ There never seem to be enough ports on a computer. If you don't want to switch cables each time you need to print or perform a HotSync, consider buying an inexpensive hub that connects multiple devices.

■ If you use an older Macintosh with a serial port (as opposed to newer machines with USB), make sure that AppleTalk is disabled before attempting to perform a HotSync: in the Chooser, select the AppleTalk Inactive radio button. AppleTalk can hog the serial port and not allow other applications, like HotSync Manager, to use it. The same is often true of fax software.

CONFIGURING HOTSYNC MANAGER

Setting Up Conduits

Each of the built-in applications, as well as the Palm OS and the program installer, has its own conduit, a software translator that specifies how records should be compared and copied between platforms. Additionally, many third-party applications, such as AvantGo, include their own conduits for manipulating their specific data.

To configure conduits:

1. Choose Custom from the HotSync menu in Windows. Under the Mac OS, launch the HotSync Manager and choose Conduit Settings from the HotSync menu, or press Command-J.

2. Highlight the conduit you wish to edit, then click the Change (Windows) or Conduit Settings (Mac) button. Double-clicking a conduit also lets you modify its settings (**Figure 3.9**).

3. Choose an action for that conduit (**Figure 3.10** and **Table 3.3**). Click the Set as default checkbox (Windows) or the Make Default button (Mac) to make the new setting permanent each time you do a HotSync. Click OK.

Under Windows, clicking the Default button in the Custom dialog box restores the conduit settings to the last default state.

✔ Tip

- Many people use PIMs such as Microsoft Outlook and Symantec's ACT! instead of Palm Desktop. In addition to the Outlook conduits included with the Palm software, a variety of third-party applications, like PocketMirror (www.chapura.com), replace the built-in conduits with ones that synchronize data with your favorite desktop PIM.

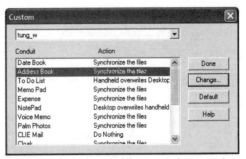

Figure 3.9 Conduits control the way each program's data is handled during a HotSync.

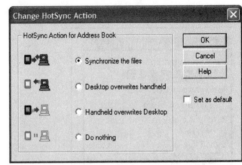

Figure 3.10 Multiple HotSync actions let you override the default synchronization settings.

Table 3.3

HotSync Conduit Actions	
SETTING	ACTION
Synchronize the files	All records are compared individually; newer records overwrite older records.
Desktop overwrites handheld	Individual records are not compared; entire desktop file replaces handheld file.
Handheld overwrites desktop	Individual records are not compared; entire handheld file replaces desktop file.
Do nothing	Records are skipped; no action is taken.

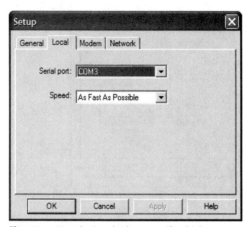

Figure 3.11 Use the Local tab to specify which port your HotSync cradle is connected to.

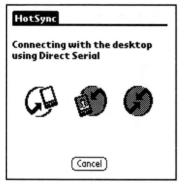

Figure 3.12 Pressing the HotSync button on the cradle activates the HotSync; the progression is visible on both the handheld and the PC.

Local HotSync

Most of your HotSync actions fall into the category of Local HotSync, in which the handheld and PC are connected directly by either a serial cable or cradle, or via infrared.

To set up a Local HotSync:

1. Launch Palm Desktop or the HotSync Manager and choose Setup from the HotSync menu.

2. Click the Local tab (Windows, **Figure 3.11**) or the Connection Settings tab (Mac).

3. Windows: From the Serial port popup menu, specify the COM port to which your HotSync cable or cradle is connected.

4. Specify the speed of the connection from the Speed popup menu. Click OK, or close the window.

5. From the Windows Taskbar popup menu, specify that Local HotSync monitoring should be activated by clicking the name; a checkmark appears. On the Macintosh, this information is available in the Connection Settings window.

✔ Tip

■ If you're having trouble maintaining a connection, reduce the speed setting in the Setup dialog box.

To perform a Local HotSync:

1. Place your device in the cradle.

2. Push the HotSync button on the front, or press the button in the HotSync application on the handheld. A short series of tones indicates a successful connection.

3. A window appears on the desktop indicating the HotSync progression. A similar screen also appears on the handheld (**Figure 3.12**). Another set of tones indicates when the synchronization is done.

Bluetooth HotSync

Forget the cradle or a USB cable—if your handheld and PC support Bluetooth, you can synchronize wirelessly. It takes a small amount of setup the first time, but connecting wirelessly is worth it (see Chapter 2 for more on configuring Bluetooth).

To set up a Bluetooth connection:

1. Launch the HotSync application on your handheld.

2. Choose Connection Setup from the Options menu.

3. Tap New, then name the connection "Bluetooth".

4. Select PC from the Connect to popup menu.

5. Change the Via popup menu selection to Bluetooth (**Figure 3.13**).

6. Tap the Device field to locate your Bluetooth-enabled PC.

7. Choose your PC from the results list.

8. Tap Done to return to HotSync.

To perform a HotSync via Bluetooth:

1. Launch HotSync on your handheld.

2. Make sure the Local button is highlighted.

3. Choose Bluetooth from the connection popup menu located under the main HotSync button (**Figure 3.14**).

4. Tap the HotSync button to synchronize.

✔ Tip

■ I find that when using a removeable Bluetooth module on my laptop, I often need to re-establish the PC as a trusted device if the HotSync operation doesn't initially work.

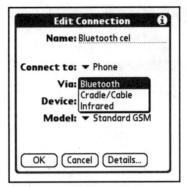

Figure 3.13 On Bluetooth-enabled devices, "Bluetooth" appears as a connection type.

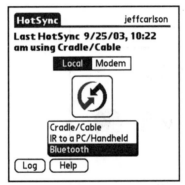

Figure 3.14 With Bluetooth set up, simply select it from the popup menu below the HotSync button before synchronizing.

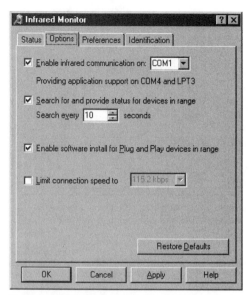

Figure 3.15 If your laptop or desktop PC is equipped with an infrared port, you can set your preferences to recognize the handheld and perform a HotSync.

Figure 3.16 Use the HotSync application on the Palm to initiate an infrared HotSync operation.

Infrared HotSync

Knowing a good opportunity when it zaps them in the head, the engineers at Palm incorporated infrared HotSync capabilities into the Palm OS. The system's IR communication is built upon the IrCOMM protocol.

To set up infrared HotSync (Mac):

1. Open the HotSync Manager, and switch to the Serial Port Settings tab.

2. Choose Infrared from the Port popup menu under Local Setup.

To set up infrared HotSync (Win):

1. Open the Infrared Monitor from the Settings folder and click the Options tab.

2. Check the box labeled Enable infrared communication on, and choose the COM port (usually COM4 or COM5) used by the infrared port (**Figure 3.15**).

3. In the HotSync Manager, choose the COM port as the Local source.

To perform an infrared HotSync:

1. Launch the HotSync application on the Palm device, and make sure that IR to a PC/ Handheld is selected from the Connection popup menu.

2. Tap the large HotSync button to begin (**Figure 3.16**).

INFRARED HOTSYNC

Modem HotSync

Make sure you have disabled any programs on your PC (such as fax software) that may cause HotSync headaches.

To set up a Modem HotSync on your computer:

1. Choose Setup from the HotSync menu to bring up the Setup dialog box.

2. Click the Modem tab (Windows, **Figure 3.17**) or the Connection Settings tab (Mac; skip to step 5).

3. From the Serial Port popup menu, specify the COM or serial port to which your modem is connected.

4. Specify the speed of the connection from the Speed popup menu. Click OK, or close the window.

5. From the Taskbar popup menu, specify that Modem HotSync monitoring should be activated by clicking the name; a checkmark appears. On the Mac, click the checkbox next to Internal Modem (**Figure 3.18**).

To set up a Modem HotSync on your Palm device:

1. Launch the HotSync application.

2. Choose Conduit Setup from the Options menu, or write ⁄-D.

3. Choose which conduits should be run by marking the checkboxes to the left of each program's name (**Figure 3.19**). Tap OK.

4. If you haven't set up your Modem preferences, choose Connection Setup from the Options menu (and see Chapter 2).

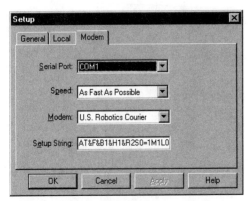

Figure 3.17 As with a Local HotSync, specify your modem's COM port and speed, as well as the model.

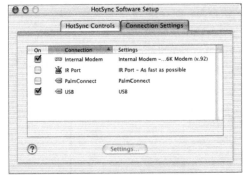

Figure 3.18 Mark the Internal Modem checkbox in the Mac Connection Settings screen.

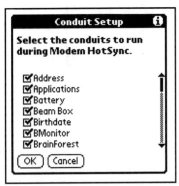

Figure 3.19 To save some connection time, mark only the conduits you want to have synchronized.

Figure 3.20 With everything configured, simply tap the HotSync button.

To perform a Modem HotSync:

1. Go to the main HotSync screen and tap the Modem button.

2. Tap the dotted Enter Phone # box (under the Connection popup menu) to specify a phone number.

3. Attach a compatible modem (connected to a phone line, of course) to your handheld.

4. If you're using a modem with a HotSync button on the case, push it to initiate the HotSync (and skip the next step). If not, launch the HotSync application on the handheld.

5. Tap the main HotSync button (**Figure 3.20**). You should hear the startup tones.

6. When the HotSync is complete, you'll hear the tones signaling the end, and the connection will terminate.

MODEM HOTSYNC

LANSync/Network HotSync

Network HotSync extends your range and flexibility by providing a method to synchronize your data from any computer on your PC network—whether it's using someone else's HotSync cradle down the hall or several states away. (Network HotSync isn't available for Macintosh computers.) If your network has dial-in remote access, you can also connect using a compatible modem.

To set up a Network HotSync:

1. Launch the HotSync application.

2. Depending on which mode you're in, pressing the HotSync icon will attempt to connect directly to the PC attached to the current HotSync cradle, or to your PC out on the network. If you're dialing in to a modem that acts as the gateway for a network, choose Modem Sync Prefs from the Options menu, or write /-O. Tap either the Network or Direct to modem button to specify the Modem Sync action (**Figure 3.21**).

   If you're connected directly to the network, choose LANSync Prefs from the Options menu, or write /-L. Choose between LANSync and Local HotSync (**Figure 3.22**).

3. Choose Primary PC Setup from the Options menu, or write /-P. In most cases, you shouldn't have to change this information, since it's downloaded from your PC when you perform a HotSync.

4. On your PC, bring up the HotSync settings by choosing Setup from either the HotSync menu within Palm Desktop or from the popup menu on the Taskbar.

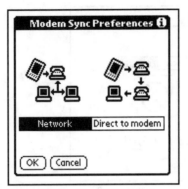

Figure 3.21 The Modem Sync Preferences dialog box lets you choose between a direct dial-up connection or a dial-up network connection.

Figure 3.22 By choosing LANSync or Local HotSync, you dictate the action of the main screen's HotSync button.

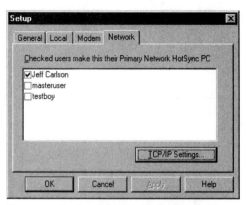

Figure 3.23 The Network tab in the HotSync Setup screen sets up your PC for LAN synchronization.

Figure 3.24 Dial up your network by tapping the Modem button, then tap the HotSync button.

5. Tap the Network tab, then place a checkmark next to the users who will have access to your machine (**Figure 3.23**).

6. If you need to adjust the TCP/IP configuration, click the TCP/IP Settings button. Otherwise, click OK.

To perform a Network HotSync:

◆ If the computer you're connecting from is on the same local area network (LAN) or wide area network (WAN), and you've set the LANSync preferences to LANSync, tap the Local button, then tap the Hot-Sync icon to connect.

◆ If you need to dial in via modem to connect to your network, and you've set the Modem Sync preferences to Network, tap the Modem button, then tap the single HotSync button. Under Palm OS 3.1, tap the Modem Sync icon to dial the number and establish a connection (**Figure 3.24**). Once connected, the HotSync operation should proceed normally.

✔ Tip

■ Wi-Fi enabled devices such as the Palm Tungsten C don't really need a cradle to HotSync. Set up a Network HotSync to your PC and synchronize using the faster 802.11b wireless network if you have one.

Viewing the HotSync Log

The details of each of the last ten HotSyncs are stored in a text file on your computer. Although the information usually isn't important, the HotSync Log is the first place to turn to if you're having HotSync problems (fortunately, most error messages are written in understandable English; **Figure 3.25**).

To view the HotSync Log:

◆ **Windows:** Choose View Log from the HotSync menu within Palm Desktop or from the HotSync popup menu located on the Taskbar (**Figure 3.26**).

◆ **Mac OS:** Choose View Log from the HotSync menu within the HotSync Manager.

◆ **Palm OS:** Tap the Log button on the main HotSync screen. However, don't get angry with me for suggesting it, since the Palm HotSync Log gives only the most basic of information (like the scintillating "OK Date Book").

◆ Alternately, open the log file itself with a word processor or text editor. You'll find the log in your user folder.

✔ Tip

■ To record a detailed log on the Macintosh (instead of the minimal log that's stored on the handheld), mark the Show more detail in HotSync log checkbox at the bottom of the HotSync Controls screen.

```
HotSync started 09/03/01 02:12:12
   - Installed file: C:\Palm\CarlsoJ\
Install\giraffe.prc
OK Install
OK Mail
OK Date Book
OK Address Book
OK To Do List
OK Memo Pad
OK Expense
ZoskSync Conduit 2.3.3 Begin:
   ZoskSync: No reports were transferred
from the handheld.
OK ZoskSync Conduit End
```

Figure 3.25 A typical HotSync Log looks like this, with plain-English comments to indicate the steps taken.

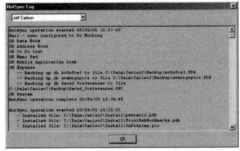

Figure 3.26 The HotSync Log can be viewed from within Palm Desktop (Windows version shown here), or you can use a word processor or text editor to read the file from your hard drive.

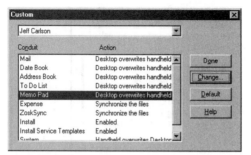

Figure 3.27 In the event of a hard reset, your first HotSync should be set so that the desktop information overwrites the handheld's data.

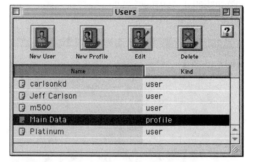

Figure 3.28 Sharing one computer with multiple Palm devices entails creating a new user account for each person. The Macintosh screen is shown here.

Multiple HotSync Options

The majority of owners use their handhelds on an individual basis: one organizer, one PC. However, there are some cases where you may want to synchronize one device with multiple machines, or several organizers on the same machine.

Since HotSync *synchronizes* your data, not overwrites it, the information on each machine should remain updated without any special work on your part. Simply Hot-Sync as you normally would; the desktop software keeps track of multiple users.

However, if you should happen to lose your handheld's data (for example, due to a hard reset), customize your first HotSync as described here.

To set up a first HotSync on an empty Palm device:

1. On your PC, choose Custom from the HotSync popup menu on the Taskbar, or from the HotSync menu in the Palm Desktop application.

2. Specify Desktop overwrites handheld for all of the conduits (**Figure 3.27**). Click Done.

3. Perform a HotSync. Your data on the handheld should be in the state it was before it was lost.

4. Before you HotSync again, change the conduit settings back to Synchronize.

To set up a new user:

1. In Palm Desktop, select Edit Users from the User submenu of the HotSync menu (Mac), or select Users from the Tools menu (Windows).

2. Click the New (Windows) or New User (Mac) button (**Figure 3.28**) and type a name, then click OK; a new user appears.

MULTIPLE HOTSYNC OPTIONS

File Link

Frequently updating memos or addresses is made simple for Windows users. Using the File Link feature, you can create a Windows file that is in plain text (.txt), comma separated (.csv), or Palm archive format that gets transferred to the handheld according to scheduled intervals (**Figure 3.29**).

To create a File Link:

1. Prepare the file you wish to link. For example, let's say everyone who accesses my PC needs each week's movie box office listing. Save it as either straight text, comma-separated, or as a Memo Pad archive (see later in this chapter for details). If you're saving a list of addresses (say, the month's new clients), save the file as either comma-separated or as an Address Book archive.

2. Choose File Link from the HotSync menu in Palm Desktop, or the HotSync popup menu on the Taskbar.

3. Select a user name, make sure the Create a new link radio button is activated, and click the Next button.

4. Choose either Memo Pad or Address Book from the Application name popup menu.

5. If you know the path to your file, type it into the File path field. Otherwise, click the Browse button to locate it.

6. Linked file data is stored in its own category to avoid conflicts with your other data. Enter a name in the Category name field (**Figure 3.30**), and click Next.

7. A dialog box confirming your link settings appears. By default, the file will be queued for HotSync whenever it changes. If this is okay, click the Done button.

Figure 3.29 Set up a File Link that points to a file filled with important information that changes often.

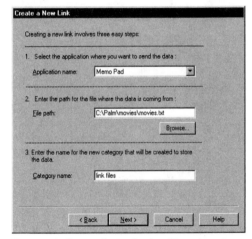

Figure 3.30 Choose the application, file path, and specify a category name to set up a File Link.

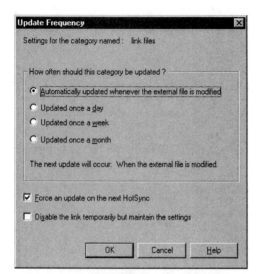

Figure 3.31 You can set the frequency at which the linked file is transferred to the handheld.

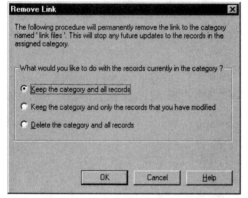

Figure 3.32 If you want to put your File Link into hibernation for a while, choose to keep the category and records, or just the category, for later.

To schedule a File Link update:

1. If you want to specify other options (such as daily, weekly, or monthly updates), click the Update Frequency button on the Confirm your Link Settings dialog.

2. Specify the interval for how often the category should be updated (**Figure 3.31**).

   If you know the file isn't going to change for a while, mark the checkbox next to Disable the link temporarily but maintain the settings.

3. Click OK to exit the Update Frequency dialog box, then click the Done button.

To remove a File Link:

1. Choose File Link from the HotSync menu in Palm Desktop, or the HotSync popup menu on the Taskbar.

2. Choose a user name, and select the option marked Modify or remove an existing link. Click the Next button.

3. Highlight the link you wish to delete and click the Remove button. The Remove Link dialog box appears.

4. Choose how you'd like to handle your existing linked data (**Figure 3.32**).

5. Click OK.

✔ Tips

- Although it may look like something's gone wrong, don't be surprised if, after you've set up a link, the category you set up appears to be empty. The linked data won't get copied to Palm Desktop until you perform a HotSync.

- Unfortunately, File Link is not available on the Macintosh.

FILE LINK

75

Working with Archived Records

When you delete a record from the handheld or the Palm Desktop, you're given the option to save it on your PC by marking the Archive deleted *program* item(s) at next HotSync checkbox (**Figure 3.33**). This is a great feature if you've accidentally deleted something, or if you need to free up some memory on your handheld, but don't want to lose the information permanently. But where does it go? And how do you get it back?

Each of the built-in applications creates an archive file (such as an Address Book archive (.aba) or Date Book archive (.dba)) for each category that contains deleted records. Those files are stored in each application's folder, although recent deleted items won't show up until you perform a HotSync (**Figure 3.34**).

To restore archived records:

1. In Palm Desktop, go to the Palm application module you want to restore records from (such as the Memo Pad). Choose Open Archive from the File menu.

2. In the Open Archive dialog box, highlight the archive file named after the category you're looking for (such as "Personal.mpa"), and click the Open button.

   Your deleted records are now visible in the main window. You'll see the name of the file, followed by "(Archive)" in the window's title bar (**Figure 3.35**).

3. Highlight the records you want to restore, and choose Copy from the Edit menu (or press Control/Command-C).

4. Switch back to your active Palm records by choosing Open Current from the File menu.

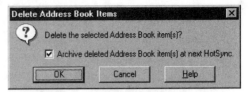

Figure 3.33 You may have seen this dialog dozens of times...but do you know where the data actually goes? If you mark the checkbox, you can retrieve deleted records from your PC's hard drive at any time.

Figure 3.34 Archives are named according to the deleted records' categories.

Archive indicators

Figure 3.35 Opening an archive file is straightforward, but the records are displayed in the main window, which can be confusing if you're not paying attention. Look to the title bar or an indicator in the lower-right to signal that an archive is currently active.

Figure 3.36 You don't have to limit yourself to using archives for resurrecting deleted data. Export selected records, or your entire set of addresses, to-do items, and memos into archive format.

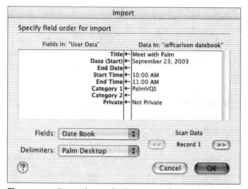

Figure 3.37 Records can be imported from tab-delimited files, in addition to Palm's archive formats.

5. Choose Paste from the Edit menu, or press Control/Command-V to paste the restored records.

6. Perform a HotSync to restore the data to your handheld.

You can also use the archive format to create customized archives, rather than just files containing deleted records. This can be useful if you need to email a batch of addresses to another Palm device owner, for example.

To export archive files in Palm Desktop:

1. Go to the Palm application module you wish to export. If you want to export only certain records, highlight them.

2. Choose Export from the File menu. In the Export As dialog box, choose Currently selected records if you're not exporting the entire contents of the application. Give the file a unique file name, then click the Export button (**Figure 3.36**).

Note that if you have private records hidden, you will need to choose Show private records from the View menu before exporting them.

To import archive files in Palm Desktop:

1. Go to the Palm application module you wish to import.

2. Choose Import from the File menu. In the Import dialog box, highlight a file and click OK (**Figure 3.37**).

✔ Tips

- You can also import records in text-only and comma-delimited file formats.

- Change the category for many records at once: export them, switch to the new category, then import them back in.

Creating HotSync Profiles

Profiles allow you to set up a group of master records that can be transferred to new Palm devices. For example, you can set up a profile containing your company's important meetings to be copied to each person's handheld. However, the profile erases any existing data, so you can only copy a profile to a brand new or empty device.

To create a HotSync profile:

1. Windows: In Palm Desktop, select Users from the Tools menu.

   Macintosh: In Palm Desktop, go to the HotSync menu and select Edit Users from the User submenu.

2. Windows: In the Users dialog box that appears, click the Profiles button to view a list of profiles. Click the New button (**Figure 3.38**).

   Macintosh: Profiles are marked in the Users window with a different icon (**Figure 3.39**). Click New Profile.

3. Windows: Highlight the name of your new profile and click OK.

   Macintosh: After your profile is created, click the close box in the upper-left corner, or press Command-W.

4. Stock your profile with the information that you want to appear on every Palm device you copy it to. Enter the data by hand, or switch between the profile and a user account to copy and paste records.

✔ Tip

- To preserve your existing categories when copying records to the profile, first set up the category names in your new profile. Then, in your user account, view by category and copy the records you want. Switch to the profile, view the similarly named category, and paste the records.

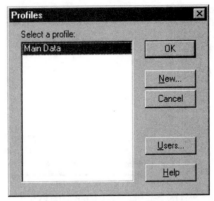

Figure 3.38 In the Profiles screen, you can toggle between the Users and the Profiles lists.

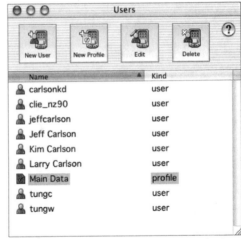

Figure 3.39 On the Mac, profiles are displayed using a separate icon. Click the Edit button to rename them.

CREATING HOTSYNC PROFILES

DATE BOOK

My mother called me at college one night to see how things were going. After updating her on my classes, friends, and the usual local intrigue, I inquired what was new with her. "Not much," she replied. "We just finished my birthday cake."

Oops. So, my brain isn't hardwired for dates and holidays—that doesn't mean I have to forever miss important events and appointments. Although Mom was good-humored about my chronological ineptitude, it made me realize that I needed more than just the rusting calendar in my head.

Now several years later, I use Date Book to store meetings, social occasions, and holidays, confident that they're quickly available at hand.

Plus, unlike the calendar that hangs in my kitchen, Date Book can remind me of events before they happen, not after. My mom should be proud.

Setting Preferences and Display Options

The 160 by 160 pixel screen on most Palm devices can display 25,600 pixels, which sounds like a lot until you consider that the minimum PC screen resolution today is 640 by 480 pixels (or a total of 307,200 pixels). It's easy to see why every effort has been made to keep the Palm's small screen uncluttered yet understandable. Even on high-resolution displays, simplicity is key. Date Book displays time in daily, weekly, and monthly views. The Agenda view, introduced in Palm OS 3.5, displays a day's events with tasks from the To Do List (**Figure 4.1**).

Changing some of the display options allows you to specify how dense or sparse your calendar will appear.

To set Date Book preferences:

1. Choose Preferences from the Options menu.

2. If you've ever wished you could set your own hours, here's your chance. Select the Start Time and End Time by tapping the arrows to the right of the time boxes (**Figure 4.2**).

3. The Preferences dialog box also contains settings for Date Book's alarm. Checking Alarm Preset specifies that each new event includes an alarm, which will go off according to the number of minutes you specify.

4. You can also specify which sound the alarm will use, how often it plays when the alarm goes off, and at what interval it will play until you dismiss it.

5. Tap OK to return to the Date Book views.

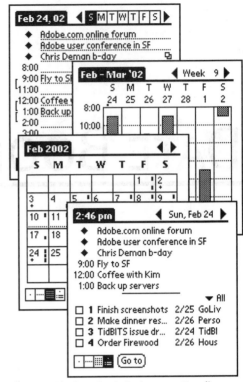

Figure 4.1 The Date Book displays your time (from top) in daily, weekly, and monthly views. The Agenda view (bottom) shows tasks as well.

Figure 4.2 Most people choose regular business hours, but for some of us that means all day long, as shown here. Checking the Alarm Preset box adds an alarm to each new event you create.

Figure 4.3 Date Book's Day view makes the best of its limited screen real estate, displaying elements such as time bars and icons while hiding unused time lines.

Figure 4.4 You can control the degree of clutter in the day and month views. I prefer to see everything.

Figure 4.5 Choose from three fonts to display the Day view records (this example uses the largest font).

Day View

Whenever you access the Date Book, either by tapping its icon from the Applications screen or by pressing the physical Date Book button at the lower-left of your device, you are presented with the Day view. From the other Date Book views, you can also tap the first box (containing one dot) in the lower-left corner of the screen. This is where you enter and edit events, and generally manage your schedule (**Figure 4.3**).

Day view features

◆ Events of the day appear on the dotted lines beside their allotted times, which adjust to conform to your schedule (a meeting ending at 10:15, for example, is marked as such, instead of displaying somewhere before 11:00). If there isn't enough space on the screen to view all your events, the Date Book removes any unused lines. To disable this feature, deselect Compress Day View in the Display Options dialog box (**Figure 4.4**).

◆ If you select Show Time Bars in the Display Options dialog box, the black brackets at left will indicate an event's time span—a handy way to see if you've scheduled overlapping events.

◆ Tap the days of the week buttons at the top of the screen to switch days. Tapping the arrows on either side of the buttons moves you forward or backward in weekly increments.

◆ The icons at right signify that an event contains a note (⌺), an alarm (⏰), or that it is a repeating event (⊡).

◆ You can also specify which font is used to display event text (**Figure 4.5**). Select Font from the Options menu (or write ╱-F) and choose from three styles.

DAY VIEW

✔ Tips

- The Day view provides a fine overview of the day, but doesn't tell you what time it is now. Tap the date tab in the upper-left corner to briefly display the current time (**Figure 4.6**). This works in each Date Book view except for the Agenda view, which shows the time by default.

  However, tapping the title bar under Palm OS 3.5 and later brings up the program's menus, so although the time appears, it's quickly obscured by the menu. Instead, tap and hold to view the time, then move your stylus off the tab (without lifting the stylus) to return to normal without engaging the menu.

- For those times when manipulating the stylus is inconvenient, or just to save time, press the Date Book button on the case to switch between views.

- In school, I knew a kid who (for whatever irrational reason) always hated those blue horizontal lines on the notebook paper we had to use. If he has a Palm device now, I'm sure he'll be happy to learn that he can get rid of the Day view's dotted lines. Set the Start Time and End Time to the same hour, and only the existing events will be displayed (**Figure 4.7**).

- On color devices, red time bars indicate time conflicts between appointments (**Figure 4.8**).

Figure 4.6 What time is it? Tap the tab in the upper-left corner to view the current time.

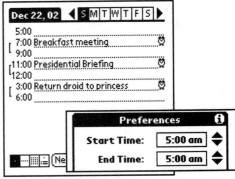

Figure 4.7 Setting the Start Time and End Time to the same hour displays only the lines that contain events.

Conflict in red

Figure 4.8 A subtle but helpful touch on color devices is the red time bar indicating conflicting appointments.

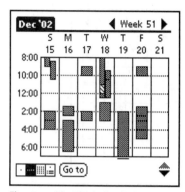

Figure 4.9 The Week view isn't necessarily a weak view: time blocks show how busy your week is, with overlapping events shown as thin bars.

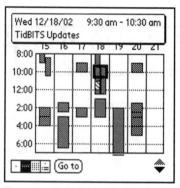

Figure 4.10 Deciphering the identity of a time block is easy—tapping one brings up its description at the top.

Week View

Viewing an entire day's schedule is helpful, but I often want to know what's coming up during the week without having to switch between multiple day views. To get an idea of my schedule's density, I display the Week view by tapping the second box (containing a line of four dots) in the lower-left corner.

Week view features

◆ Events in the Week view are represented by gray bars that span vertically across the displayed hours. If the appointments overlap, the bars become narrower and sit side-by-side on the week's grid. If you have several items happening at once, subsequent events are displayed with a diagonal pattern (**Figure 4.9**), or in red on some color devices.

◆ To see what a particular bar indicates, tap it once to bring up a floating window at the top of the screen containing the description you entered in the Day view, and its specific time span (**Figure 4.10**).

◆ Tapping the arrows in the upper-right corner of the screen moves you forward or backward one week, indicating the week's number in the year. Pressing the up or down button on the device case also shifts between weeks.

◆ Tapping the weekday abbreviations at the top of the screen switches to the Day view for that day. The current day is bold.

◆ Unlike the Day view, the week grid does not compress to fit all events onto one screen. Items appearing before or after the visible 11-hour period are indicated by a solid horizontal line appearing above or below the day's column. A dot at the top indicates an untimed event. You can scroll to these events by tapping the arrows in the lower-right corner.

WEEK VIEW

Month View

So, you're the type of person who likes to see the big picture? The Month view is your viewfinder, although at first glance you may think you've stumbled upon Morse code: who added all those dots? Tap the third box in the lower-left corner (containing a grid of 16 dots) to switch to the Month view.

Month view features

◆ This screen displays the entire month in a typical calendar format, with the days of the week running along the top of each column. Today's date, if you're viewing the current month, shows up as white text within a black square (**Figure 4.11**).

◆ To move forward and backward among months, tap the arrows at the top-right corner of the screen, or press the up and down buttons on the handheld case.

◆ Event blocks are indicated by black bars on the day in which they occur. Due to a lack of space, events are noted by the period of the day they occur: morning, midday, and evening. Similar to the Week view, this gives you an idea of the density of your schedule (**Figure 4.12**). Note that the day's month view will only display one bar for that part of the day, even if you have multiple appointments.

◆ If you have selected the Show Daily Repeating Evts box in the Display Options window, repeating events show up as a line of dots running along the bottom of the days they occupy. This option, the equivalent to "banners" in most desktop calendar programs, is off by default.

◆ If you have selected Show Untimed Events in the Display Options dialog box, these items are shown as little plus-signs at the bottom left of the day's square.

Figure 4.11 Your entire schedule is displayed using a minimum of space.

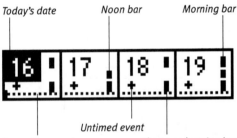

Today's date   Noon bar   Morning bar

Repeating event   Untimed event   Afternoon/evening bar

Figure 4.12 Realizing the limitations of their screen, Palm's designers opted for a "less is more" approach to the Date Book's Month view.

Figure 4.13 View the day's events and to do items in the Agenda view.

Agenda View

Recognizing that what you do is often tied to when you do it, Palm's programmers added a fourth view to Date Book in Palm OS 3.5. The Agenda view is similar to the Day view, but also contains the day's tasks from the To Do List in the lower half of the screen (**Figure 4.13**). Tap the fourth box in the lower-left corner to bring up the Agenda view.

Agenda view features

◆ Tap an appointment to switch to the Day view, where it will be actively selected. Similarly, tapping a task switches to that record in the To Do List.

◆ Tap the horizontal scroll arrows at the top of the screen to move forward or backward one day.

◆ The to do items are displayed just as they appear in the To Do List. To see data such as the due date or category name, enable those options in the To Do List.

◆ View different To Do List categories by selecting them from the category popup menu above the to do items.

✔ Tip

■ If you have the Agenda view displayed, then switch to another application, the Agenda will appear when you come back to the Date Book. Normally, the Date Book returns to the Day view when you switch back to it. To keep the Agenda view, make sure it's active before you exit Date Book.

Date Book Navigation: Jumping Through Time

I've become so dependent upon my handheld for scheduling that if an event isn't in Date Book, then it isn't happening. (This approach has prevented several event conflicts!) As a result, I find myself frequently looking ahead to specific dates, a process the Palm designers have streamlined pretty well.

To jump to specific dates:

1. From any Date Book view, tap the Go To button. The Go to Date dialog box is context sensitive based on your previous view. So, the Day view gives you the option to jump to a specific day, the Week view jumps to weeks, and the Month view jumps to months (**Figure 4.14**).

2. Select a year using the arrows at the top of the page.

3. Select a month and a date or week. (If you came from the month view, selecting the month will take you there immediately.)

   If you've been time-traveling and want to get back to the present, tap the Today, This Week, or This Month button.

✔ Tip

■ A faster method of jumping to today's date is to press the Date Book button on the handheld's case—the first press will return you to today's Day view from anywhere in the Date Book (except the Agenda view under Palm OS 3.5 or later; see the previous page).

Figure 4.14 Tapping the Go To button brings up the day (top), week (middle), and month (bottom) navigation screens, depending on your previous view.

Figure 4.15 Splitting the time into two vertical bars may appear odd at first, but this approach puts the controls in a smooth path for your stylus.

Figure 4.16 After exiting the Set Time window, go ahead and give your event a descriptive title.

Entering and Deleting Date Book Events

I'm sure Mrs. Wilson, my second-grade teacher, would pale at the sight of my handwriting. All that cursive training, wasted! Date Book allows me to enter legible events quickly, using a variety of methods—and delete them just as easily without the mess of strikethroughs and scribbles.

To enter an event using the New button:

1. In the Day view, tap the New button to bring up the Set Time dialog box. You can also choose New Event from the Record menu, or write ╱-N in Graffiti.

2. Specify a starting time. If you tap the Start Time box, the day's beginning time (from Date Book's Preferences) is entered by default. The time in the End Time box automatically sets to one hour after the Start Time. Tap on an hour and minute (the first and second vertical columns) to change the Start Time (**Figure 4.15**). The All Day button enters the time span you set up in the preferences.

   You can also elect to create an untimed event by tapping OK before specifying Start and End Times, or by tapping the No Time button if those fields are already filled. Birthdays, anniversaries, and other holidays work best as untimed events.

3. Change the End Time, if desired, and tap OK.

4. Write a descriptive title (**Figure 4.16**).

✔ Tip

■ A slightly faster way to enter an event is to tap directly on one of the times running down the left side of the display.

To enter an event by naming it on the appropriate line:

1. The quickest method for creating a new record is to tap the line belonging to the time you wish to use. Date Book creates a one-hour event and positions the text cursor on the line for you to name the record; no dialog boxes or OK buttons are involved (**Figure 4.17**).

2. Tap on a null area of the screen to enter your new event. To modify the event's time, tap either the time itself or the Details button.

To enter events in the Week view:

1. In the Week view, tap on a day and time for your new event—a black rectangle appears (**Figure 4.18**).

2. When you remove the stylus from the screen, Date Book changes to the Day view and automatically enters an untitled record at the time you specified.

✔ Tips

■ If you're feeling like a hunter-gatherer while poking at all of these buttons and locations, consider using a more expressive method to enter Date Book events. In the Day view, begin writing your event's Start Time using Graffiti's number-entry area (the right portion). A new record will be created at that time.

■ A similar approach is to just start writing the title of a new appointment in Graffiti. An untimed event appears; use the Details button or tap the time to schedule it.

■ Also, if you're tired of pecking at the vertical hour and minute columns in the Set Time dialog box, you can write Graffiti numerals that will show up in the Start Time box (and also in the End Time box after selecting it).

Figure 4.17 Tap directly on the time you wish to create an event for, and bypass the Set Time dialog box.

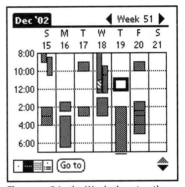

Figure 4.18 In the Week view, tap the time for a new event (indicated by the box with a dark border).

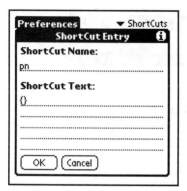

Figure 4.19a Set up your "pencil-in" notation by creating a ShortCut in the Palm OS Preferences application.

Figure 4.19b Write the Graffiti characters you set up as a ShortCut, then enter the event's title.

Figure 4.19c Your event is now easily recognizable as a temporary date/time. After confirming the specifics, remove the "pencil-in" notation.

"Pencil-in" Events

One capability I miss from paper-based organizers is being able to "pencil-in" an event, which you can then confirm later. In the Date Book, temporary and confirmed appointments show up the same. What I'd really like to see is the ability to write an event in gray, but until that day comes, here's a simple workaround using the Palm OS's ShortCut feature (**Figures 4.19a**, **4.19b**, and **4.19c**).

To add a "pencil-in" event:

1. From the Applications screen, launch the Prefs utility and select ShortCuts from the popup menu in the upper-right corner.

2. Tap New and name your ShortCut something like "pn".

3. Figure out how you'd like penciled items to display—I've always liked the curly brackets, so I enter both characters under ShortCut Text.

4. Tap OK and return to Date Book.

5. When you want to create a penciled-in event, preface its title with the shortcut you just created. In my case, the brackets appear and I either tap to put my cursor between them, or use the Graffiti cursor-left stroke (↜).

6. When the event is confirmed, remember to remove the "pencil-in" notation.

✔ Tip

■ I hoped that Palm OS 3.5's color support would let me create events in gray, but that's still not yet the case, even under Palm OS 5.2. However, DateBk5 (www. pimlicosoftware.com) can: create an event, tap the Details button, then tap the Font field to set the color. You can also set up a template to create new penciled-in events. (See later in this chapter for more on DateBk5.)

"PENCIL-IN" EVENTS

Editing and Deleting Existing Events

Once created, events aren't set in stone. The ways to change their attributes are as varied as creating new appointments.

To change an event's time and/or date (the long way):

1. In the Day view, tap a record to select it, then tap the Details button.

2. In the Event Details window, tap the Time field or the Date field (**Figure 4.20**).

3. Adjust the time in the Set Time window, and the date in the Set Date window.

To change an event's time (the short way):

1. In the Day view, tap on the time to the left of the event you wish to edit.

2. Adjust the time in the Set Time window.

To change an event's time and/or date (the shortest way):

1. In the Week view, tap and hold the event you wish to edit (**Figure 4.21**).

2. Drag the event to its new time and/or date (within the same week).

To delete an event:

1. In the Day view, tap the event to select it and then tap the Details button.

2. In the Event Details window, tap Delete, choose Delete Event from the Record menu, or write ╱-D .

3. If you want the record to be saved on your PC the next time you perform a HotSync, be sure to mark the Save archive copy on PC option; uncheck the box to banish it forever (**Figure 4.22**).

Figure 4.20 You can easily change the date and time of any event by accessing the Event Details window.

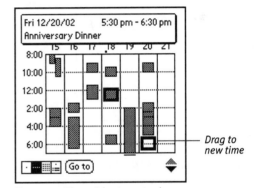

Drag to new time

Figure 4.21 The quickest way to change an event's time and date is to tap and drag it in the Week view.

Figure 4.22 If you don't want an event taking up valuable memory in your handheld, you can keep a copy of it on your PC's hard drive.

Figure 4.23 Traffic likely to be bad? Specify a longer time period for the alarm to go off before an event.

Figure 4.24 The alarm's Reminder screen appears before an event, accompanied by a cheerful chime (Palm OS 4.0 shown here).

Figure 4.25 Date Book gives you several options for alarms, including repeating reminders and seven different sounds.

Setting Alarms

Remember the days of carrying a travel alarm clock? They're long gone, my friend.

To set an alarm:

1. After you've created an event, tap Details and mark the Alarm checkbox.

2. Choose the amount of time before the event that the alarm should go off. Minutes is the default, but you can also select Hours or Days (**Figure 4.23**).

To respond to an alarm:

◆ Tap OK to dismiss the Reminder screen when the alarm activates (**Figure 4.24**).

◆ Under Palm OS 3.5 or later, tap the Snooze button to give yourself a few extra minutes before the alarm goes off again. Palm OS 4.0 and later displays a small indicator at the upper-left corner of the screen to indicate the impending alarm.

◆ Tap the Go To button to display the event in Date Book.

To change alarm options:

1. Go to the Date Book Preferences dialog box (choose Preferences from the Options menu, or write ╱-R).

2. Choose your favorite Alarm Sound.

3. Choose the "snooze" options: Remind Me specifies how often the alarm will go off before you dismiss it. Play Every sets the time between reminders (**Figure 4.25**).

✔ Tip

■ If you've missed multiple alarms, Palm OS 4.0 and later displays a screen summarizing them, which you can clear individually or all at once. Previous versions forced you to tap OK on several screens before you could use the handheld again.

SETTING ALARMS

Creating Repeating Events

Scheduling meetings, appointments, and reminders is a great use for Date Book, but one of the primary reasons I wanted an electronic organizer was to keep track of those recurring events that I never seem to remember: birthdays, holidays, weekly meetings, and the like. Date Book's repeating events feature allows me to do just that.

To create a repeating event:

1. Select an event and tap the Details button.

2. Next to the word Repeat, tap None. This brings up the Change Repeat dialog box (**Figure 4.26**).

3. Specify if the event is a daily, weekly, monthly, or yearly event by tapping one of the boxes at the top of the screen.

4. Write the numerical frequency of the event in the Every field.

5. If the event stops repeating on a certain date, select Choose Date from the End on popup menu; otherwise, leave it set to No End Date.

6. Depending on your selection in step 3, you can specify additional event criteria.

   Weekly events can be set to repeat on certain days by tapping in the appropriate Repeat on boxes.

   Monthly events can be repeated by day ("The 1st Wednesday of every month"), or by date ("The 5th of every month") (**Figure 4.27**).

   Yearly events, by default, are set to repeat according to the date of the first event.

7. Tap OK to exit the dialog; you'll see the repeating event icon appear to the right of your record in the Day view, and a dotted line in the Month view if Show Untimed Events is selected in Display Options (**Figure 4.28**).

Figure 4.26 Why manually add the same events over and over? Repeating events allow you to specify multiple days of the week, among other options.

Figure 4.27 Date Book is smart enough to base the repeated event upon the date that's selected.

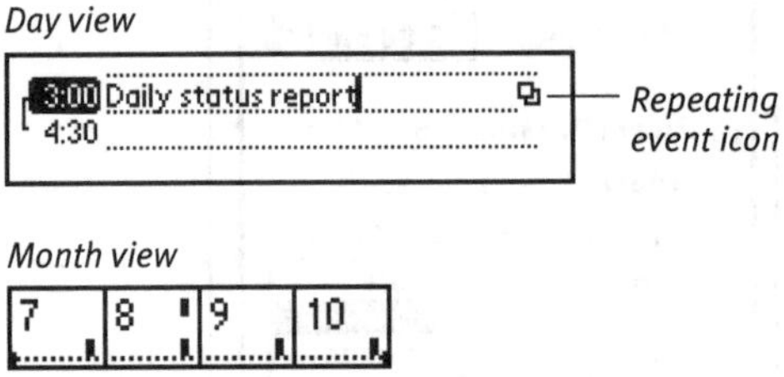

Day view

3:00 Daily status report — Repeating event icon
4:30

Month view

7 8 9 10

Figure 4.28 Repeated events are shown with an icon in the Day view, and a dotted line in the Month view.

Figure 4.29 If you change an existing repeating event, you're asked how you prefer to implement the changes.

Figure 4.30 Yearly occasions that fall on a particular day of the week can be set up as monthly, not yearly, repeating events, such as Thanksgiving.

To change a repeating event:

1. Tap any occurrence (you don't have to edit the first record you create) to select it, then tap the Details button.

2. Make any changes you like, including time, date, or attached notes, then tap OK.

3. Choose whether you wish to apply the change to the Current record, All occurrences of the event, or if you'd rather Cancel (**Figure 4.29**).

The Future option leaves past occurrences intact and deletes only the current and future repetitions.

If you only change the title of the event, the change is automatically applied to all occurrences without displaying the Repeating Event dialog box.

✔ Tips

■ What about those events, like Thanksgiving, that occur yearly but are based on a particular day of the week? Since the yearly repeat option only specifies the event's date, you have to out-think Date Book. Set up a monthly repeat that occurs every 12 months, and choose Repeat by Day (**Figure 4.30**).

■ One of my biggest scheduling problems is not being aware of an event, such as a birthday, until the day is upon me. One workaround is to set alarms to go off several days before the event. Another solution is to install Birthdate (www.birthdate.com), a shareware utility that collects birthdates from other areas of the Palm OS (such as the Address Book) and optionally notifies you when they are coming up.

CREATING REPEATING EVENTS

Attaching and Deleting Notes

Initially, I thought the ability to attach notes was a superfluous add-on, best used when you wanted to record snide (er, I mean "constructive") comments during a meeting.

Since then, I've seen the light. Not only are they good for jotting random thoughts in context, but they have become indispensable for storing information that I know I will need at a particular time.

To attach a note to an event:

1. Tap an event to select it.

2. Tap the Details button, then tap Note. Alternately, choose Attach Note from the Record menu, or write ╱-A.

3. Compose your note using Graffiti or the onscreen keyboard (**Figure 4.31** and **4.32**).

4. When you are finished, tap Done.

✔ Tip

- To edit the attached note later, follow the steps above to access the note. If you want a quicker method, however, go to the Day view and tap the note icon (▯) to the right of the event's name.

Navigating a note

- If your note occupies more than one screen, use the scroll bar on the right side of the screen to move within the text.

Figure 4.31 Tap the Note button in the Event Details window to attach more text to an event.

Figure 4.32 A new note presents you with a slightly limited version of the Memo Pad application.

Figure 4.33 Move through a long note quickly by "select-scrolling" the stylus through the text.

Figure 4.34 When you no longer need a note, delete it—keep in mind that you don't have the option to archive it to your PC, as you do with memos.

✔ Tip

■ A quicker option, though harder to navigate, is to "select-scroll" through long notes (**Figure 4.33**). Position your cursor somewhere in the middle of the text, and, without lifting the stylus from the screen, drag down the screen. The text will be highlighted, and soon you'll find yourself at the bottom of the note (or whichever point you chose to lift the stylus).

To delete a note:

1. In the Day view, choose Delete Note from the Record menu, or write ╱-O.

   Or, if you're on the note editing screen, tap the Delete button. The Delete Note dialog box appears.

2. Click Yes or No to confirm if you really want to delete the note (**Figure 4.34**).

ATTACHING AND DELETING NOTES

Performing a Phone Lookup

Luckily for those of us who value good data, the built-in applications don't live independently of each other. One of the handier features employed in the Palm OS is the ability to perform phone number lookups from the Address Book.

To perform a phone lookup:

1. If you know the name of the person you're scheduling an event with (such as "Coffee with Pedro Finn"), write his or her name into a field in the Day view.

   If you don't know the person's name, just leave that part blank (i.e., "Coffee with ").

2. Choose Phone Lookup from the Options menu, or write ╱-L.

3. If a name in your Address Book matches the name you wrote, the phone number will be added to your event's description. If not, or if you didn't specify a name, scroll through the list of names and highlight the one you want (**Figure 4.35**).

4. Tap Add to include the phone number in the Date Book record (**Figure 4.36**).

✔ Tip

■ The Palm OS searches for last names when performing a lookup, so you can write a person's last name and, if theirs is the only instance of that name, the phone number will appear without making a trip to the Address Book screen.

Figure 4.35 Finally, contact information that's convenient to contact. Performing a phone lookup lists the names in your Address Book with phone numbers.

Figure 4.36 The looked-up number automatically gets added to the time line you created.

PERFORMING A PHONE LOOKUP

Figure 4.37a Tap the Private checkbox to keep an event safe from curious onlookers.

Figure 4.37b If the Current Privacy setting in the Security application is set to Show Records, you are reminded that the event is not yet hidden.

Figure 4.38 Under Palm OS 3.5 and later, changing the security setting alters it in every application.

Marking Events Private

I have a tendency to show my handheld to anyone who asks, but I don't always want them to see everything in my schedule. (Okay, so maybe I don't have very much information that needs to be kept secret, but it's good to know I can when I need to.)

When you mark Date Book events as Private, their appearance depends on the state of the Current Privacy option in the Palm OS's Security application. If you've specified an alarm for a hidden private record, a Reminder screen will still appear when scheduled.

To mark events Private:

1. Select an event and tap the Details button.

2. In the Event Details dialog box, mark the Private checkbox (**Figure 4.37a**). If the Show/Hide Private Records setting is switched to Show, you will receive a warning dialog about how to hide private records after you tap OK (**Figure 4.37b**).

To change the security setting:

1. Choose Security from the Options menu, write ∕-H, or tap the lock icon from the command bar. The Change Security dialog box appears.

2. From the Current Privacy popup menu, choose Show Records, Mask Records, or Hide Records (**Figure 4.38**). This changes the security setting in all applications on your handheld.

✔ Tip

■ To easily read a masked record under Palm OS 4.0 and later, tap it and enter your password. When finished it becomes masked again.

Beaming Events

In the movies, conspirators are always synchronizing their watches to make sure everyone's on the same schedule. In the real world, I use the Palm OS to beam appointments to colleagues and family members, and thereby avoid having anyone say, "Why didn't you tell me there's a meeting today?"

To beam an event:

1. Tap an event to select it.

2. Choose Beam from the Record menu, write /-B, or tap the Beam Event icon (☏) from the command bar (**Figure 4.39**). If the recipient's Beam Receive preference is set to On and the IR ports are aimed at each other, the record will be transferred (**Figure 4.40**).

To receive a beamed event:

1. Make sure your Beam Receive preference is set to On. Aim your IR port at the other person's Palm device.

2. After you've received the beamed record, you will be asked if you wish to add it to the Date Book. Tap Yes or No.

Figure 4.39 Palm devices equipped with infrared capabilities can beam records to one another easily.

Figure 4.40 Be sure your Palm device is pointed at the recipient, and within seconds the record is transferred.

Figure 4.41 Some people choose to leave their past behind them—select Purge to wipe away old events.

Figure 4.42 I know people who have saved every event for as long as they've been able. Others wipe the old information and store it on their PCs.

Purging Old Events

Although the Palm OS has been written to accommodate very small file sizes, there comes a point at which the volume of past events begins to eat into your available memory. Will you have to shoulder the weight of the past forever? Luckily, you don't have to.

Date Book gives you the option to permanently delete older records from your device, while still maintaining an archive of the past on your PC.

To purge old events:

1. From the Day view, choose Purge from the Record menu, or write ╱-E in the Graffiti area (**Figure 4.41**). The Purge dialog box appears.

2. Choose the time frame of records that will be purged by selecting an item on the Delete events older than: popup menu. You can select 1 Week, 2 Weeks, 3 Weeks, or 1 Month (**Figure 4.42**).

3. If you want to maintain a copy of the purged records on your PC, be sure the checkbox next to Save archive copy on PC is marked; otherwise, uncheck the box. Tap OK.

Handspring's Date Book+

In many ways, Handspring's Treo is just a Palm device in a different package (and which also happens to be a phone, of course). It runs the Palm OS, which includes the built-in applications found on any Palm handheld. However, Handspring chose to add Date Book+, an application that gives it the features Date Book should have included long ago.

Date Book+ adds three new views, plus an assortment of features like floating events (i.e., scheduled to do items), a daily journal, the ability to view tasks and appointments on the same screen (like the Date Book's Agenda view), plus other tweaks and improvements (**Figure 4.43**).

Figure 4.43 Date Book+ looks like the original Date Book, but includes more views, activated at lower left. Also note the appearance of to do items from the To Do List at the top of the screen.

Date Book+ Week View with Text View

The standard Week view can be helpful, but its assortment of dots and dashes is often too cryptic. The Week View with Text view displays as many event and to do titles as can fit (**Figure 4.44**). Tap the third button from the left to access this view.

Figure 4.44 The awkwardly named Week View with Text view offers a better idea of your schedule.

Features of the Week View with Text view

- Tap any day area to switch to the Day view.

- Tap the numbered box at the top of the screen to switch between viewing one week or two weeks (**Figure 4.45**).

- If you have a mix of morning and afternoon appointments, tap the arrow button next to the Go button to display those portions of the day.

Figure 4.45 View two weeks on the same screen, though it's not as readable.

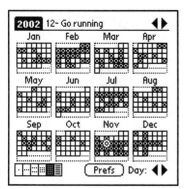

Figure 4.46 The Year view is handy for getting a sense of how crowded your schedule is.

Figure 4.47 Date Book doesn't need to get fancy displaying calendars when a list will do just as well.

Figure 4.48 Tap the up arrow in the List view to choose a range of time to jump back through.

Date Book+ Year View

The Year view offers an even bigger picture of your schedule, but doesn't pull out many details (**Figure 4.46**). Tap the fifth button in the lower-left corner.

Features of the Year view

◆ Tap a box on the calendar to view that day's date and the first appointment.

◆ The scroll arrows at the top of the screen advance or go back one year per tap; the scroll arrows at the lower-right corner move one day at a time. Pressing the scroll buttons does the same thing.

Date Book+ List View

Sometimes I just want to see a list of what's coming up. Tap the rightmost box at the lower-left corner of the screen to activate the List view (**Figure 4.47**).

Features of the List view

◆ Tap an event to display its start and end times in the title bar.

◆ Double-tap an event to view it in the Day view.

◆ If you've used the Go button to view a different day, tap the List view button to return to the current day.

◆ Tap the up arrow at the top-right corner of the screen to specify which increment (day, week, month) to move up the list, or pick a date in the past (**Figure 4.48**). The down arrow advances a full screen.

◆ Tap the Prefs button to specify which records appear in the list.

✔ Tip

■ From the List Preferences screen, you can filter the list by entering text on the Find field under Filter by Text.

Date Book+ Preferences

With more features come more preferences, and Date Book+ is loaded with options. These settings define global behavior (**Figure 4.49**).

Important Date Book+ Preferences

◆ By default, new events appear with a one hour duration. In Date Book+, specify any time span from zero to 23 hours and 55 minutes by tapping the Event Duration field and setting the amount.

◆ Use the Initial View preference to set the view displayed when you enter the application. The Day view is the default.

◆ Pressing the Date Book button on the Treo's case shuttles you through the different Date Book+ views. Deselect views you don't scroll through by tapping them in the Button Views preference.

◆ Gone are the days of the standardized workweek. If you want your weeks to begin on a certain day, like Tuesday, choose it from the Week Start popup menu. Every calendar view is affected (**Figure 4.50**).

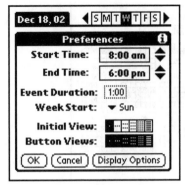

Figure 4.49 Choose the options you wish to use in Date Book+.

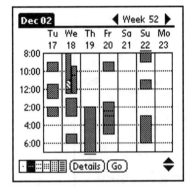

Figure 4.50 Setting a different day to begin the week changes the calendar layout throughout Date Book+.

Figure 4.51 The easy way to create new records in Date Book+ is to select from the menu that appears when you tap the New button.

Entering Date Book+ Events

Since Date Book+ can display more than just appointments, it adds an easy method of entering new records. Yes, you can choose their commands from the Record menu, write their Graffiti shortcut strokes, or start typing on the keypad, but there's a much easier way.

To enter a new Date Book+ event (the easy way):

1. With no records selected, tap the New button; a popup menu appears, listing the types of records available (**Figure 4.51**).

2. Choose Floating Event, To Do, Daily Journal, Template, or Appointment. A new untimed record appears (or in the case of the journal, a new note screen appears with a time stamp).

3. Fill in the record's title and other pertinent information as you normally would.

To duplicate a Date Book+ event:

1. Select an existing record in the Day view.

2. Choose Duplicate Item from the Record menu, or write ✓-Y.

3. Change the new item's settings in the Details screen, then tap OK to return to the Day view.

Date Book+ Floating Events

There are times when I need to make sure I do something at a certain time. Floating events can be scheduled like any event, but carry over until the next day if they're not marked completed.

To work with floating events:

1. Create a new floating event from the New popup menu, or by choosing New Floating Event from the Record menu, or by writing ╱-B. Assign it a title and time. It will be identified by a circle to the left or right of the name, depending on whether it's scheduled or not (**Figure 4.52**).

2. Tap the circle to indicate that the task is completed, or tap Details and select the Done option under Type. If left alone, it will display the following day.

Date Book+ Journal Entries

For an easy method of keeping track of thoughts and ideas, use the Daily Journal.

To create a journal entry:

1. Choose Daily Journal from the New button's popup menu, or New Journal Entry from the Record menu, or write ╱-J. A new note screen appears with the current time entered (**Figure 4.53**).

2. Insert pithy thought, wry observation, erudite comment, or overheard joke.

3. Tap Done to return to the Day view. Journal records appear as untimed records at the top of the screen (**Figure 4.54**).

4. If, at the end of your scribblings, you decide to delete what you've written (or if you wrote over a previous record), tap the Restore... button to revert to the state at which you first entered the journal.

Figure 4.52 Floating events are really just scheduled to-do items.

Figure 4.53 A timestamp is automatically added to the bottom of the day's journal record.

Figure 4.54 The Daily Journal is really just an untimed record with an attached note, but it's a quick method of jotting down ideas and snippets of information.

Figure 4.55 Templates store all the data about a selected event.

Figure 4.56 Set up templates for frequently used events to avoid having to enter the same info time and again.

Date Book+ Templates

The template feature in Date Book+ exemplifies yet another aspect of the Palm philosophy of saving time and avoiding repetition. When you make a template from an existing record, it retains all of the event's settings like alarm, privacy, and attached note.

To create a template:

1. Create a record that you want to use as a template.

2. Select the record and choose Create Template from the Record menu, or write ∕-V (**Figure 4.55**).

To use a template:

1. Tap the New button and choose Template from the popup menu.

2. Select a template from the Appointment Templates screen, then tap OK to place the event (**Figure 4.56**).

To edit a template:

1. Tap the New button and choose Template from the popup menu.

2. Select a template and tap the Details or Edit button to change its properties.

3. Tap OK to return to the Day view.

Restoring Archived Events

If you leave the Save archive copy on PC checkbox marked when you delete records, there's a way to get them back.

To restore archived events:

Select UnDelete from Archive from the Record menu. The records appear in reverse order based on when they were deleted. Repeat the command until you've restored the record you want.

Palm Desktop Special Features

For the most part, you'll find that working within Palm Desktop's Date Book is similar to using the Palm OS Date Book: click New Event to create new events, Edit Event to change them, and view them using either the Day, Week, Month, or Year views. However, the desktop software also includes several features that make it easier to create and modify appointment times, and add events based on phone lookups. And because it operates on your PC, you can print your calendar.

To edit events in the Day view:

1. Select the day you need in the calendar to the right.

2. Click on the time that you'd like to schedule your event. You can click either the time numerals in the left column, or click an empty area in the right column.

3. Type your event's description, then press Enter.

4. To add an alarm or a note, right-click on the event to bring up a contextual menu. You can also delete the record here, as well as access the main Edit dialog box.

5. To quickly move the event to another date, drag it to the calendar in the pane at right. It retains the same time.

To edit events in the Week view:

◆ Click on an empty time slot, or click the time numerals, to create a new event.

◆ As in the Day view, drag events to new times and dates using the event handle, or reschedule lengths using the duration handle (**Figures 4.57, 4.58,** and **4.59**).

◆ Right-click on any event to bring up the editing contextual menu.

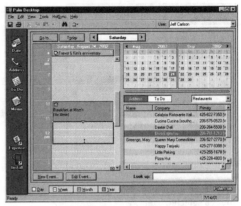

Figure 4.57 Click and drag an appointment's bottom handle to change its time span; click and drag the right-side event handle to reschedule its time or date.

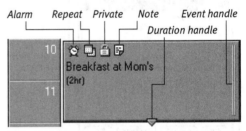

Figure 4.58 Events are more configurable in the desktop Day view than in the Palm OS Day view.

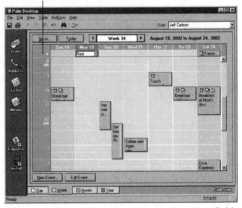

Figure 4.59 Untimed events appear in the upper field marked by a diamond. The field expands to accommodate the number of untimed events.

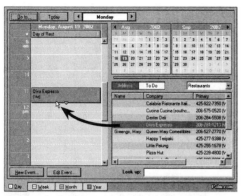

Figure 4.60 Quickly create an appointment with a phone lookup by dragging a name from the Address pane at lower right to the time of the event.

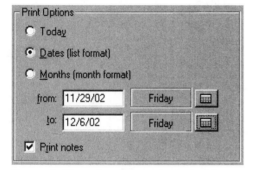

Figure 4.61 Choose how you want your schedule printed. Clicking on the tiny calendar icons gives you a popup calendar to specify the date ranges.

To perform a phone lookup in Palm Desktop:

1. Switch to the Day view, and select the date on which you wish to create an event.

2. Click Address in the lower-right pane to display your Address Book entries.

3. Locate the contact either by scrolling through the names, or typing in the Look up field.

4. Drag the contact's name to the time of the appointment (**Figure 4.60**).

✔ Tips

- For whatever reason, Palm Desktop 4.1 doesn't include the phone number in the title of an event that's been created by dragging a contact.

- You can also drag a To Do item from the lower-right pane onto your day to schedule a task. Although the records aren't linked (changing the date on one won't affect the other), this capability is good for setting aside blocks of time to complete your tasks.

To print your appointments:

1. In any Date Book view, select Print from the File menu, or press Control-P. The Print Options dialog box appears.

2. Choose a print option: Today's appointments, a list of Dates, or a time span in Months format (**Figure 4.61**).

3. If printing in month format, you can use the small calendar icons to specify which days you want to print.

Macintosh Palm Desktop Special Features

Most cross-platform applications share the same interface and features, but that's not the case with the Macintosh Palm Desktop software. Because it's built on top of Claris Organizer (see Chapter 1), you'll find many features that don't exist in the Windows version of Palm Desktop.

Navigating Palm Desktop for Macintosh

One of the first things you'll notice is the presence of a toolbar at the upper-left corner of the screen (**Figure 4.62**). Clicking on the buttons offers a quick alternative to common actions, such as:

◆ **Create Event** (or press Command-Option-E). This opens the Appointment dialog box, allowing you to enter the schedule information without finding the time and date on the calendar first (useful when you're entering several events at different times). Click Add Another to stay in the dialog box and enter multiple events instead of switching back to the calendar view (**Figure 4.63**).

◆ **Create Untimed Event** (or press Command-Option-U). See the next page for details.

◆ **Go To Date** (or press Command-R). This jumps to a specific date (**Figure 4.64**).

◆ **Go To Today** (or press Command-T). Jump to the current date. *Carpe diem*, etc.

◆ **Show Date Book** (or press Command-Shift-B). If you're viewing to do items or contacts, clicking this button takes you to the last calendar view you were using.

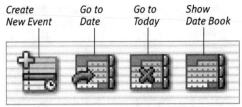

Create New Event · Go to Date · Go to Today · Show Date Book

Figure 4.62 Palm Desktop for Macintosh features a floating toolbar with buttons to work within the Date Book module.

Figure 4.63 Click the Add Another button to create a new event without exiting the dialog box.

Figure 4.64 Go To Date switches your current calendar view to the date you specify. This small window is also handy when you're viewing the Day or Week views, giving you a monthly calendar without switching to the Month view.

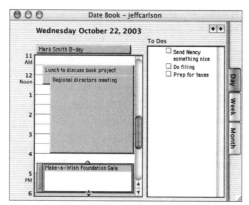

Figure 4.65 Click and drag within the Day or Week views to create a new event.

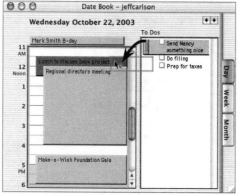

Figure 4.66 Attach to do items in the Tasks pane to events in the Day and Week views by dragging-and-dropping them. Existing links can be viewed by clicking the folder icon that is created after linking.

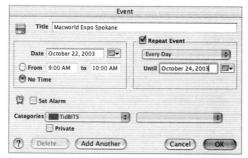

Figure 4.67 Create repeating events by setting up event banners, which can be assigned categories and sub-categories.

To create and edit events:

◆ Double-click in one of the calendar views to bring up the Event dialog box.

◆ Click and drag on the event's time. Unlike the Windows version of Palm Desktop, the Mac software allows you to create an event with one click that spans its full duration (**Figure 4.65**).

◆ Choose Event from the Create menu, or press Command-Option-E.

To edit an existing event, double-click it in any calendar view, or single-click it and select Edit Event from the Edit menu.

You can also attach related records to other records (such as to do items attached to events, or contacts attached to events—the Mac equivalent of phone lookups).

To attach records to events:

◆ If both records are visible, drag and drop one to the other. A link is created in both records (**Figure 4.66**).

◆ Click the folder icon (🗎▼) and choose Attach To from the popup menu.

Repeating events are known as banners in Palm Desktop for Macintosh.

To create a repeating event:

1. Choose Untimed Event from the Create menu, or press Command-Option-U. The Event dialog box appears.

2. Set the starting date in the Date field (or use the popup calendar to the right).

3. Click the Repeat Event checkbox (**Figure 4.67**).

4. Specify a time interval from the Repeat Event popup menu, and optionally set an end date in the Until field. Click OK when you're finished.

MAC PALM DESKTOP SPECIAL FEATURES

Attaching Notes in Mac Palm Desktop

The one truly bizarre thing about the Macintosh Palm Desktop software is the roundabout manner of attaching notes to records. Although you can attach records to events (see previous page), that's not the same as adding a note to a record (as discussed at the beginning of this chapter). Fortunately, there is a way to attach notes to events so they show up properly on the handheld device.

To attach notes in Mac Palm Desktop:

1. Attached notes are considered memos just as if you had written them into the Memo Pad. So, create a new memo and write your text.

2. In the Title field, type "Handheld Note: Date Book" exactly (**Figure 4.68**).

3. Locate the calendar entry to which you want to add your note. Drag the note's title bar icon to the calendar entry (**Figure 4.69**).

✔ Tips

■ There's a faster way of making attachments that will appear on the handheld. With a blank note visible, write "Handheld Note: Date Book" in the Title field as you did above. Now, choose New Template from the Create menu, and enter a name; if you want, choose a Command-key number from the ⌘ popup menu. From now on, choose one of the templates from the Create menu or press the Command-key to display a new formatted note window (**Figure 4.70**).

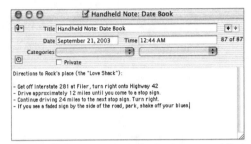

Figure 4.68 To create an attached note, you must first create the note separately (unlike in the Palm OS).

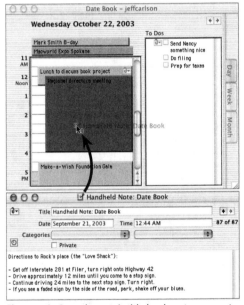

Figure 4.69 Drag the note's title bar icon to an event to attach the note.

Figure 4.70 Create notes easily with templates.

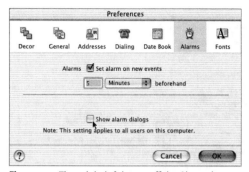

Figure 4.71 Though helpful, turn off the Show alarm dialogs option to avoid interruptions on your Mac.

Drag tasks to the calendar

Figure 4.72 Quickly schedule tasks by dragging them from the Tasks pane to the calendar.

■ In the Palm OS Date Book, performing an address lookup puts a person's name and phone number in the title of an event. On the Mac, however, dragging a contact to an event only creates a link between the two on the desktop. Instead, you'll have to manually cut and paste the person's phone information for it to appear in the title.

■ In the calendar's Daily view, double-click the date to bring up the Go To dialog.

■ The Daily view also displays the day's active tasks in the right-hand pane; click the word "Tasks" to send completed tasks to the bottom of the list.

■ In the Daily and Weekly views, pressing Command and the right or left arrow key advances or goes back one day. Hold down Option or Shift to move in one-week increments.

■ In the Monthly view, you can choose to display Appointments, Tasks, or both (or none). Go to the View menu, then choose the options under the Calendar submenu.

■ Palm Desktop for Macintosh includes a feature for displaying an alarm onscreen (**Figure 4.71**).

■ You can create scheduled to do items easily in the Daily or Weekly views. Simply drag a task from the Tasks pane to a time in the calendar. The item's title becomes the appointment's title, and any attached notes are copied over as well. The text "Work on" appears in the title, and an attachment link is created between the task and the new calendar item (**Figure 4.72**).

DateBk5: The Supercharged Date Book

The Palm OS's built-in applications haven't changed much over the past few years, in accordance with Palm's mandate to keep its handhelds simple and useful. As long as appointments are scheduled, tasks recorded, and phone numbers easily looked up, most users don't require more than the basics. But we don't all qualify as "most users." For the most full-featured calendar application on the Palm OS, look to Pimlico Software's DateBk5 (www.pimlicosoftware.com).

DateBk5 essentially adds all the features that you've wanted (or didn't know you've wanted) in Date Book. DateBk5 sports six calendar views, displays to do items as well as events, and features a daily journal, floating events, and templates. In addition, DateBk5 adds categories, icons, time zone support, color, and the ability to set font styles for any record, not just the entire application (**Figure 4.73**).

But that's not all. You can split the Day view screen and choose the contents for the new window pane. To do items are usually listed, but you can also view your Address Book records, or memos, and then filter the lists based on any text you specify. Color device owners have good reason to install DateBk5: unlike the built-in applications, this program enables you to color-code categories or individual records, making it easier to quickly differentiate between events (**Figure 4.74**). And if that's not enough, you can also link records between the built-in applications (though you have to view them within DateBk5).

What's the dark side to this miracle application? The only serious criticism is its size: around 669K, which is huge by Palm OS standards. For users who don't have that much free space available, Pimlico also offers a previous version, DateBk3, which weighs in at 247K. Of all the applications I've installed on my Palm devices, DateBk5 remains a permanent fixture.

DateBk5 costs $24.95 (all of which goes to the developer's organization, Gorilla Haven, a non-profit preserve that provides a secure temporary holding facility for gorillas awaiting permanent zoo housing, and helps ensure the welfare and genetic diversity of the species).

Figure 4.73 DateBk5 adds more features to the built-in Date Book database than any three programs combined.

Figure 4.74 This is the reason to buy a color handheld: events can be categorized and displayed in different colors for easy recognition—a capability missing from the initial color implementation from Palm.

ADDRESS BOOK

My first attempt at organizing the contact information I had collected over several years was a slick (or so I thought at the time) system involving a Personal Information Manager (PIM) program on my desktop computer and a cheap little three-ring notebook. I would print my addresses onto standard copy paper, cut the pages into 6.5-inch by 8.5-inch sections, and punch holes in the sides with a hole-punch I had modified to accommodate the binder's rings. This was my low-cost, no-hassle method of keeping contacts handy.

Well, my system had more holes than its resulting pages. Whenever an address changed, or I added someone to my list, that information would get written in barely-legible pen in the margins. Every week or so, I'd update the PIM and have to print out fresh copies of the whole thing.

The Palm's built-in Address Book, by comparison, is such a dramatic improvement that I can only look back and blame the inexperience of my youth. With Address Book, you can store more than just names and addresses: office and home phone numbers, email addresses, driving directions, birthdays, and more.

Viewing Addresses

The Address List is another example of how Palm devices can store and present a great deal of information without cluttering up the limited screen.

Address List and Address View

◆ Contacts are listed alphabetically either by last name or by company name down the left side of the screen (**Figure 5.1**).

◆ The right-hand column lists each person's primary contact information; the letter at the end of each line indicates which type of information is displayed (for example, W equals Work, H equals Home, and E equals E-mail).

◆ A note icon (☐) at the far right indicates that the record includes an attached note.

◆ The triangular arrows in the lower-right corner scroll up and down the contact list. You can also use the scroll buttons on the handheld case or jog dial (on some models), which move through the list one screen at a time.

◆ When you tap a record to view it, the Address View shows you that contact's details (**Figure 5.2**). Scroll up or down to view the details by tapping the arrows, pressing the scroll buttons, or using the jog dial.

✔ Tip

■ Press the physical scroll buttons when you're at the beginning or the end of the current record to jump to the next one.

Figure 5.1 The Address List displays names and preferred phone numbers— you may not even have to tap a name to get the number you need.

Figure 5.2 Tapping a name brings up the contact information; fields left blank (such as Fax number) are hidden to conserve space.

VIEWING ADDRESSES

Figure 5.3 Two options are available for sorting the Address List, depending on whether you're looking for companies or people's names.

Figure 5.4 Sorting by Company, Last Name reorders the list alphabetically by company, and truncates longer names to show more information.

Figure 5.5 Specify a preferred number by using the Show in List popup menu.

Changing the Sort Order

Since there isn't much space on the screen, you can't tell if, for example, Thomas Silvestri was the guy you met at last month's conference, or if he's your genius financial adviser. Fortunately, you can choose how you want the records listed.

To change the sort order:

1. Select Preferences from the Options menu.

2. Choose either Last Name, First Name or Company, Last Name from the List By box, then tap OK (**Figures 5.3 and 5.4**).

Specifying a Preferred Number

Suppose you want to view someone's home number instead of their work phone in the Address List. The Address Book provides a way to do it, although it's slightly buried.

To specify a preferred number:

1. Tap the record you wish to change. This takes you to the Address View screen.

2. Tap the Edit button, or tap anywhere within the Address View to go into the Address Edit screen.

3. Tap Details.

4. Choose the field you want to appear in the main list by tapping the Show in List popup menu (**Figure 5.5**). Tap OK to return to the edit screen, then tap Done.

✔ Tip

- If you know ahead of time which field you want to appear in the Address List, write that number first when you're entering the address. By default, the contact information shown in the Address List is the first contact field entered.

CHANGING THE SORT ORDER

Changing the Display Font

You have three options for changing fonts: within the Address List, within the Address View, and within the Address Edit screen.

To change the display font:

1. Select Font from the Options menu.

2. Tap one of the font styles in the Select Font window (**Figure 5.6**). Tap OK.

✔ Tips

■ Some high-resolution devices, such as Palm's Tungsten line, feature four text sizes, while others include three sizes.

■ The Treo display includes a contact's phone number on a separate line, which makes it easier to tap for dialing (see Chapter 9). I prefer to set the list display to the largest font size when using a Treo (**Figure 5.7**).

Figure 5.6 Choose the font to display contact information. The larger fonts are more readable, but show less data.

Figure 5.7 The Treo's Address List shows phone numbers on separate lines, which works better in a larger font size.

Figure 5.8 Begin writing the last name of your contact in the Look Up field to jump to the closest match.

Figure 5.9 The Find function can be helpful when searching for text located within a record.

Address	▼ Restaurants
Figaro Bistro	206-284-6465 W
Greengo, Mary	206-527-2770 W
Happy Teriyaki	425-277-9388 W
I Luv Teriyaki	425-235-2160 W
Little Peking	425-255-1678 W
Pizza Hut	425-228-4800 W
Ristorante Paradis	425-889-8601 W
Sabai Sabai Thai Cu	206-524-2500 W
Starbucks-Factoria	206-747-9441 W
Taco Del Mar	206-545-8001 W
Thai Ocean	206-526-5023 W

Look Up: **S A**

Figure 5.10 Use the Navigator to look up contacts one-handed.

Looking Up Contacts

There's a better way to find the person you're looking for than scrolling through the list.

To search using Look Up:

1. In the Look Up field, write the first letter of the last name (or company name, depending on the sort order) you're looking for; the first match will be highlighted (**Figure 5.8**).

2. If the first letter doesn't match the intended name, keep writing letters until you get a match. If you know you're close, use the arrows in the lower-right corner to scroll through the list by individual record, or the scroll buttons (or jog dial) on the case to scroll by screen.

To perform a find:

1. If you're looking for a word located within a record or a record's attached note, tap the silkscreened Find icon.

2. Enter the text you're searching for, then tap OK. The results (including matches in other programs) appear in a new window. Tap the match you want (**Figure 5.9**).

✔ Tips

- Find will begin its search within the application you're currently running.

- To quickly clear the Look Up field, press either the up or down scroll button.

- On my work phone with Caller ID, if an unfamiliar number is displayed, I do a quick Find for part of the number to see if it matches someone in my Address Book.

- On Palm Tungsten and Zire 71 models, press the right navigation button to display a name selector. Scroll up or down to select letters, then press right again to go to the next letter (**Figure 5.10**).

Entering and Deleting Address Records

Graffiti is a great method for entering text into a handheld, but I won't pretend it's always the best option. If you need to create lots of new records, you're better off typing them into Palm Desktop on your PC. But for one or two, here's how to enter them quickly.

To create a new record:

1. From the Address List or the Address View screen, tap the New button.

2. Fill in the fields using Graffiti or the built-in keypad (**Figure 5.11**). Tap Done.

✔ Tips

■ Write the next field Graffiti character (᛭) to go to the next field without moving the stylus from the Graffiti area. Or, on devices with keypads, press the Tab key.

■ You can enter more than one line of text into each field. Write a carriage return (╱) and add another line of information; it stays in the same field (**Figure 5.12**).

To create a new record using Palm Desktop (Windows):

1. Click the Contacts button to view the Address Book.

2. Click the New Contact button, select New Contact from the Edit menu, or press Control-N.

3. Enter the text in the appropriate fields, then click OK (**Figure 5.13**).

✔ Tip

■ To create another contact without leaving the New Contact dialog, click the New button.

Figure 5.11 After tapping New, write the contact's information in the fields.

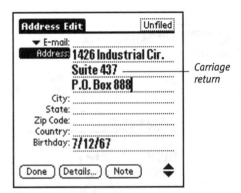

Figure 5.12 Don't worry if there aren't enough fields (such as a second address field): simply write a carriage return to make a new line.

Figure 5.13 The New Address dialog includes all contact info on one screen. Press Ctrl-Tab to easily switch to the Note tab if you want to add more information.

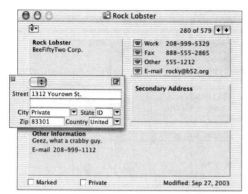

Figure 5.14 The Macintosh Palm Organizer features information areas that pop up entry fields when you click on them.

Figure 5.15 Sometimes we lose track of people who were once dear to us. Check Save archive copy on PC to save deleted records at the next HotSync.

To create a new record using Palm Desktop (Macintosh):

1. Click the Addresses button from the toolbar, choose Address List from the View menu, or press Command-Shift-A.

2. Click the New Address button, select Address from the Create menu, or press Command-Option-A (the keyboard shortcut works anywhere in the program, not just with the Address List viewed).

3. Click on an information area to access the entry fields (**Figure 5.14**). When you're finished, close the window or press Command-W.

✔ Tips

- You can jump between the information fields by pressing the Tab key.

- If you're typing something that's been entered before, such as a city name, Palm Desktop automatically completes the word for you.

- Two areas are provided for entering an email address: the E-mail field in the Other Information area, or as a popup item in the Phones fields. Choose one, or use them to list more than one email address.

To delete a contact (Palm):

1. Tap the contact to select it.

2. Select Delete Address from the Record menu, or write ╱-D.

   You can also tap Edit, then Details, then the Delete button—but who has that kind of time?

3. If you want to store the record in the PC's Palm archive files, be sure to check Save archive copy on PC. Click OK to delete (**Figure 5.15**).

ENTERING AND DELETING ADDRESS RECORDS

Duplicating Records

Palm OS 3.5 introduced a welcome change to the Address Book: the ability to duplicate existing records. This is especially helpful when you're adding several people who work at the same company, for example.

To duplicate an existing record:

1. Select an Address Book record from the Address List or tap it to open the Address View screen.

2. Select Duplicate Address from the Record menu, or write ╱-T (**Figure 5.16**). The new record adds the word "Copy" at the end of the text in the First name field (**Figure 5.17**).

✔ Tips

■ If you've accidentally made more duplicates than you intended, or if for some reason your records have been duplicated during a bad HotSync, Palm Desktop for Windows offers a solution. From the Tools menu, choose Delete Duplicates from the Addins submenu. Or, click the Delete Duplicates button on the toolbar (to the left of the user field). The Delete Duplicates dialog appears, which you can use to search for and remove any duplicate records (it also searches Date Book, To Do List, and Memo Pad).

■ Need to duplicate a record but aren't running Palm OS 3.5 or later? You can make a copy by beaming it to yourself! In any text field, write ℒ- · -T (shortcut stroke, period, T). Then, select the record to duplicate and select Beam Address from the Record menu. Write ℒ- · -T again to deactivate the beaming feature.

Figure 5.16 Duplicate records, don't re-enter the same information again.

Figure 5.17 When a record is duplicated, Address Book adds the text "Copy" to the First name field.

DUPLICATING RECORDS

Figure 5.18 If your device supports Quick Connect, an icon appears at the top of the Address List window.

Figure 5.19 Tap a phone number to dial it, or an email address to create a new message in supported email software.

Figure 5.20 Choose which programs handle which Quick Connect tasks.

Using Quick Connect

Palm handhelds no longer exist alone—they can communicate with the outside world with the help of Quick Connect. Depending on the capabilities of your device, you can dial a phone number; send an email, fax, or instant message; or locate an address on a GPS-assisted map.

To use Quick Connect:

1. Tap an Address Book record.

2. Choose Connect from the Record menu, write ╱-I, or tap the Quick Connect icon at the top of the screen (**Figure 5.18**).

3. Tap a number in the Quick Connect list to activate it (**Figure 5.19**). Only supported actions appear (for example, an email address won't show up if you have no compatible email software installed).

To configure Quick Connect settings:

1. At the Quick Connect list (see step 3 above), tap the Settings button.

2. Tap a popup menu next to the type of action you want to define. For example, if you have multiple compatible email programs installed, choose one from the E-mail popup list (**Figure 5.20**).

3. If a phone number requires a dialing prefix (such as dialing an international number), tap the Number Prefix box and enter the prefix text in the field provided.

✔ Tip

■ To dial a number without going to the Quick Connect list, turn on Tap-to-Connect mode. In the Address Book preferences, mark the Enable Tap-to-Connect checkbox. This disables the capability to edit a record by tapping anywhere on the screen, but you can still tap the Edit button to make changes.

Changing and Editing Phone Field Labels

Although there are five fields for contact numbers such as work and home phones, many of us have more access numbers than that. Address Book includes eight labels accessible via popup menus.

To change phone field labels:

1. Tap on a record to view it, then tap the Edit button (**Figure 5.21**).

2. Tap the popup menu next to the number you want to change. With the menu active, choose from Work, Home, Fax, Other, E-mail, Main, Pager, or Mobile.

3. Tap Done to exit the Address Edit screen.

To edit phone field labels in Palm Desktop (Windows):

1. Highlight a name and click Edit Address, or double click the name.

2. In the Contact Info area (**Figure 5.22**), click the field name next to the number you want to change, and choose the desired label from the popup menu.

3. Click the radio button to the left of the popup menu for the number you wish to appear in the Address List.

To set default phone field options in Palm Desktop (Windows):

1. Choose Preferences from the Tools menu.

2. Change the labels in the Default Labels area as described above (**Figure 5.23**).

3. Click OK.

Figure 5.21 The popup phone label options provide for more than just work and home numbers.

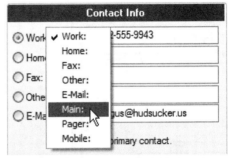

Figure 5.22 Changing the phone field names in Palm Desktop for Windows works the same as in the Palm OS.

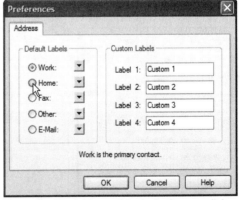

Figure 5.23 The Address tab in the Preferences dialog sets the default labels for all new contacts.

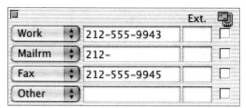

Figure 5.24 The Phones box in Palm Desktop for Macintosh features popup menus to label the fields, plus an option for adding numbers to the Instant Palm Desktop menu.

Figure 5.25 A phone field in Palm Desktop for Macintosh can have any name, though it appears as Other on the device if it's not one of the existing labels.

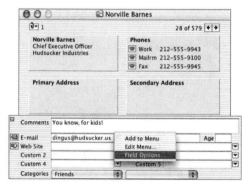

Figure 5.26 Email shows up in the Other Information field instead of in Phones like on the Palm OS and under Windows.

To edit phone field labels in Palm Desktop (Macintosh):

1. Click the Phones box within a Contact window to edit the phone fields.

2. Choose a label from the popup windows to the left of each field (**Figure 5.24**).

3. If you want that contact's name and a number to appear in the Instant Palm Desktop menu (see the end of this chapter for more information), mark the box to the far right of the desired number.

To customize phone field labels in Palm Desktop (Macintosh):

1. Choose Other from the popup menu to create a custom field name.

2. To permanently add a custom label to the menu, choose Edit Menu (**Figure 5.25**).

3. Enter a new name and click OK.

✔ Tips

- If you enter an extension into the Ext. field, it appears on the same line as the number in the Palm OS.

- Only a maximum of four fields appear in a contact's Phones section, but there are five on the handheld. The fifth field is the Email field, found in the Other Information area (**Figure 5.26**). An Email option appears on the phone field popup menu as well, giving you a way to record multiple email addresses for contacts.

- You can use any name to describe a phone field, but keep in mind that anything not matching the predefined labels will appear as Other on the handheld.

Renaming the Custom Field Labels

In addition to standard fields such as Address and City, four custom fields are available for text input. Since "Custom 1" is a boring label, you can change the names to anything else.

To rename custom field labels:

1. Choose Rename Custom Fields from the Options menu to display the Rename Custom Fields dialog box (**Figure 5.27**). In Palm Desktop for Windows, select Preferences under the Tools menu (**Figure 5.28**).

    If you're using Palm Desktop for Macintosh, getting there is a little more tricky: open a contact by double-clicking on it, then click in the Other Information area. Choose the field you want to edit, click the popup menu to the right, and select Field Options; or, just double-click the name of the field (**Figure 5.29**).

2. Type the words or phrases you'd like to use. I find that Birthdate, Web, and Anniversary are essential labels; other possibilities include Spouse, Children (remember, you can type more than one item in the fields by writing a return character in the edit screen), or even Known Allergies.

3. Tap OK to exit.

✔ Tip

■ Remember that if you beam a contact to another Palm device, your custom label names won't transfer with the record. So, any data in these fields might confuse someone who uses different labels.

Figure 5.27 Name the custom fields according to the information that's most important to you.

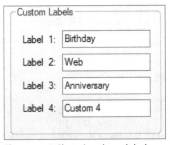

Figure 5.28 Changing these labels applies them to every record in the Address Book.

Figure 5.29 Change the field names from within an active record by selecting Field Options from a field's popup menu.

Figure 5.30 From the Address Edit screen, attach a note by tapping the Note button.

Figure 5.31 An attached note appears in the record as if it was a regular field. Use the scroll arrows to read more.

Attaching and Deleting Notes

The Palm OS's notes feature gives you a blank slate to add all sorts of information about a person or company, from a favorite movie to invaluable driving directions.

To attach a note to a contact:

1. Tap a contact to select it.

2. Tap the Edit button to bring up the Address Edit screen, then tap Note (**Figure 5.30**). Or, select Attach Note from the Record menu, or write ╱-A.

3. Compose your note using Graffiti or the onscreen keyboard.

4. When you are finished, tap Done.

✔ Tips

■ To edit the attached note later, follow the steps above to access the note. If you want a quicker method, however, tap the note icon (▯) to the right of the contact's preferred phone number.

■ You don't have to open the note separately to view it. The text appears at the bottom of the contact's Address View, and can be read using the scroll arrows (**Figure 5.31**).

■ A quick way to scroll, though harder to navigate, is to "select-scroll" through long notes. Position your cursor somewhere in the text and, without lifting the stylus, drag down the screen.

To delete a note:

1. In the Address View or Address Edit screens, select Delete Note from the Record menu, or write ✓-O.

2. If you're on the note editing screen, tap the Delete button.

3. You will be asked to confirm your choice. Tap Yes or No (**Figure 5.32**).

To attach a note (Windows):

1. Double-click a contact or click the Edit button to view the Edit Record screen.

2. Click the Note tab, or press Control-Tab to switch to it.

3. Type the text of your note, then click OK.

To attach a note (Macintosh):

1. Create a new note by clicking the New Memo button, or pressing Command-Option-N.

2. Write "Handheld Note: Address Book" in the Title field.

3. Type the text of your note.

4. Link the new Memo record to the desired address by dragging the memo icon in the window's title bar to the Address window (**Figure 5.33**). (See later in this chapter for information on linking records.)

✔ Tips

- The memo icon in the title bar is hard to handle (not to mention awkward). Click and hold on the icon before you start dragging it.

- I'll never be lost again! I used to keep a tattered library of paper scraps in my car containing driving directions. Now, I store directions in notes attached to people's addresses (**Figure 5.34**).

ATTACHING AND DELETING NOTES

Figure 5.32 When you delete a note, you will be asked to verify your action.

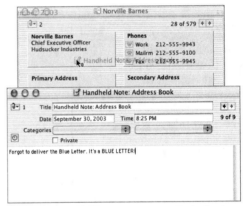

Figure 5.33 On the Mac, create a new attached note by dragging the memo icon to the intended contact.

Figure 5.34 Attach driving directions to contacts and impress your relatives.

Figure 5.35 The option to edit your categories is strategically placed at the bottom of the popup category list.

Figure 5.36 Create or rename categories using up to 15 characters.

Figure 5.37 Address Book prefers to show you every contact whenever it's launched, unless you select Remember last category in the Preferences dialog.

Setting Up Custom Categories

The categories that are preset in the Palm OS barely hint at the value of organizing records by category. In addition to preventing data confusion, it makes it easier to view your data in comprehensible chunks, rather than one big list.

To create a custom category:

1. Select Edit Categories from the category popup menu in the upper-right corner of the screen (**Figure 5.35**).

2. Tap New and give your category a name (**Figure 5.36**).

3. Tap OK to return to the list.

To specify the last category viewed:

1. Select Preferences from the Options menu, or write ⁄-R.

2. Mark the Remember last category box, then tap OK (**Figure 5.37**).

✔ Tips

- To quickly switch to the next category, press the Address Book button on the handheld's case. If you've created a category that currently has no records assigned to it, Address Book skips to the next category containing records. Highly annoying, however, is that the Unfiled category is skipped using this method.

- Create several records that share the same category by displaying that category and tapping New from the Address List; each new record will remain assigned to the current category.

- Palm Desktop for Macintosh doesn't store categories for each built-in application, so you can only have a total of 15 categories shared among those programs.

Marking Contacts as Private

It's fun to show off your handheld sometimes, but you don't want everyone to have unlimited access to your private information. It's easy to hide records from wandering eyes.

To mark contacts as private:

1. Tap the record you wish to mark as private, then tap the Edit button.

2. Tap the Details button.

3. Mark the Private checkbox, then tap OK (**Figure 5.38**).

4. Tap Done when finished (**Figure 5.39**).

To mark contacts as private (Windows and Macintosh):

1. Select a record in the Address List, then double-click it to display the contact's information window.

2. Mark the Private checkbox (**Figure 5.40**).

3. Click OK (Windows) or close the information window (Macintosh).

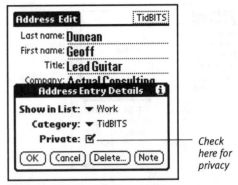

Check here for privacy

Figure 5.38 It takes a few taps to get to the Address Entry Details dialog, but it's worth it if you want to ensure that your private records are hidden or masked.

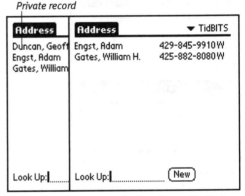

Private record

Figure 5.39 When you set the Security application's settings to Hide Records, private records disappear in the Address List.

Figure 5.40 A checkbox appears in Palm Desktop to mark private records.

Figure 5.41 Change the Security setting from within any application.

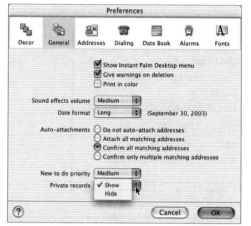

Figure 5.42 Palm Desktop for Macintosh can only show or hide private records.

Changing the Security Setting

Private records can be either hidden entirely or masked. Although the procedure below changes the display option throughout the system, you can change the Security setting from within any of the built-in applications.

To change the security setting:

1. Select Security from the Options menu, write ∕-H, or tap the Security icon in the command toolbar.

2. Select an option from the Current Privacy popup menu: Show Records, Mask Records, or Hide Records (**Figure 5.41**).

3. Tap OK.

To change the security setting (Windows):

In Palm Desktop for Windows, choose a setting from the View menu, or click the small lock icon on the toolbar to choose a setting: Show Private Records, Mask Private Records, or Hide Private Records.

To change the security setting (Macintosh):

1. Choose Preferences from the Palm Desktop menu (Mac OS X) or from the Edit menu (Mac OS 9).

2. In the Preferences dialog box, switch to the General preferences.

3. Click the Privacy Records popup menu and choose either Show or Hide (**Figure 5.42**). Palm Desktop for Macintosh does not support masked records.

Beaming Addresses

Every Palm device includes an infrared (IR) port for beaming data from one device to another. The most common usage of IR is to swap electronic business cards directly into other people's Address Books. If you've ever returned from a conference or trade show with a stack of business cards (and then lost them), you'll appreciate how useful beaming can be. Simply create a record for yourself and be prepared to amaze onlookers.

To specify your business card:

1. Find yourself (in the Address List—we can talk more about philosophy later). Tap the record to select it.

2. Choose Select Business Card from the Record menu (**Figure 5.43**).

3. If you're sure, tap Yes in the confirmation dialog. A special icon appears next to the Address View and Address Edit tabs (**Figure 5.44**).

To beam your business card:

Choose Beam Business Card from the Record menu, or just press and hold the Address Book button on the handheld's case.

To beam an Address record:

1. Tap the record you wish to beam.

2. Choose Beam Address from the Record menu, or write ∕-B. Private records become public when beamed individually.

To beam a category:

1. Make your chosen category visible in the Address List.

2. Choose Beam Category from the Record menu. All records in that category, except Private records, will be transferred.

Figure 5.43 Choose the record you want for your business card (preferably the one with your name on it), then activate it from the Record menu.

Figure 5.44 The record designated as your business card displays a "beaming file card" icon next to the Address View tab. The best way to zap it to another IR-equipped Palm device is to just hold down the Address Book button on the front of the handheld.

BEAMING ADDRESSES

Figure 5.45 Find a record and beam it from the Address List using the Beam Address icon on the command bar.

Figure 5.46 You can choose to keep the Beam Receive option turned off, knowing that there's a shortcut for turning it on without coming back to Preferences.

✔ Tips

- You don't have to view a record before beaming it. Use the Look Up field to find a record, which highlights the match in the Address List (**Figure 5.45**). Write the command stroke (∕) to view the command toolbar, then tap the Beam Address icon (📡).

- When you transfer a category, the category's name does not appear on the recipient's Palm device. However, if they're running Palm OS 3.5 or later, they can choose which of their categories to assign to the group of incoming records, or they can create a new category.

- Some people prefer to leave the Beam Receive option off in the Preferences application to conserve battery life (see Chapter 2). If you fall into that camp, but need to receive beamed business cards from other Palm users, there are two ways to activate Beam Receive without making a side trip to the Preferences application (**Figure 5.46**).

  In a text field, write ℓ- · -I to temporarily enable Beam Receive for five seconds.

  The other option is to press and hold the Address Book button on the handheld's case as if you were going to beam your business card. After you beam your information (or tap Cancel), you'll be asked if you want to turn Beam Receive on.

- It's possible to "spread-beam" records to multiple handhelds at once. This is great if you're in a small group of Palm users and exchanging business cards; as long as the recipients are in range of the IR beam, they will all receive your business card even if you send it only once.

Importing Contacts into Palm Desktop

There's a good chance that you already have a stash of contact information stored in a desktop PIM program, or maybe even a customized database or Excel spreadsheet. If so, you should be able to transfer your records into Palm Desktop with a minimum of fuss.

To import contacts from a PIM:

1. In your existing PIM, select the export function—most programs include something like Export under the File menu.

2. Export the file as a tab-delimited text file; if you are presented with the option to include field names (such as "Last Name" or "City"), go ahead and include them.

3. In Palm Desktop, choose Import from the File menu.

4. Click and drag the field labels in the left-hand pane of the Specify Import Fields (Windows) or Import (Macintosh) dialog box to match the data in the right pane (**Figures 5.47** and **5.48**).

5. When the data looks right to you, click OK to begin the import process. After a few seconds, the records will be available to use.

✔ Tips

■ If you have the option of including field names when you export the data from your original PIM, do it—you can save some time by matching the label names instead of guessing the order.

■ If you select a category from the Contact List's category popup menu before you import, the new records will belong to that category after being imported.

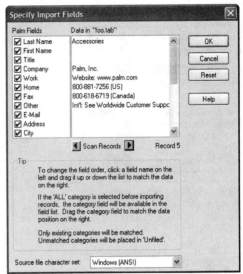

Figure 5.47 In Windows Palm Desktop, drag the field labels to match the record's field-mapping order.

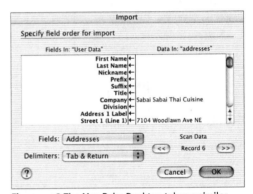

Figure 5.48 The Mac Palm Desktop takes a similar approach to Windows. This step can be slightly monotonous, but you'll appreciate it later on.

Figure 5.49 Let the computer do the work for you—never memorize a phone number again!

Select which records to print
Choose how much information will be printed

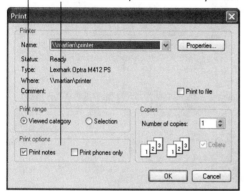

Figure 5.50 Printing Address Book records requires only two specialized fields in the standard Print dialog.

Palm Desktop Special Features

In general, the desktop software mirrors the Palm OS in functionality. However, there are also a few features of Palm Desktop that add functionality, such as dialing phone numbers (if your PC is connected to the phone line you use for making calls), printing records, and sharing data with other applications.

To dial phone numbers:

1. In the Address List, click the contact you wish to call.

2. In Windows, choose Dial from the Edit menu, or right-click the contact and select Dial from the popup menu that appears. In Palm Desktop for Macintosh, open the contact's information and click the dial button (**Figure 5.49**). (In Mac OS X, you can dial only through the computer's speaker, however.)

3. Pick up the phone after the number begins dialing, and press the Talk button (Windows) or the Release button (Mac OS 9 version).

To print records:

1. Choose which records you want to print. If you want only a few, select them by Control/Command-clicking their names. To print an entire category, select it from the category popup menu. To print all records, select the All category.

2. Choose Print from the File menu, or press Control/Command-P. The Print dialog box appears (**Figure 5.50**).

3. Set the print range to either Viewed category or Selection, and specify full records or just phone numbers to be printed.

PALM DESKTOP SPECIAL FEATURES

To create vCards:

If you use an email program that supports vCards (a method of attaching contact information to an email message), select a contact and choose Forward as vCard from the Edit menu. A new message is created with the vCard information attached.

You can also create a standalone vCard file (.vcf) by choosing Export vCard from the File menu.

To change the Address Book view:

With the Address Book visible, click the tabs at the bottom of the screen. The default view is the List view, but you can also arrange your contacts in the easier-to-read Business Card view (**Figure 5.51**) or the Large Icons and Small Icons views (**Figure 5.52**).

The Hide Details button allows you to display more contacts by removing the details pane, and becomes the Show Details button when the pane is hidden.

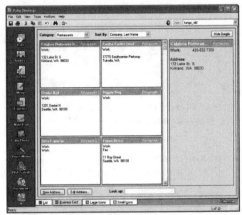

Figure 5.51 Some people find it easier to use the Business Card view to browse contact information.

Figure 5.52 Using the Large Icons (shown here) and Small Icons views means you never have to feel left out of the crowd.

PALM DESKTOP SPECIAL FEATURES

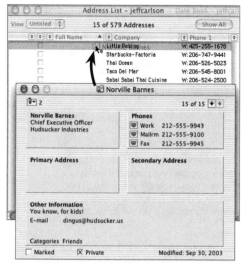

Figure 5.53 Create relational links between records by dragging them onto one another.

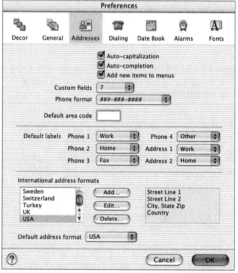

Figure 5.54 Palm Desktop offers several options for working with Address Book data.

Macintosh Palm Desktop Special Features

Palm Desktop for Macintosh includes several features not found in the Windows software. For example, it offers the ability to attach not only notes to records, but also to create links between related records. Unfortunately, the links don't transfer over to the handheld.

To link records:

1. Open an Address record by selecting it and pressing Return, or double-clicking it.

2. Grab the title bar icon (🔲) in the upper-left corner and drag it to the contact you wish to link. You can drag contacts onto events, to do items, and memos as well (**Figure 5.53**). You can also just drag one record in the Address List onto another without viewing the details of either.

   Alternately, click the attachment popup menu (🔲▼) and choose an item from the Attach To submenu.

To set Addresses preferences:

1. Choose Preferences from the Palm Desktop menu (Mac OS X) or the Edit menu (Mac OS 9). The Preferences dialog box appears (**Figure 5.54**).

2. Click the Addresses button. Notable preferences here include:

   ▲ **Phone popup menu.** No matter how you type the number, it will be formatted according to this selection.

   ▲ **Auto-capitalization.** Similar to the Palm OS, Palm Desktop capitalizes information within Addresses fields.

   ▲ **Auto-completion.** Palm Desktop stores lists of field contents; when you're entering information, it searches for a match and displays the likely result as you type.

To find addresses:

1. Choose Find from the Locate menu, or press Command-F to display the Find dialog box (**Figure 5.55**).

2. Begin typing the name you're searching for. If you're looking for text within a contact, but it isn't a name or company name, click Display Results in List Window.

3. Click Display when it's found.

To sort records:

◆ To sort each list according to a column's contents, click the column's title (it will become underlined to indicate it's the active method) or choose Sort from each title's popup menu (**Figure 5.56**).

◆ You can also edit the columns to customize your display. Click and drag a column's right border to change its width. To rearrange the columns' order, click and hold in the area next to a column name, then drag left or right to position it (**Figure 5.57**). To choose which columns are displayed, select Columns from the View menu and mark the ones you want.

✔ Tips

■ Palm Desktop has the added ability to sort using secondary criteria as well. For example, if you want to sort a list of people within a specific company, click the Company column title, then Shift-click the Full Name column title.

■ The Mark checkbox (**Figure 5.58**) enables you to mark records from multiple categories, then quickly view them without creating a filter by choosing Marked from the popup menu in the column head. When printing, you can opt to print only the marked records without first locating them in the Contact List.

Figure 5.55 The Find command displays matches containing the entire text in the Starts With field. Type more letters to narrow the search if several items appear.

Click name to sort...   ... or choose popup menu item.

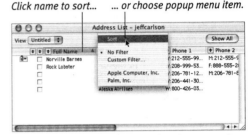

Figure 5.56 Sort the list by any column's contents by either clicking on the column's name, or choosing Sort from the popup menus.

Click and hold here

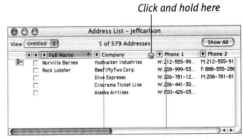

Figure 5.57 Click in the title area and drag to change the order of the visible columns.

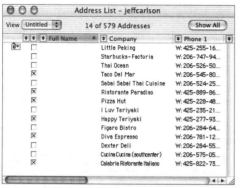

Figure 5.58 Mark records that you use frequently to view and print them quickly, without creating a filter.

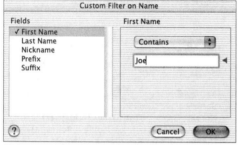

Figure 5.59 Create custom filters to display only the contacts matching specified criteria.

Figure 5.60 The custom fields can be customized even further. Here, the E-mail field is set to create a pre-addressed message in Eudora Pro.

To filter specific data:

You can also configure the sorting method by choosing Custom Filter from the popup menus, which displays only the items that meet the filter's criteria. For example, if you want to list only the phone calls you need to make, set up a filter that searches for the words "call" or "phone" (**Figure 5.59**).

To save memorized views:

When you've set up a sort order and specific filters, choose Memorize View from the View popup menu to save it. This way, you can see related tasks and notes without repeating the sorting steps above. To see the full list again, click the Show All button.

To create a pre-addressed email message:

1. In a record's Address window, click the Other Information area.

2. Click the email button (   ) beside the E-mail field in the Other Information section. A blank email message is created in your email program with the contact's email address in the To: field.

✔ Tip

■ You can change the email client that's tied into the E-mail field's button. Choose Field Options from the field's popup menu, then choose your email client from the Script File popup menu (**Figure 5.60**).

Using the Instant Palm Desktop Menu

The Instant Palm Desktop menu appears in the Dock icon for Palm Desktop in Mac OS X (**Figure 5.61**), or next to the Mac OS's Application menu in Mac OS 9. It allows you to access addresses and other records quickly.

To access contact information using the Instant Palm Desktop:

◆ Click the menu and highlight a contact to view or edit its details; or, choose Open Palm Desktop to launch the program.

◆ Search for an address by selecting Find Address (**Figure 5.62**). To make a contact appear permanently on the menu, click the Add to Menu button. You can also dial phone numbers directly from the contact detail window (**Figure 5.63**).

◆ Create new addresses, events, to do items, memos, and event banners from the Create submenu.

To add contacts to the Instant Palm Desktop:

In a record's Instant Palm Desktop contact view, or the Address window within Palm Desktop, check the box to the right of the phone number you want to appear in the Instant Palm Desktop menu.

To remove contacts from the Instant Palm Desktop:

In the Address window, uncheck the box to the right of the phone number.

✔ Tip

■ If you find yourself writing your address frequently in letters or email, put yourself in the Instant Palm Desktop menu, then click the Copy All button to get the info.

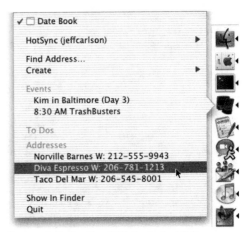

Figure 5.61 Under Mac OS X, the Instant Palm Desktop is accessible from the Dock.

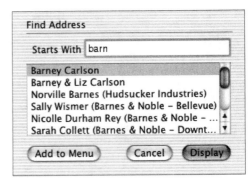

Figure 5.62 Search your Address Book using the Instant Palm Desktop's Find Address feature.

Figure 5.63 All of Palm Desktop's information is available when you select a record from the Instant Palm Desktop menu.

Alternatives to Using the Built-In Address Book

The Address Book offers a lot of power in a svelte package, but what if you want to supercharge your address list? Although there are plenty of alternatives, the two I'm most impressed with are Super Names (www.standalone.com) and PopUp Names (www.benc.hr/popnames.htm). Both programs use the Address Book's database as their data source, which means your contacts are still synchronized with your PC.

Super Names

I was dubious of Super Names at first, mostly because I respond strongly to interfaces. A quick look at the Super Names main screen shows how crowded it can be (**Figure 5.64**). But notice what's there: categories appear as tabs across the top of the screen; an alphabet running beneath the tabs lets you tap a letter to jump to that range of contacts; an optional panel below the Address List previews the highlighted name, with icons to specify which info appears.

In addition to cramming a lot of useful information on one screen, Super Names lets you link contacts to other contacts, or even to records from Date Book, the To Do List, or the Memo Pad (**Figure 5.65**). Linked records can be displayed by tapping a paper-clip icon at the top of the screen.

PopUp Names

PopUp Names shows more contact information on its main screen, but it has the distinction of being viewed from within any application on your handheld. PopUp Names is actually a system hack (see Chapter 8); when enabled, you can write a stroke in the silkscreened area (the default is to draw a line from the Calculator icon to the Find icon) to bring up the PopUp Names window (**Figure 5.66**).

You can even perform Address Book functions, like beaming your business card or other contacts, just as if you've launched the Address Book application itself.

Figure 5.64 Once you get the hang of the Super Names interface, you'll like how easy it is to view contact info.

Figure 5.65 Link contacts or other records to view them quickly next time.

Figure 5.66 PopUp Names is available from any application on your handheld.

To Do List, Memos, and Notes

When I tell people about Palm handhelds, most seem to get excited about the Date Book and Address Book, two applications that can greatly decrease the amount of paper they carry. But when I was first considering whether to buy a handheld, it was the To Do List that thrilled me. I need to *see* tasks that must be accomplished, or else I risk forgetting about them until it's too late. A digital to-do list that keeps reminding me of tasks not yet finished was irresistible.

The Memo Pad, on the other hand, was low on my list of required features. I mean, it's a necessary element (what's the point of having a palmtop device if you can't jot down quick notes?), but light bulbs are also necessary elements, and you don't see me drooling over the latest 100-watt GE soft-white bulb.

Now, both applications are essential to me: I can track my tasks with the To Do List (and make them disappear when completed), and I can use Memo Pad to store information that I had never considered before.

TO DO LIST, MEMOS, AND NOTES

Viewing Options

The To Do List (**Figure 6.1**) can be as sparse or as detailed as you want. Tap the Show button to access the To Do Preferences window, which provides the following options (**Figure 6.2**).

◆ If you prefer to see the items you've accomplished, mark the Show Completed Items checkbox.

If you uncheck this option to hide completed items, the records are still held in the device's memory until you manually purge them (see "Purging Records" later in this chapter).

◆ The To Do List, by default, displays all upcoming tasks, even if they're several years away. If you would rather live for today, mark Show Only Due Items.

◆ Marking Record Completion Date changes an item's due date to the date it was checked off when finished.

◆ Show Due Dates, when marked, adds a date column to the right of the task names; items with no due date specified are represented by dashes.

◆ Marking Show Priorities displays a column of numbers, representing the importance of each task (1 is highest, 5 is lowest), between the checkboxes and item names.

◆ As with the Address Book and Memo Pad, To Do List records can be assigned to categories. Show Categories adds a category column to the right side of the screen.

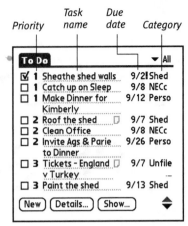

Figure 6.1 The To Do List, with all aspects visible, includes each task, plus its priority, due date, and category.

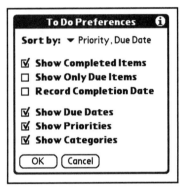

Figure 6.2 Depending on your tolerance for visual clutter, you may want more options visible.

Figure 6.3 Choose how your private records are displayed.

Figure 6.4 The Sort by popup menu organizes tasks to fit your preferences.

Changing Security View

Beginning with Palm OS 3.5, private records can be displayed, masked (grayed out), or (as in previous versions) hidden from within the To Do List.

To change the Security view:

1. Select Security from the Options menu.

2. Tap the Current Privacy popup menu to choose one of three methods: Show Records, Mask Records, or Hide Records (**Figure 6.3**).

3. Tap OK to exit.

Setting the Sort Order

Once you've decided which elements will be visible, you need to figure out how to sort the To Do records. Feel free to experiment with each setting for a few days to get a sense of what works best for you.

To set the sort order:

1. Tap Show to bring up the To Do Preferences window (**Figure 6.4**).

2. Tap the Sort by popup menu to choose one of four methods: Priority, Due Date; Due Date, Priority; Category, Priority; or Category, Due Date (**Figure 6.5**).

3. Tap OK to exit.

✔ Tip

■ I can't stress how much I love to check off a To Do item and have it *disappear*. In college, I carried spiral notebooks filled with to-do lists—or rather, I carried notebooks filled with scribbles and marked-out scribbles. Ick. I can understand that people like to see what they've accomplished, but to me it's all just clutter. Show Completed Items is therefore never marked on my handheld.

To Do   ▼ All

☐ 3 Call Herman Boren   9/17 Busin
☐ 1 Catch up on Sleep   9/8 NECc
☐ 2 Clean Office   9/8 NECc
☐ 3 Invent Insanely   1/2 NECc
      Successful Device
☐ 1 Make Dinner for   9/12 Perso
      Kimberly
☐ 2 Invite Ags & Parie 9/26 Perso
      to Dinner
☐ 2 Roof the shed   9/7 Shed
☐ 3 Paint the shed   9/13 Shed

(New) (Details...) (Show...)   ◆

Figure 6.5 Sorting by Category, Due Date can do funky things with dates: the task for "Invent... device" is really set for January 2, 2004, three months after "Make dinner..." because they belong to different categories.

Entering To Do Items

Creating new To Do items takes more than just having someone say, "Do this!" over your shoulder. But not much more.

To create a new To Do item:

1. Tap the New button. A flashing cursor will appear on a blank line.

2. Write the name of your task—feel free to use multiple lines (**Figure 6.6**). Tap anywhere in a "null" area of the screen (such as the lower-right corner) to deselect your new task.

✔ Tips

- You don't have to tap the New button to create a new To Do item. With nothing selected, start writing in the Graffiti area; a new record will be created automatically (**Figure 6.7**).

- The default settings for new To Do items are Unfiled, no date, with a priority of 1. If you want a new task to share attributes of an existing item, you can maintain category, priority, and/or due date by highlighting an existing record and then tapping New.

- If one category is displayed (versus viewing All), any new records are assigned to that category.

Figure 6.6 Tapping the New button creates a blank record for you to name.

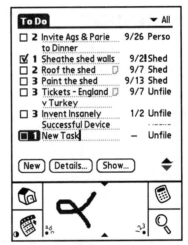

Figure 6.7 If you know what you want to add, just write it! Entering Graffiti characters with nothing selected creates a new To Do List item.

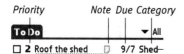

Figure 6.8 You can edit most aspects of a task without leaving the To Do List by tapping these areas.

Figure 6.9 Tap the Details button to bring up a dialog box where you can change any aspect of a To Do item.

Figure 6.10 The only aspect of a task you can't edit from the main list is an item's privacy state.

Editing To Do Items

Depending on which options you've chosen to show, almost every aspect of a To Do item can be changed from the main To Do screen. However, if you prefer a cleaner window, the options are no more than two taps away (**Figure 6.8**).

To prioritize a task:

1. If visible, tap the priority column to the left of the task name and choose a different priority level. Or, tap the To Do item, then tap the Details button.

2. Choose a priority from the buttons at the top of the To Do Item Details window. Tap OK to make the change.

To change a task's category:

1. If visible, tap the category column at the far right of the screen and choose a new category. Or, tap the To Do item, then tap the Details button.

2. Tap the Category popup menu and select a new category (**Figure 6.9**). To add or edit categories, see "Categorizing To Do Items and Memos" later in this chapter. Tap OK.

To make a task private:

1. Tap the To Do item, then tap the Details button.

2. Mark the Private checkbox (**Figure 6.10**). If you've chosen Hide Records or Mask Records from the Security application, the record's text will not be visible when you tap OK. (See Chapter 2 for information on hiding and showing private records.)

To change a task's due date:

1. If visible, tap the due date column and choose a new date. Otherwise, tap the To Do item, then tap the Details button.

2. Tap the Due Date popup menu. The frequently used commands Today, Tomorrow, and One week later make it easy to reschedule tasks (**Figure 6.11**).

3. If you need to switch to a specific date, tap Choose Date and select a new day (**Figure 6.12**). Tap OK.

To mark a task completed:

The moment you've been waiting for—tap the checkbox at left to mark the task completed (**Figure 6.13**).

✔ Tip

■ The To Do application indicates a missed deadline by displaying an exclamation point (!) in the due date column (see "Take out trash" in **Figure 6.13**).

Figure 6.11 Your handheld knows how you work: four common date options are included in the popup menu.

Figure 6.12 If you select Choose Date from the popup menu, you can tap your intended date on the calendar.

Completed task

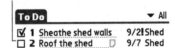

Figure 6.13 Tap the checkbox to mark a task completed. Feels good, doesn't it?

EDITING TO DO ITEMS

Figure 6.14 Tap the Note button to add important information to a task.

Figure 6.15 To delete a note attached to a To Do item, tap the delete button, then confirm the deletion.

Adding and Deleting Notes to To Do Items

To attach a note to a task:

1. Tap an item to select it.

2. Tap the Details button, then tap the Note button (**Figure 6.14**).

   Alternately, select Attach Note from the Record menu, or write ╱-A.

3. Compose your note using Graffiti or the onscreen keyboard. Tap Done when you are finished.

✔ Tip

■ To edit the attached note later, follow the steps above to access the note. If you want a quicker method, tap the note icon (▭) to the right of the task's name.

To navigate a note:

Use the scroll bar on the right side of the screen, the physical scroll buttons, or directional rocker (if your handheld has this) to move through the text.

To delete a note (from main list):

1. Tap the To Do item to select it.

2. Select Delete Note from the Record menu, or write ╱-O. Confirm its deletion by tapping Yes or No.

To delete a note (standard method):

1. Tap Details, then the Note button.

2. Tap Delete in the Note window. Confirm whether you want to delete it by tapping Yes or No (**Figure 6.15**).

Purging Records

It may bring you a measure of satisfaction to know there are dozens, maybe hundreds, of completed tasks in your handheld. Unfortunately, that means they're also taking up RAM. To free up some memory, purge those aging To Do items (**Figure 6.16**).

To purge old records:

1. From the To Do List, select Purge from the Records menu, or write ╱-E.

2. If you want to remove the items from your handheld, but keep them stored on your computer's hard drive, mark the Save archive copy on PC checkbox (**Figure 6.17**). They will be transferred at the next HotSync operation, and removed from your handheld.

3. Tap OK.

Figure 6.16 You can see how much space your completed and pending To Do items are filling by going to the Applications screen and selecting Info from the App menu. Here, the amount of free memory has increased dramatically following a purge.

Figure 6.17 The urge to keep all those successfully completed To Do items can be overpowering, but at some point you'll need to free up some memory on your handheld. Mark Save archive copy on PC to ensure that the tasks aren't lost forever.

PURGING RECORDS

Figure 6.18 Memo Pad lets you store all those random scraps of information.

Figure 6.19 The text on the first line of your memo becomes its title. From there, write your memo, or paste the text in from the clipboard.

Creating and Editing Memos

The Memo Pad is straightforward, yet surprisingly useful. Imagine all of your Post-it notes—plus the crumpled papers discovered in last week's laundry—stored in one location (**Figure 6.18**). The power here is not in the number of features the Memo Pad offers, but in its overall utility.

To create a new memo:

1. Tap the New button, or start writing in the Graffiti area.

2. Start writing. The first line of your memo will become its title, so don't write something generic like "Note" (**Figure 6.19**).

3. Tap Done when you're, well, done.

✔ Tip

■ Move between memos using the right/left arrows at the top of the screen or using the directional rocker.

To edit a memo:

1. Tap once on the title of a memo.

2. To change the memo's category, select one from the category field in the upper-right corner. Or, tap the Details button.

3. Tap Done.

To make a memo private:

1. After tapping the memo you want, tap the Details button to display the Memo Details dialog box.

2. Mark the Private checkbox. If the Security preferences are set to hide private records, the memo will not appear in any of the Memo Pad category lists.

3. Tap Done.

Sorting Memos

Information, unlike dark socks, begs to be sorted. Some prefer alphabetical listings, while others are quite content with chaos. Although the Memo Pad doesn't claim to be the storehouse of the world's information, its sorting capabilities—though limited—can appeal to both extremes.

To sort memos:

1. Select Preferences from the Options menu, or write ╱-R, to display the Memo Preferences dialog box (**Figure 6.20**).

2. Choose a sorting method from the Sort by popup menu. Alphabetic lists items based on their first letters; Manual gives you the power to list items randomly, or by your own secret sorting code. Tap OK.

Note that you must first select Manual sorting before you can begin moving items within the Memo List (**Figure 6.21**). If you've been manually sorting and want to switch back to Alphabetic, you will lose your sort order. Unfortunately, the sorting method you choose applies to all memos, so you can't have some categories sorted manually and others sorted alphabetically.

✔ Tip

■ If you want to type on the road, consider the Palm Portable Keyboard (store. palm.com). See Chapter 1 for more on these keyboards.

Figure 6.20 The Memo Pad gives you two options for sorting the Memo List.

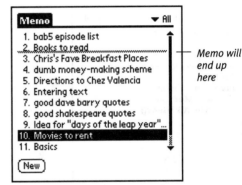

Memo will end up here

Figure 6.21 With sorting set to Manual, tap and drag a memo to a new location. A gray line indicates where it will end up when you lift the stylus.

Navigating Memos

Moving around in memos isn't much different than navigating notes (see "To navigate a note" earlier in this chapter), but a few aspects do stand out.

To navigate memos:

◆ Use the scroll bar at right (if the memo extends past one screen length) to move up and down the text.

◆ Press the directional rocker or plastic up and down buttons (on older models) on the handheld's case. One added benefit of this approach is that you can jump to the next or previous memo, without returning to the main Memo List.

◆ If you're running Palm OS 3.1, jump quickly from the top to the bottom (and vice-versa) by choosing either Go to Top of Page or Go to Bottom of Page from the Options menu. Unfortunately, this capability was removed in Palm OS 3.5.

✔ Tip

■ Although the Go to Top of Page and Go to Bottom of Page commands were removed in Palm OS 3.5, there's still an easy workaround to zap through your text: tap and drag up or down to select the text and quickly go to the top or bottom. It may not be the most elegant solution, but it's easy and it works.

Is Memo Pad Good Enough for Taking Notes?

You'd think that having a palm-sized device to write with would make people want to ditch paper forever. Although some people use their handhelds as note-taking machines, I've found that writing longer texts takes more effort and headache than regular ink and wood pulp.

The advantage of writing longhand is that you can write several letters with one stroke (depending on your handwriting style, of course), whereas Graffiti requires that each character be a separate entity. Plus, extended Graffiti writing tends to aggravate my hands and wrists, which have had their share of repetitive strain injuries (RSIs) in the past (**Figure 6.22**).

I prefer to use the Memo Pad as a great place to store information, not necessarily create it.

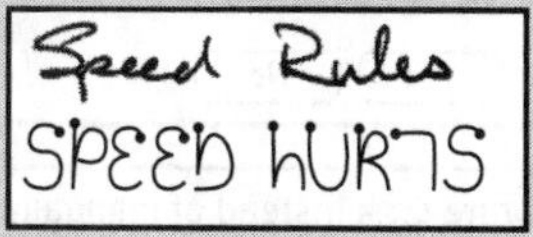

Figure 6.22 Longhand text is a little easier on the hands and wrists than Graffiti.

Categorizing To Do Items and Memos

To assign a To Do List category:

1. If Show Categories is selected in the To Do Preferences, tap the category name to the right of a record and choose a new category from the popup menu that appears (**Figure 6.23**).

   If categories are not visible, select the record and tap Details.

2. Select a name from the Category popup menu. Tap OK to return to the list.

To assign a category to a memo:

1. Tap a memo to open it.

2. Select a category name from the popup menu in the upper-right corner of the screen. Or, tap Details and choose an item from the Category popup menu there.

To set up custom categories:

1. In both the To Do List and the Memo Pad, tap the category popup menu in the upper-right corner. Select Edit Categories from the bottom of the list to bring up the Edit Categories dialog box.

2. Tap the New or Rename button and write the category name (**Figure 6.24**) or tap a name and Delete to remove a category.

✔ Tips

- To create multiple records sharing the same category, go to that category's screen, then create your records there.

- You can merge categories without changing each record individually. Simply rename the categories so they share the same name; you will receive a dialog box confirming your action (**Figure 6.25**).

Figure 6.23 Assign categories quickly by tapping the category column.

Figure 6.24 You can specify up to 15 categories for each of the four built-in applications.

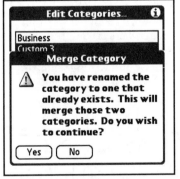

Figure 6.25 Instead of manually reassigning a category to multiple records, merge two existing categories into one.

CATEGORIZING TO DO ITEMS AND MEMOS

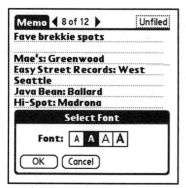

Figure 6.26 Selecting a font changes the setting for all memo records, not just the one currently viewed.

Figure 6.27 Tap the Beam icon in the command bar under Palm OS 3.5 or later.

Changing the Font

In the To Do List and Memo List, you can set a different font for list and record views.

To change the font:

1. In either the list view or the record view, select Font from the Options menu, or write ╱-F. The Select Font dialog box appears.

2. Choose the font from the boxes provided, and tap OK (**Figure 6.26**).

Beaming Records

Save a friend some writing time and transfer your to do items or memos via infrared.

To beam a To Do item or memo:

1. Tap the record that you want to beam. The Memo Pad will display the entire memo; the To Do List will position your cursor in the record's text.

2. Select Beam Item (To Do List) or Beam Memo (Memo Pad) from the Record menu, or write ╱-B; you can also choose the Beam icon (🔝) from the command toolbar under Palm OS 3.5 or later (**Figure 6.27**).

To beam a category:

1. With no records selected, select the category you wish to beam from the category popup menu at the top-right corner. To beam all categories, choose All.

2. Select Beam Category from the Record menu. Note, however, that your categories will appear as Unfiled on the recipient's Palm device. (Starting with Palm OS 3.5, he or she can choose a category for the received records.)

Working in Palm Desktop for Windows

Using the To Do List and the Memo Pad within Palm Desktop is, for the most part, the same as working on the handheld (**Figure 6.28**). There are also a few features that can only be accessed on your PC.

To print records:

1. Choose the items you want to print, or choose the category to print.

2. Choose Print from the File menu, or press Control-P.

3. Specify how you want the data to appear in the Print Options box. Click OK to create a printout (**Figure 6.29**).

To share To Do items with other applications using Send To/Send To:

1. Select the to do items to transfer.

2. In Palm Desktop 4.0, go to the Edit menu and choose an option from the Send To submenu. You can also right-click the selection to access the same submenu.

   If you're running Palm Desktop 3.1, drag the selected records to the Drag To icons in the lower-right corner.

3. If you chose Word, you are given the option to format the data as a Task Progress Report, a Task Delegation Form, or just Leave Data as a Table. When the transfer is complete and the data is formatted, it will be available in Word.

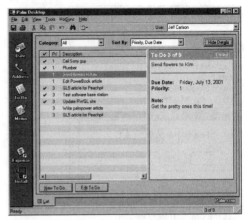

Figure 6.28 The To Do List within Palm Desktop presents all of your options on one main screen.

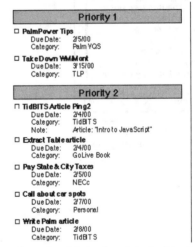

Figure 6.29 Printing from Palm Desktop isn't sexy, but it works. The layout of tasks depends on the sort order you've specified using the Show button.

Figure 6.30 Memo contents are displayed in the pane at right. The contextual menu offers the Send To command.

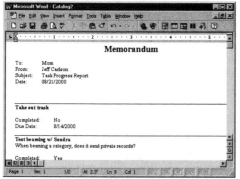

Figure 6.31 The Send To MS Word action activates a set of macros that formats your data using handy templates.

To share memos with other applications using Drag To/Send To:

1. Select the memos you wish to transfer.

2. In Palm Desktop 4.0, go to the Edit menu and choose an option from the Send To submenu. You can also right-click the selection to access the same submenu (**Figure 6.30**).

    If you're running Palm Desktop 3.1, drag the selected records to the Drag To icons in the lower-right corner.

3. Format your information in the program you chose (**Figure 6.31**).

✔ Tips

■ In addition to clicking the application buttons at left, you can press the F4 key to view the To Do List, and the F5 key to bring up the Memo Pad. F1 launches the Palm Desktop online help.

■ In Palm Desktop 3.1, you can quickly access the Note Editor from the To Do List by clicking either a note icon (🗋) to the right of a task, or the blank space where the icon would appear, which will take you to the Note Editor. Palm Desktop 4.0 has unfortunately removed this handy shortcut.

■ When adding records in Palm Desktop 3.1, you can press the Apply button to deactivate the current record. If you're adding multiple records, however, forget about the Apply button and instead just press New to begin the next record—your previous entry will be added automatically to the list.

WORKING IN PALM DESKTOP FOR WINDOWS

Working in Palm Desktop for Macintosh

In essence, the To Do section of Palm Desktop for Macintosh (referred to as the To Do List) provides the same functionality and features as its Windows counterpart, even though it looks quite a bit different.

To view To Do items or memos:

◆ In Palm Desktop 4.1, select To Do List or Memo List from the View menu , or press Command-Shift-T or Command-Shift-N. In Palm Desktop 3.5, To Do and Memo are replaced by Task and Note.

◆ Click the To Dos or Memos button on the Toolbar (**Figure 6.32**).

To create new To Do items and memos:

◆ Double-click an unused portion of the Task List window or Note List window (**Figure 6.33**). You can also double-click the Task pane of the Daily calendar view.

◆ Choose To Do or Memo from the Create menu, or press Command-Option-T (To Do item) or Command-Option-N (memo).

◆ You can also click the New To Do or New Memo button on the Toolbar.

✔ Tips

■ The Daily calendar window also displays tasks for that day only. The only time I ever need the full To Do List is if I'm looking ahead at future To Do items.

■ In the Daily calendar window, set aside a block of time to work on a task by dragging it to the day's schedule. Palm Desktop adds "Work on" to the task name—or "Celebrate" if it's a birthday reminder created by Palm Desktop (**Figure 6.34**)!

Figure 6.32 The Toolbar offers quick access to the To Do and Memo controls.

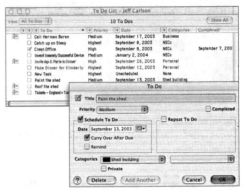

Figure 6.33 Double-clicking in the To Do List brings up a new To Do window.

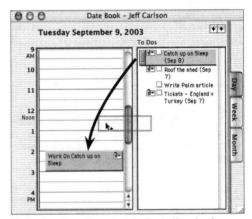

Figure 6.34 Dragging a task to the Daily calendar blocks out time for needed work.

Click name to sort... ...or choose a popup menu item.

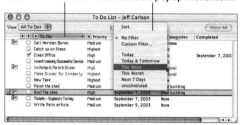

Figure 6.35 Sort the list by any column's contents by either clicking on the column's name, or choosing Sort from the popup menus.

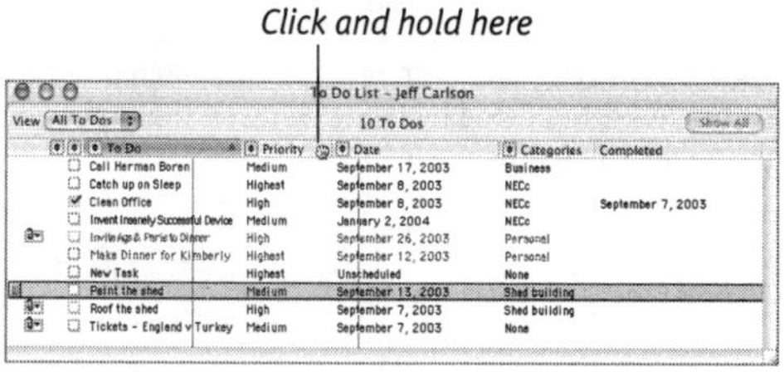

Click and hold here

Figure 6.36 Click in the title area and drag to change the order of the visible columns.

Figure 6.37 Create custom filters to display only the tasks or memos that match specified criteria.

To sort records:

◆ To sort each list according to a column's contents, click the column's title (it will become underlined to indicate it's the active method) or choose Sort from each title's popup menu (**Figure 6.35**).

◆ You can also edit the columns to customize your display. Click and drag a column's right border to change its width. To rearrange the columns' order, click and hold in the area next to a column name, then drag left or right to position it (**Figure 6.36**). To choose which columns are displayed, select Columns from the View menu and mark the ones you want.

To filter specific data:

You can also configure the sorting method by choosing Custom Filter from the popup menus, which displays only the items that meet the filter's criteria. For example, if you want to list only the phone calls you need to make, set up a filter that searches for the words "call" or "phone" (**Figure 6.37**).

To save memorized views:

When you've set up a sort order and specific filters, choose Memorize View from the View popup menu to save it. This way, you can see related tasks and notes without repeating the sorting steps above. To see the full list again, click the Show All button.

✔ Tips

■ You can sort a list according to multiple criteria. Click a column name to perform the first sort, then Shift-click another column name to then sort the sorted results.

■ In the Daily calendar view, sort the day's To Do List according to completion by clicking the word "To Dos" above the list.

WORKING IN PALM DESKTOP FOR MACINTOSH

157

You can attach related records to other records (such as memos attached to To Do items). Although this linkage does not transfer to the handheld, it can be a valuable way of working with your data on the desktop.

To attach records to To Do items and memos:

◆ If both records are visible, drag and drop one to the other. A link is created in both records (**Figure 6.38**).

◆ Click the folder icon (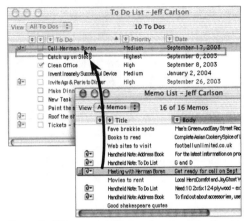) and choose Attach To from the popup menu.

The biggest confusion arising from Macintosh Palm Desktop is the way it handles notes belonging to records (such as in the Date Book or Address Book). Whereas the Windows Palm Desktop treats attached notes as separate entities, the Mac software uses its Memos feature to handle attached notes.

Each note attached to a To Do item exists as a separate record in the Mac Palm Desktop Memo List, and each is titled, "Handheld Note: To Do List." It is then linked to its associated record using the Palm Desktop's attachment feature explained above. With that in mind, it becomes relatively easy to attach new notes on the desktop.

To attach notes to To Do items:

1. Click the New Memo icon or press Command-Option-N.

2. Type "Handheld Note: To Do List" exactly as shown in the Title field.

3. Write the text of your note.

4. In Palm Desktop 4.1, click and hold the note icon in the title bar, then link the note by dragging it to its associated task (**Figure 6.39**).

Figure 6.38 Drag and drop records onto each other to create links, indicated by the folder icon that appears to the left of records.

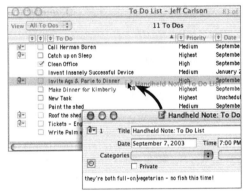

Figure 6.39 Drag the note icon in a memo's title bar to associate it with a task. Be sure to use the title "Handheld Note: To Do List" to ensure that your note will appear as an attached note on your handheld.

WORKING IN PALM DESKTOP FOR MACINTOSH

Figure 6.40 You don't even need to open Palm Desktop to access its features; the Instant Palm Desktop menu is a quick method of accessing or creating records.

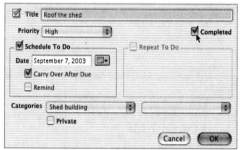

Figure 6.41 Experience the joy of completing a task without even launching Palm Desktop to mark it done.

Instant Palm Desktop menu

The day's current tasks are also listed in the Instant Palm Desktop menu, from which you can edit or create tasks without switching to the Palm Desktop application. You can access it in Mac OS X by right-clicking the Palm Desktop icon in the dock (**Figure 6.40**), or in Mac OS 9 via the icon at the right side of the menu bar.

◆ Highlight an item to view or edit its details, or choose Open Palm Desktop or Switch to Palm Desktop (if it's already running) to launch the program.

◆ To mark an item as done, highlight it to open the Task dialog box. Click the Completed checkbox and click OK (**Figure 6.41**).

◆ Create new To Do items by selecting Task from the Create submenu.

✔ Tip

■ In Mac OS 9, you can edit tasks without launching the Palm Desktop. However, with Mac OS X, the application has to be open in order to access Instant Palm Desktop.

WORKING IN PALM DESKTOP FOR MACINTOSH

Using Note Pad

Beginning with the Palm m100 and m500 series models, the Palm OS has included Note Pad, a handy way to jot messages in a Post-it note fashion. Unlike Memo Pad, the records in Note Pad are simple drawings; a separate Note Pad application displays the pictures on your Mac or Windows PC.

To create a new note:

1. Launch Note Pad from the Applications screen, or press the Note Pad button on the handheld (it's the rightmost one). A new blank record is created and named according to the date and time.

2. Write on the screen. Tap the pencil icon at lower-right to change the thickness of the line, or select the eraser icon to remove what you've drawn (**Figure 6.42**).

3. If you want a more descriptive title than the timestamp, highlight the title field and write a title using Graffiti.

4. Tap Done when you're finished. Tap New to immediately create a new note. Or, of course, you can destroy your masterpiece by tapping Delete.

   When you HotSync your device, you can view or copy your notes using the Note Pad application on your computer (**Figure 6.43**).

To set Note Pad alarms:

1. With a Note Pad record open, choose Alarm from the Options menu, or write ╱-A. The Set Alarm dialog appears.

2. Select a day and time. Unlike the Date Book, where you specify a lead time before an event, the time chosen here is the actual time the alarm will sound.

3. When the alarm goes off, the note is displayed; tap OK (**Figure 6.44**).

Figure 6.42 Select a line weight and then draw words or pictures.

Figure 6.43 View your notes on the computer using the basic Note Pad application.

Figure 6.44 Note Pad is a quick and easy method of creating simple alarms.

USING NOTE PAD

CALCULATOR, EXPENSE, & CLOCK

Remember when having one of those calculator watches was the coolest? Imagine! A whole calculator on your wrist—and if you could just sneak it into math class without anyone suspecting....

The screen is now bigger than the old calculator watches (and the buttons are certainly larger!), but the utility of having a calculator on my handheld has been helpful for those times when this former English major has found himself awash in numbers.

The number fun doesn't stop at the calculator, though. If you have to keep track of expenses for work, the included Expense application should save you a headache at month's end when you're trying to explain to your boss where that $100 went in Las Vegas.

If you're a global day trader, you can also keep track of stock market openings across the globe with the World Clock application, new to Palm OS 5.

Using the Calculator

Admittedly, the Palm OS's built-in calculator isn't what you'd call comprehensive (especially if you're a real number cruncher). It adds, subtracts, multiplies, and divides. It has big buttons so you can use your finger instead of the stylus if you want to. And it reinforces the Palm philosophy that something doesn't have to be complicated and bloated with features in order to be useful.

Still, several things lurk just below the surface of the Calculator application that make it better than a cheapo math machine hiding somewhere in the back of your desk drawer.

To perform calculations:

1. Launch the Calculator application by tapping the silk-screened icon (on devices that include it), or the Calculator icon from within Applications (**Figure 7.1**).

2. Tap the buttons to enter numbers and basic mathematical operations.

3. Tap the percentage button to convert a number to a decimal percentage (for example: **2 5 %** = 0.25).

4. Tap the **+/-** button to make a number either positive or negative.

To clear the results field:

1. Tapping **c** clears the entire calculation.

2. Tapping **CE** clears the last number you entered without wiping out everything.

✔ Tip

■ You can operate the calculator by writing in the Graffiti area (**Table 7.1**). I'm not sure why exactly you'd want to, but at the very least it's good Graffiti practice!

Figure 7.1 There's no mistaking that this is a calculator, right down to the finger-friendly buttons.

Table 7.1 Yes, it's true! Use the Calculator without tapping buttons by writing numbers and symbols in the Graffiti area.

Graffiti Calculator?			
Button	**Graffiti**	**Button**	**Graffiti**
1	I	CE	ε
2	2	C	C
3	3	MC	m
4	L	MR	R
5	5	M+	p
6	6	%	·/
7	7	+/-	·\
8	8	÷	\◊◊
9	9	×	·◊
0	O	−	·—
.	··	=	\Z
		+	\∝

Figure 7.2 View the last several steps in an operation by bringing up the Recent Calculations screen.

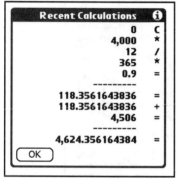

Figure 7.3 The Calculator's "tape" makes it easier to see where mistakes are made, although it only stores one screen full of information.

To memorize calculation results:

1. Tap the **M+** button to store the current result in memory; a small "m" will appear in the number field. If you tap the button again later, the new result is added to the stored number, instead of replacing it.

2. Tap **MR** to display the stored number; you can use it as part of a calculation in progress.

3. Tap **MC** to clear the contents of the stored memory.

To view "the tape":

1. You can access a list of the most recent numbers in a calculation by choosing Recent Calculations from the Options menu, or by writing ╱-I (**Figure 7.2**).

2. You'll see the numbers of the current calculation in a list running down the right side of the screen (**Figure 7.3**). Note that only what you see is stored; you can't scroll up to an earlier number.

USING THE CALCULATOR

Copying and Pasting Calculations

Being able to take your calculation results to another application is one of the reasons I said that Calculator is more useful than most calculators. Sure, you can write the numbers on paper, but that's just *so* 1995.

To copy and paste calculations:

◆ On the main screen, choose Copy from the Edit menu (or write ╱-C) to copy the current number to the Palm OS's Clipboard for pasting into other programs. Similarly, you can copy a number from another application and choose Paste (or write ╱-P) to add it to your calculation.

◆ In the Recent Calculations screen, choose Copy from the Edit menu (or write ╱-C) to grab the visible list of calculations for pasting elsewhere (**Figure 7.4**).

✔ Tips

■ If you make a calculation, then switch to another application, the calculation result is held in memory. However, the last set of operations normally viewed by the Recent Calculations screen gets erased! If you're going to need the full transcript of a calculation later, copy it first before exiting the Calculator. You may want to set up a Memo Pad record to paste in your results before moving on to the next task.

■ There are several calculators you can download that should be able to handle whatever you throw at them (**Figure 7.5**). For example, RPN (www.nthlab.com) is an advanced calculator that also accepts plug-ins written by other developers. PowerOne Finance (www.infinitysw.com) specializes in financial calculations.

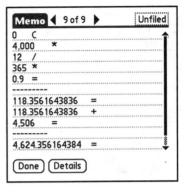

Figure 7.4 Paste calculations or results into other applications, like Memo Pad, shown here.

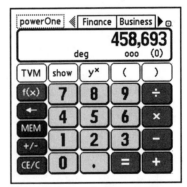

Figure 7.5 Other calculators, such as RPN (top) and PowerOne Finance (bottom) take over where the built-in Calculator leaves off.

Figure 7.6 Expense records are shown in a basic list that's easy to read and quick to access.

Figure 7.7 Choose from 28 different expense types when creating records.

Using Expense

Business people who are continually on the move have adopted the Palm OS platform in droves. Not only can they retrieve their valuable information quickly, they can manage one of the most dreaded aspects of modern business: expense reporting. Keeping track of charges that will be reimbursed by your company is often no more involved than three or four Graffiti strokes. At the end of the month, the data can be transferred easily to a Microsoft Excel file.

To create new Expense items:

1. Launch Expense from the Applications screen by tapping its icon.

2. Tap the New button (**Figure 7.6**). A new record is created with today's date, the temporary title "-Expense type-", and a field for entering the expense amount.

3. Write the amount in the numbers section of the Graffiti area. Expense will automatically enter ".00" after the number if you don't specify a cent value.

4. Tap a title to access the type popup menu, then select from a list of 28 expense types (**Figure 7.7**). If none of them match your expense, select Other; unfortunately, you can't edit the type list. Don't just leave "-Expense type-" as the type—the record won't be saved!

5. Tap on a blank area of the screen to deselect the record.

To edit Expense records:

1. Tap a record to select it; the date will become highlighted to indicate your selection.

2. To modify the date, expense type, or amount, tap those elements and make the change directly (**Figure 7.8**).

3. Tap a blank area of the screen to deselect the record.

To toggle the "automatic fill" feature:

1. Choose Preferences from the Options menu, or write /-R. The Preferences window appears.

2. Mark or unmark the Use automatic fill when entering data checkbox, then tap OK (**Figure 7.9**).

✔ Tips

- Once Expense is launched, you can avoid the New button entirely by writing the expense amount in the Graffiti area. A new record will be created automatically with the numbers in place.

- Additionally, you can begin writing the name of an expense type in the Graffiti area. If you have the automatic fill feature turned on (see below), the first match will be selected (**Figure 7.10**).

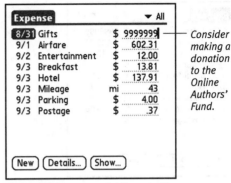

Consider making a donation to the Online Authors' Fund.

Figure 7.8 The amount fields can hold a maximum of seven characters. (And if that's not enough, why do you have to expense it?)

Figure 7.9 The automatic fill feature can dramatically decrease the time it takes to enter an expense record.

Figure 7.10 Create records by writing the first letter of an expense type in Graffiti.

USING EXPENSE

Figure 7.11 The Receipt Details screen is where you find the bulk of your expense information. Taxi rides and plane trips are good times to flesh out your expense information.

Editing Expense Details

The Receipt Details screen lets you specify more information about an expense (**Figure 7.11**)—but don't feel compelled to fill in everything if it doesn't apply (such as the City field, if you never travel).

To edit Expense details:

1. With a record selected, tap the Details button to bring up the Receipt Details window.

2. Select a category from the Category popup menu. Choose Edit Categories to set up new ones.

3. If you didn't select an expense type in the main screen, tap the Type popup menu to choose one.

4. Select the method of payment from the Payment popup menu.

5. Select other currencies from the Currency popup menu.

6. Write the name of the payee in the Vendor field. With automatic fill activated, Expense will display previous vendors that match letters alphabetically as you write them (for example, writing D would bring up "Dan's Café," but writing Di would switch to "Diva Espresso").

7. Write the city name in the City field. The automatic fill feature works here, as well.

Recording Attendees and Notes

Expense offers the ability to easily add notes, such as who was present at a lunch.

To record attendees:

1. In the Receipt Details window, tap the dotted box beside Attendees (if no attendees are listed, the box reads Who).

2. Write the names of the people present. If their names are located in your Address Book, tap the Lookup button (only contacts with data in the Company field are shown). Selecting a person copies the name, title, and company information to the Attendees screen (**Figure 7.12**).

To add and delete notes:

1. Tap the Note button on the Receipt Details screen to open a Memo Pad-like window where you can jot down miscellaneous details about the expense (**Figure 7.13**).

2. Change the typeface by selecting Font from the Options menu (or writing ╱-F).

3. You can record a person's name and phone number by choosing Phone Lookup from the Options menu (or writing ╱-L).

4. Tap the Delete button to kill the note, or tap Done to complete your edits.

✔ Tips

- Although you can specify a separate note for each expense record, you can also write notes in the Attendees screen, consolidating some of your information in one place.

- Put a space in the Company field to make a record show up in the Lookup list.

Figure 7.12 Use the Lookup button on the Attendees screen to quickly record the participants of a meeting.

Figure 7.13 The Note feature is very much like Attendees, but sticks closer to a Memo Pad record.

Figure 7.14 Sort your list of expenses by Date or Type. If you drive often, note whether you want to use Miles or Kilometers to record your travel.

Figure 7.15 Mileage is the only expense type that doesn't show a currency indicator next to the amount.

Viewing Options

One problem with keeping track of expenses is that they all tend to blur together at a certain point (specifically, just before you need to compile them and turn them in). As you're reviewing expenses, choose to view them chronologically or by type, as well as display distance and currency indicators.

To change the sort order:

1. Tap the Show button on the main Expense screen to display the Show Options window (**Figure 7.14**).

2. Tap the Sort by popup menu to sort by Date or Type.

To change the distance measurement:

1. Tap the Show button on the main Expense screen to display the Show Options window.

2. Tap the Distance popup menu and choose either Miles or Kilometers.

3. When you choose Mileage as the type, either mi or km appears instead of a currency symbol, depending on your choice (**Figure 7.15**).

Specifying Currency

The default currency type is set to dollars ($), but Expense also includes English pounds (£), German deutschemarks (DM), and the Euro ( ) on its Currency popup menus (you can add others).

To set the default currency:

1. Choose Preferences from the Options menu, or write ╱-R.

2. Tap the Default Currency popup menu to choose a currency type, then tap OK.

To add countries to the Currency popup menus:

1. Choose Edit Currencies from any Currency popup menu (found in the Preferences and Receipt Details windows).

2. Specify countries for up to five currency list items by tapping the popup menus to the right of each currency slot (**Figure 7.16**). Tap OK when finished.

To create custom currencies:

1. Choose Custom Currencies from the Options menu, or write ╱-Y.

2. Tap a dotted box to specify a new country (**Figure 7.17**).

3. In the Currency Properties window that appears, write the name of the country and its symbol (**Figure 7.18**). Tap OK.

4. You can create up to four currencies. Tap OK to return to the main window.

✔ Tip

■ If you use only one type of currency, or you're just tired of seeing that dollar sign on every record, you can opt to hide the currency symbol. Tap the Show button on the main Expense screen and unmark the Show currency checkbox. Press OK.

Figure 7.16 View up to five countries in the Currency popup menu by specifying them here.

Figure 7.17 Is the currency list missing a few countries? Enter them at the Custom Currencies screen.

Figure 7.18 Be omnipotent! Create countries out of thin air and...assign them currency symbols.

Click here to "launch" Expense.

Figure 7.19 Your Expense records are just a simple click away in Palm Desktop for Windows.

Figure 7.20 If you're a more visual person, use one of the Icon views to sort through your records.

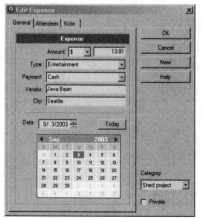

Figure 7.21 Edit all details, including attendee information and additional notes, from the Edit Expense dialog box.

Expense in Palm Desktop

In previous versions, clicking the Expense button in Palm desktop began a complex tango with Microsoft Excel, where macros formatted the data into a spreadsheet. Happily, Palm Desktop 4.1 provides Expense as its own built-in application, though you can still export to Excel for serious number crunching.

Unfortunately, this still only applies to Palm Desktop for Windows. There is no built-in support for Expense in the Mac software.

To open Expense:

◆ In Palm Desktop, choose Expense from the View menu or click the Expense button at left (**Figure 7.19**).

To view Expense records:

◆ Expense offers three different views—List, Large Icons, and Small Icons—found in tabs at the bottom of the window. Each view displays information in the same manner: select the record to see details in a column at right (**Figure 7.20**).

To edit or create new Expense records:

◆ To edit an existing Expense record, select a record and either double-click it or click the Edit Expense button. Alternatively, double-click the details box (referred to as the Record Pane).

◆ To create a new Expense record, click the New Expense button or an empty area of the Expense application's View Pane.

Either of the actions above will open the Edit Expense dialog box, from which you can edit General information (amount, type, date, etc.), Attendees, and a Note about the expense (**Figure 7.21**).

To export to Excel or Word:

1. Select a record or multiple records within any view of the Palm Desktop Expense application.

2. Go to the Edit menu and choose either MS Excel or MS Word from the Send To submenu. You can also right-click the selection to access the same submenu. (**Figure 7.22**).

3. Format the data in your program of choice. (**Figure 7.23**).

✔ Tips

- Clicking the New button in the Edit Expense dialog box creates a new expense record with the same category of the viewed record.

- By default, not every piece of information from an expense record shows up in the list view. To add more data (such as city, vendor, or payment), right-click the top row and select Show Columns to see a list of available columns. If you've got too much information, select Remove Columns.

- Like other applications within Palm Desktop for Windows, sorting is limited to just the two choices in the Sort By drop-down menu: Date and Type.

- Selecting an individual category from the drop-down menu displays only those records, as well as the expense amount for that category in the Total section at the bottom of the application (**Figure 7.24**).

- If you're looking for a more robust expense tracking program, WalletWare's ExpensePlus for Palm (www.walletware. com) offers more features than Palm's Expense application, plus conduits for both Macintosh and Windows.

Figure 7.22 Importing to Microsoft Word or Excel is a breeze in Palm Desktop 4.1.

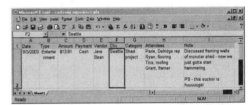

Figure 7.23 Expense can be very useful in Palm Desktop, but you'll be able to ramp up the formatting in Excel for the expense report you turn in.

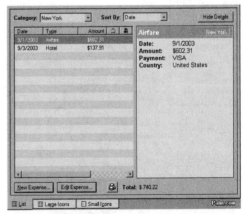

Figure 7.24 The Total section at the bottom of the Expense application calculates just the selected records.

Figure 7.25 Clock shows you the current date and time, without having to launch the Date Book application.

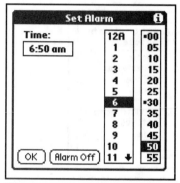

Figure 7.26 Unlike Date Book, the alarm in Clock occurs at the time specified, not at a time prior to an event.

Figure 7.27 The Alarm Preferences works independently of the volume controls in the Palm OS preferences.

Using Clock

Recent devices include Clock, a simple application that gives you quick access to the current date and time (**Figure 7.25**). It can also be used as an alarm clock.

To view the time with Clock:

◆ Launch Clock from the Applications screen.

◆ Tap the Clock icon in the upper-left corner of the silkscreen area, next to the Applications icon.

◆ On m100 series handhelds, press the scroll up button on the device's case when the power is turned off.

To set an alarm:

1. Tap the field next to Alarm to bring up the Set Alarm dialog box.

2. Choose a time by tapping the hour and minute columns (**Figure 7.26**).

3. Tap OK to finish. If you're cancelling an alarm, tap the Alarm Off button.

✔ Tips

■ On the main Clock screen, the Set Date & Time button takes you to the Preferences application (see Chapter 2).

■ Choose Alarm Preferences from the Options menu to change the alarm sound and volume (**Figure 7.27**).

■ After an alarm occurs, the alarm feature is turned off. For repeating alarms (such as a meeting that happens each day at the same time), use Date Book to schedule a repeating event (see Chapter 4).

Using World Clock

Palm OS 5 and higher devices include the World Clock application, which provides date and time views for up to three locations. It uses the same procedure as Clock for setting and using alarms.

To view the time with World Clock:

◆ Launch World Clock from the Applications screen or by tapping the clock icon in the upper-left corner of the silkscreen area (**Figure 7.28**).

◆ On devices with five-way Navigator directional buttons, press the center one when the power is turned off.

To set time and date:

◆ On the main World Clock screen, tap the Set Date & Time button to set your location as well as current date and time.

To change and edit locations:

1. Tap any of the displayed cities, and choose a city from the available popup list.

   If a city from your desired time zone isn't in the list, tap Edit List.

2. In the Edit List screen, tap the Add button to place another city into your active list. Select a city from the list in the Locations screen (**Figure 7.29**).

3. To change location details, tap a city in the Edit List screen, then tap the Edit button. In the Edit Location screen, you can modify the city's name as well as daylight saving time details (**Figure 7.30**).

✔ Tip

■ You can only select from the cities World Clock includes in its location list. Thus, while you can't choose Birmingham, England, you can choose a city within the same time zone, such as London.

Figure 7.28 View the current date and time in up to three time zones with World Clock.

Figure 7.29 Add a city to your active list from the Locations screen. Your home town might not be on this list, so choose another city within your time zone.

Figure 7.30 Add notes to city names (or rename them completely).

USING WORLD CLOCK

Part 2
Communicating

Extending Your Handheld's Reach

Palm OS devices were designed as extensions of the personal computer, not replacements for it. And despite the fact that handhelds are immensely portable, your data is really only being transported from one computing box to a smaller box. Now, with the addition of a modem or network connection, you can have the world's information literally in the palm of your hand using electronic communication hardware and software.

Chapter 8, **The Organizer as Phone**, explores an intriguing hybrid: the cellular phone with a Palm organizer built in (or is it the other way around?).

Chapter 9, **Email**, covers what you need to access your email from Palm OS handhelds.

Chapter 10, **Web Access**, gets you surfing the World Wide Web on a tiny screen—but the screen size is less limiting than you may think.

The Organizer as Phone

8

When you leave the house in the morning, do you wear a Batman-style utility belt of dangling gadgets? Handheld, pager, cellular phone... even though our modern organizational tools continue to get smaller and more portable, it's still a problem to juggle them all. I'm sure my neighbors get plenty of entertainment watching me stagger to my car each day, encumbered by these tools plus a laptop case and coffee.

Although you could just get rid of the gadgets entirely and hole up in a cabin (a tempting alternative some days), another solution is afoot: keep the functionality, but reduce the number of devices by incorporating the phone into the organizer (or is it the organizer into the phone?). A few of these hybrids are available today, including the Handspring Treo, Kyocera Smartphone, Samsung i500, and the Palm Tungsten W.

Not only does a "smartphone" (as the category is now being called) reduce the number of items you need to carry, it adds something exceptional to the field: a decent cellular phone user interface. If you've spent any time at all trying to look up numbers in a typical cellular phone's address book, or attempted to set up a three-way conference call, you know how frustrating it can be.

Smartphone Basics

Smartphones come in two flavors of wireless network access: CDMA (Code Division Multiple Access), which covers most of the United States, and GSM (Global System for Mobile communications) network, which is predominant throughout much of the world and is finally gaining ground in the United States. In addition to making and receiving calls, GSM phones can take advantage of SMS (Short Message Service) text messaging and create data connections like a regular modem.

You can hold one up to your ear like any other phone (**Figures 8.1** and **8.2**); or, better, plug in the included headset to talk hands-free and continue using the device's other applications.

I'll use the Handspring Treo as the example for this chapter.

✔ Tips

■ If you already own a GSM phone, you can simply pull out its SIM card and put it into a GSM smartphone. Your phone number and billing won't change. However, be aware that buying one of these units without a service plan (such as through T-Mobile, AT&T, or Sprint) is a significantly more expensive purchase.

■ I highly recommend using the included headset adapter. Not only is it safer, but (to be honest) you won't smudge up the screen with oil from your skin.

Figure 8.1 The Handspring Treo is a compact organizer that works as a cellular phone.

Figure 8.2 Kyocera's 7135 Smartphone incorporates a Graffiti silkscreen area above its number keys.

Figure 8.3 You can assign up to 50 speed dial buttons. Note that two spaces show the date and time.

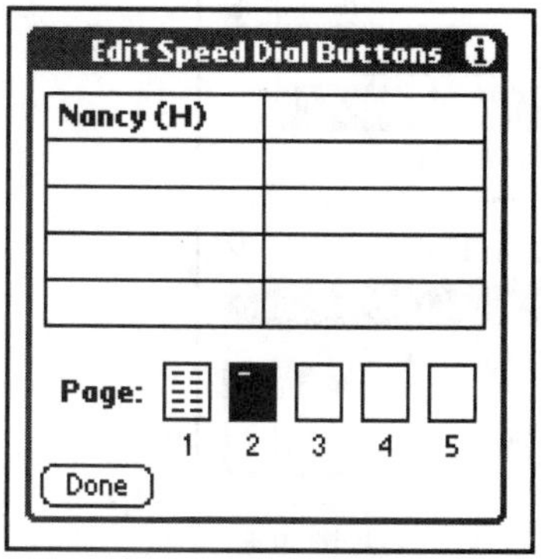

Figure 8.4 Tap an empty button to add a speed dial number to it.

Edit Entry

Name: **Nancy (H)**

Number: **1-716-555-8454**

Extra Digits:

Done   Cancel   Lookup

Figure 8.5 Use the Edit Entry dialog to customize how the name appears, or add any extra digits to dial.

Making Calls

Instead of going through the process of setting up the Treo (which is explained in the manual), let's jump to making calls. You'll likely use the Speed Dial screen most, but a trusty Keypad screen is also available.

✔ Tips

■ Press the Phone button repeatedly to switch among the Speed Dial, Keypad, and Contacts screens.

■ You don't have to stay in the Phone application. Your device can turn off, or you can use other programs during a call.

Speed Dial

At the Speed Dial screen, you can assign up to 50 buttons for your most-dialed numbers (**Figure 8.3**). Simply tap an assigned button to start dialing its number.

To set up speed dial numbers:

1. If a button is empty, tap it to display the Edit Speed Dial Buttons screen; or, select Edit Speed Dial from the Edit menu, then tap an empty slot (**Figure 8.4**).

2. Write the button name, number, and any extra digits to be dialed in the corresponding fields. Or, tap the Lookup button to get the name and number from the Address Book (**Figure 8.5**).

3. Tap OK or Done (depending on which screen brought you to the editing screen) to return to the Speed Dial screen.

✔ Tips

■ Use the Treo's scroll buttons to page through the five Speed Dial screens.

■ On the Edit Speed Dial Buttons screen, drag buttons to other slots to rearrange them. Dragging one name atop another causes the two to trade positions.

MAKING CALLS

179

Keypad

Although it's possible to dial numbers by writing them in Graffiti, we non-aliens prefer the numeric keypad (**Figure 8.6**).

To dial from the Keypad:

1. Tap the Keypad icon in the lower-left corner of the screen.

2. Tap the numbered buttons to dial. The back-arrow button clears the last-entered digit.

3. Tap the Send button (designated by a phone handset icon) to place the call.

Dialing from the Address Book

What's the point of having an organizer/phone hybrid if you can't use all those numbers stored in the Address Book?

To dial from the Address Book:

1. Tap the Contacts icon in the lower-left corner of the screen.

2. Scroll through the list of names and numbers and select the number to dial. You can also use the Look Up feature to search for names (see Chapter 5).

3. Tap the number you wish to dial. A confirmation dialog appears.

4. Tap the Dial button to call (**Figure 8.7**).

✔ Tip

■ In the Address List, tap the phone number instead of the contact's name to jump immediately to the Dial screen.

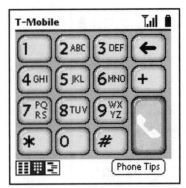

Figure 8.6 All thumbs? Forget those teeny buttons on most cellular phones.

Figure 8.7 In the Contacts list, tap a number from the address list to dial it.

MAKING CALLS

Figure 8.8 Look at those big buttons! During a call, the Treo's comparatively large screen offers lots of information.

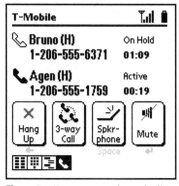

Figure 8.9 Keep two people on the line either by swapping between them or by enabling a 3-way call.

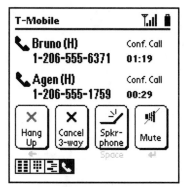

Figure 8.10 Remember all those prompts of "Are you still there?" while trying to set up conference calls on other phones? Forget 'em. Note that each call timer remains independent.

Multiple calls

When you're in the middle of a call, the Phone application displays the recipient's phone number (and name, if it came from your Address Book), the status and time of the call, plus buttons for actions you can take depending on the call (**Figure 8.8**). In addition to offering obvious commands like Hang Up and Hold, the Treo makes it easy to juggle multiple callers and establish 3-way conference calls.

To make a 3-way call:

1. Call the first party ("Bruno," for example), then put him on hold by tapping Hold.

2. Tap the 2nd Call button that appears, and call the second party ("Agen").

3. Tap the 3-way Call button to begin the conference (**Figure 8.9**).

During the call, use the following options (**Figure 8.10**).

◆ Tap the Mute button to put both parties on hold.

◆ Tap the Cancel 3-way button to put Bruno on hold and talk to Agen. You can then tap the Swap button to switch between the two callers.

◆ Tap Hang Up to end the call.

◆ Tap Spkr-phone to put the call into speaker phone mode.

MAKING CALLS

Receiving Calls

Just as Christmas isn't only about giving, using a cellular phone isn't just about making calls. When your fans start calling, the Treo can help you out. If your cellular service plan includes Caller ID, the phone compares the incoming phone number with your Address Book and displays the caller's name if it finds a match.

To answer an incoming call:

◆ Lift the device's lid, or, if it's already up, tap the Answer button to speak to the caller.

◆ Press the Scroll Up button or tap the Ignore button to direct the caller to your cellular service's voice mail system (**Figure 8.11**).

◆ If you do nothing, the Missed Call screen gives you the option to call the person back or just forget it (**Figure 8.12**).

Call History

The Treo records details of the previous 1,000 incoming or outgoing calls, which are accessible from the Call History list. Tap the third icon in the lower-left corner of the screen to view your calls (**Figure 8.13**).

The triangle to the left of each item indicates outgoing (◀), incoming (▶), and missed (≫) calls. To dial a number (if present), select an entry and tap the Dial button. Or, tap the Details button to view information about the call (**Figure 8.14**).

Figure 8.11 Tapping the Ignore button transfers the caller to your voice mail.

Figure 8.12 The Call Back button saves time spent looking up the caller.

Figure 8.13 See where your talk time is going at a glance.

Figure 8.14 The Call History records details of each call, and provides a Dial button to quickly get that person on the horn.

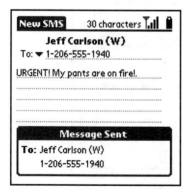

Figure 8.15 Use included templates to quickly write text messages.

Figure 8.16 Messages can be sent immediately, or saved for editing later.

SMS Text Messaging

I don't mind a good long conversation now and then, but sometimes I need to keep things short. Using SMS, you can send brief text messages to other GSM-capable phones or to Internet email addresses.

To send an SMS text message:

1. Press the SMS Message Manager button (normally the Memo Pad or Note Pad button on other Palm devices) or launch the SMS application. It acts much like the built-in Mail program, with mailboxes for new, sent, saved, and pending messages.

2. Tap the New button to create a new message. Enter the recipient's phone number in the To field, or tap the popup menu to view a list of recent numbers.

3. Begin writing your message in the Text field, or tap its popup menu to access a list of frequently used phrases. Some templates provide more options for customizing a frequently used note, such as "Call my mobile." Tap OK to accept the text (**Figure 8.15**).

4. Tap the Send button to dispatch the message immediately, or tap Save to store it for later (**Figure 8.16**).

✔ Tips

- You can insert predefined greetings and a signature to your messages. Choose Boilerplate Text from the Options menu, and add your custom text.

- Each message can be up to 160 characters (which are counted in the upper-right corner of the screen). Longer texts are sent as multiple messages.

- Press the SMS Message Manager button repeatedly to switch between message mailboxes.

To send an SMS email message:

1. Create a new message just as you would for sending to a phone, but select Address by Email Address from the To field popup menu.

2. In the Text field, enter the text message.

3. Tap Send to zap it on its way.

Selected Preferences

Here are a few options for customizing your experience.

To set ringer preferences:

1. Choose Ringer Preferences from the Options menu.

2. Set options for the two settings offered by the ringer slider switch on top of the Treo (**Figure 8.17**).

To set call preferences:

1. Choose Call Preferences from the Options menu. These settings are read from your cellular service provider.

2. If you know you're going to be out of your calling area, specify a forwarding number in the Forward all calls popup menu.

   You can also disable the call waiting feature of your phone, or prevent your phone number from being broadcast to the recipient when you make a call, by marking the other two checkboxes in this screen (**Figure 8.18**).

To select a different cellular network:

If you're traveling and need to use a cellular service other than your own, choose Select Network from the Options menu. The Treo queries available networks and gives you the opportunity to choose which one to use (**Figure 8.19**).

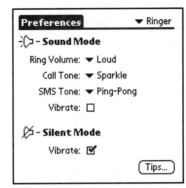

Figure 8.17 Two ringer preferences let you switch between obnoxious and polite notifications.

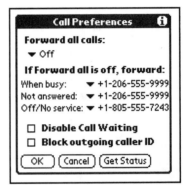

Figure 8.18 These call preferences apply to your cellular service account.

Figure 8.19 If you're out of your home area, or want to try for better reception, try changing networks.

9

EMAIL

As a freelance writer and designer, I've learned the value of "flexible portability." I alternate my working time between my office at home, an office space I share with several colleagues, and an assortment of coffeehouses in the Seattle area. A large part of that portability (both in importance and size) is my laptop, an invaluable tool that allows me to work just about anywhere. However, it can be heavy and awkward to lug around.

My Palm organizer, on the other hand, is easily the most portable device I own. It fits into my shirt pocket, weighs almost nothing, runs for months on the same battery charge, and continues to spark spontaneous conversations from nearby gawkers. Yet despite these advantages, it remained—until recently—a second-class citizen to my laptop because it lacked the ability to connect directly with two of the lifebloods of my business: email and the World Wide Web.

Now, with several alternatives on the market for expanding my handheld's communications abilities, I can often leave my laptop at home or on my desk at the office, and still be connected to the information I need.

Making the Connection

Before you can retrieve email, you'll need a modem of some sort to connect to the Internet.

Palm modems

Snap one of these portable add-ons to your Palm device, connect a phone line, and you're ready to get online or perform a Modem HotSync with your computer back at the office. The modems are powered by their own pair of AAA batteries and operate at speeds of up to 56Kbps—not as fast as the DSL connection at the office, but acceptable.

Figure 9.1 Many newer cellular phones include infrared or Bluetooth receivers, which you can use to dial your ISP from the handheld.

Cellular phones

A growing number of cellular companies are offering Internet-access services with their phones via infrared or cable connections to the Palm device. Using Palm's Mobile Internet Connection Kit (www.palm.com/software/mik/), I get online using a Nokia 8290 cellular phone (**Figure 9.1**), while others I know use Bluetooth-enabled phones to communicate with Bluetooth handhelds.

Palm VII, VIIx, i705, Tungsten W

Using the built-in wireless circuitry of these devices, you can grab email and information from the Web without requiring a single phone line. Someday, every handheld will offer built-in wireless communication, but until then these remain the darling devices of people who need their information long before they get back to the office (**Figure 9.2**).

Figure 9.2 The i705's built-in antenna automatically connects with the Palm.net wireless Internet service.

Your PC and modem

That's right, your computer is actually the Palm OS method of choice for sending and receiving email. See the next page for details.

MAKING THE CONNECTION

Matching mail records

Figure 9.3 Palm's VersaMail synchronizes with your Windows email client during each HotSync operation.

Figure 9.4 Direct-dial makes connecting easier, if you have the hardware.

Getting Online: Two Approaches

Connecting via HotSync

In keeping with its philosophy of simplicity, Palm's VersaMail program acts as an extension of your desktop email software.

When you perform a HotSync operation, the data in VersaMail and in your desktop application are synchronized (**Figure 9.3**); the next time you check your email, you send out what was composed on the handheld. A few Web browsing applications, such as AvantGo (see Chapter 10), use HotSync to transfer content to your handheld for later viewing.

Direct connection

The second method, which is probably more familiar, is to establish an active Internet connection directly from the handheld, avoiding the need to HotSync the data before any action can be taken (**Figure 9.4**).

A direct connection can be more convenient, but it also requires a device that can make direct connections to the Internet (either built-in, like the Palm Tungsten W, or via Bluetooth, infrared, or external modem hardware). If you have those, VersaMail can get online without connecting to a PC, or you can use third-party email clients such as Eudora (www.eudora.com) to send and receive mail on the fly.

✔ Tips

- If VersaMail isn't already on your handheld, check your installation CD for an installer.

- Other handheld makers may include different email software; I'm using VersaMail as an example, but the basic functionality is similar.

Email via HotSync

If you want to print a record that's on your handheld, you have to transfer that information to your PC and print from there. Using the VersaMail works the same way: any emails you create on the handheld must first pass to your desktop email application to be dispatched out to the Internet.

To configure VersaMail on your PC:

1. Choose Custom from the HotSync Manager in the Windows Taskbar.

2. Locate VersaMail in the list and click the Change button.

3. Make sure Synchronize Active Accounts is selected, and click the Configure Accounts button (**Figure 9.5**).

4. Create a new email account on the Palm by clicking the Add Account button, naming it, and clicking OK.

5. Switch to the tab labeled [*account name*] Settings.

6. Click the first checkbox, which enables the ability to synchronize the account during a HotSync (**Figure 9.6**).

7. From the Mail Client popup menu, select the email program you use on the PC. If you don't check your email on that machine, select the Direct IMAP or Direct POP options; the VersaMail conduit will then check email for you and transfer it to your handheld.

8. Choose a name to use from the Mail Profile popup menu, and provide your password in the Mail Password field.

9. Optionally, change the Sync Mail Restrictions settings to limit how much data gets transferred to the handheld.

10. Click OK to exit the window.

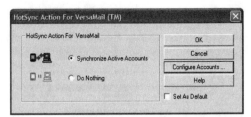

Figure 9.5 The VersaMail HotSync conduit offers more preferences than most.

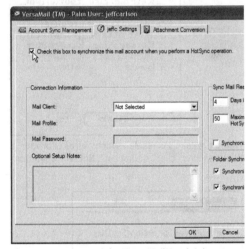

Figure 9.6 Make sure the VersaMail conduit is set up to synchronize your mail when you HotSync.

Mail on the Macintosh

Palm has never supported synchronizing email with the Macintosh, leaving many Mac users with another icon to ignore in the Applications screen. Palm's VersaMail Web page says that you can install VersaMail under Mac OS X 10.1.3 or later, but it won't synchronize mail.

Figure 9.7 Mail lists your incoming messages along with the names of their senders.

Figure 9.8 VersaMail can display more columns, but sometimes at the expense of readability.

Using VersaMail

When you open VersaMail, you're presented with the contents of your Inbox (**Figure 9.7**). The left column displays the message titles, and the right column lists the senders' names. Unread emails are marked in bold type. Use the scrollbar or the plastic up and down buttons to scroll through messages.

VersaMail includes five built-in mailbox folders: Inbox, Outbox, Drafts, Sent, and Trash. Tap the popup menu in the upper-right corner of the screen and select the one you want to view. Note that the Trash folder is functionally equivalent to the other folders until you perform a HotSync, at which point its contents are removed.

By default, messages are listed according to the date they were received.

To change the sort order and date column visibility:

1. Tap the Show button in any folder view. The Show Options dialog appears.

2. Tap the two Sort by popup menus to organize the list by Date, Sender, or Subject, and whether the listing is descending or ascending (**Figure 9.8**). This setting applies to all folders, not just the active one.

3. If you want to view other columns, mark the checkbox next to Date or Size in the Show category.

4. Tap a Font button to change the text size in the list.

Most people who use email specify a block of text that appears at the bottom of every message they write, known as a signature. This is good for including contact information, quotations, or even as a substitute for signing their names at the end of each email.

To specify a signature:

1. Choose Preferences from the Options menu, or write ╱-R.

2. Tap the Signature button, and write your signature text on the lines provided (**Figure 9.9**). A blank line will automatically be inserted between a message's body text and signature. Tap OK.

To create a new VersaMail message:

1. From any folder view, tap the New button; you can also choose New Message from the Message window, or write ╱-N.

2. Write the email address(es) of the email's recipient(s) in the To field, separated by commas.

   To make entering addresses easier, VersaMail inserts a name from the Address Book based on the text you write. If the matches aren't correct, just keep typing an email address.

3. If you want to CC ("carbon copy") other recipients, write their email addresses in the CC field, or perform a lookup.

4. Write a descriptive title in the "Subj" field.

5. In the Body field, write the text of your message (**Figure 9.10**).

✔ Tip

■ If you're sending to more addresses than are visible, tap a field's title (such as To or Subj) to view it in a full-screen. Here you can look up addresses using the Lookup button. When you're done adding names, tap the Done button.

Figure 9.9 Signatures can be added to each outgoing message, giving you space to list contact information or even a favorite quote.

Figure 9.10 Write your message's text and addresses in the New Message window. If you need more room to write, tap the name of the field for a full-screen, Memo Pad-like interface.

Figure 9.11 Sure, you don't see as much on a smaller Palm screen, but email text is still easy to read.

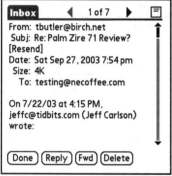

Figure 9.12 Tapping the icon in the upper-right corner shows more header information (compared to the previous figure).

To "send" a message:

When you've written your message and specified its options, tap Send (or Outbox, if you're connecting via HotSync).

If the message isn't quite ready to be sent, choose Save Draft (✎-W) from the Message menu to store it in the Draft folder.

To edit a saved outgoing message:

1. Tap the folder popup menu and choose Outbox or Draft.

2. Tap the message you want to modify.

3. Tap the Edit button.

4. If you've edited a draft message, tap the Send button to move it to the Outbox when it's ready to be sent.

To read messages:

1. Tap an email's subject or author to read its contents (**Figure 9.11**).

2. Use the scrollbar at right to scan down the full text of the message.

3. The arrows at the top of the screen take you to the previous (left arrow) and next (right arrow) emails in the list, without having to return to the main screen.

Due to the limited screen space, only the sender's name and the subject line are shown at the top of each message you read.

To view email header information:

Tap the Complete Header icon (the rightmost one) in the upper-right corner (**Figure 9.12**). To return to the shorter view, tap the Abbreviated Header icon. The option you choose applies to all messages, not just the current email.

USING VERSAMAIL

To reply to a message:

1. After you've read a message, tap the Reply button to respond to the author.

2. The Reply Options window will appear (**Figure 9.13**). Choose whether you want to reply to the Sender of the message, or to All recipients who received it (including the sender).

3. Mark the Include Original Text checkbox to send the full message in your reply. The text appears with a greater-than symbol (>) before each line of the existing message to differentiate between the original author and your remarks (**Figure 9.14**).

4. Specify the recipients in the To and CC fields, write your message, then tap Send.

To file a message:

1. To store a message in a different folder, choose Move To from the Options menu, or write ╱-V.

2. If you want to create a new folder for storing mail, tap the Edit Folders button (**Figure 9.15**).

3. In the Edit Folders dialog, tap New to create a folder, or Rename to edit an existing folder, then tap OK.

4. Select the name of a folder and tap OK to move the message.

To delete a message:

1. Tap the Delete button after reading a message to send it to the Trash folder.

2. You will be asked if you really want to delete the message. If you'd also like to instruct your email client to delete the message on the mail server, mark the checkbox labeled, appropriately, Also delete message(s) on server.

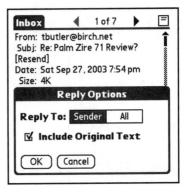

Figure 9.13 The Reply options save you the trouble of retyping each address of the people who received the original.

Figure 9.14 Replying gives you the option of including a copy of the original message, so your recipient can view your comments in context.

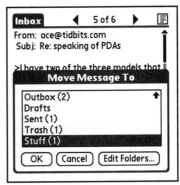

Figure 9.15 Create other folders where you can file your mail (and not clog up your Inbox).

Figure 9.16 Tap the space to the left of each message to mark several in a group.

Figure 9.17 Get rid of some of the cruft from your email folders by deleting old messages.

Deleted messages remain in the Deleted folder until you HotSync, at which point they're gone for good. This lets you go back and pull them out if you inadvertently killed the wrong messages. That means, however, that the ones you really wanted erased are still taking up memory until you HotSync.

To move or delete multiple messages:

1. In a folder list, tap the small diamond icon to the left of a message to mark it; the diamond becomes a checkmark (**Figure 9.16**).

   You can also select or deselect all messages by choosing Select All (✓-S) or Deselect All (✓-Z) from the Message menu.

2. Choose Delete (/-D) from the Message menu. The messages are moved to the Trash folder until the next HotSync.

To purge deleted messages:

If you need to free some space on your handheld, select Empty Trash from the Message menu (✓-E). Tap Yes to confirm your action.

To delete older messages:

1. If you just want to cull your Inbox (or any other folder) of old messages, choose Delete Old from the Message menu.

2. Choose a folder from the Folder popup menu.

3. Select a date range from the Older than popup menu (**Figure 9.17**). You can delete mail older than one week, one month, or you can choose a cutoff date.

To filter incoming messages:

1. Choose Filters from the Options menu. This feature lets you set certain criteria for which emails get transferred from your desktop based on message content.

2. Tap New to create a new filter, then give it a name.

3. In the section labeled "If the," tap the first popup menu to choose an email header (To, From, Subject, cc, Date, or Size).

4. Tap the second popup menu to define the state of the email header (Contains, Starts with, or Does NOT Contain).

5. Enter the filter strings that VersaMail will use when analyzing the incoming messages in the text field.

6. Define an action by choosing a folder name under the heading Then get mail and move to (**Figure 9.18**).

7. Tap OK to save the filter, then tap OK to exit the Filters screen.

✔ Tip

- You can assign different filter settings for when you're using an active connection versus a HotSync connection. A more stringent set of filters for when you're on the road, for example, can save you money if you're paying hotel phone rates or using a calling card to connect to your desktop computer at home. Choose either Connected or Synchronize from the popup menu at the top of the Filters screen.

Figure 9.18 Filters can help by organizing your mail as you receive it, instead of requiring your time to process it.

Direct Connection Email

Sending and receiving email with the help of your PC is a great way to have it available for browsing and answering later. But suppose you're sitting in a taxi, stuck in the rush-hour crush of vehicles, and you realize that the most important email of your career is sitting dormant on the computer at the office? You could jump out of the cab in a rage and run screaming into the night—but that still does not solve the problem (and, depending on the city you live in, might not draw much attention). If you have a wireless-enabled handheld, however, you could compose and send the email, save your job, and catch up on the personal letters you haven't had time to write lately. It's not science fiction; the capability to send and receive email almost anywhere is here.

In this section, I'm going to cover some of the basic elements required for setting up direct-dial email connections, rather than try to hit every feature of every email client. Again, I'm using VersaMail as the sample program to keep things simple, but note that the following features are available in other applications. Once you have a grasp of the basics, you'll be able to pick up the specifics of each program with no problems.

Setting Up a Direct Connection

To check email, you'll need a POP or IMAP server: the machine that you connect to when checking for new incoming email. Check your desktop email application for these settings, or contact your ISP or system administrator.

To send email, you need to access an SMTP (Simple Mail Transport Protocol) server that directs your messages through the complicated paths of the Internet. This server is often the same machine that you specified in the POP or IMAP setup, but not always (as you can see, it's worth setting up a good relationship with your ISP to handle questions).

Also, be sure your general modem or network settings are ready to go; see Chapter 2.

To set up mail servers:

1. Choose Mail Servers from the Options menu.

2. If you have multiple accounts set up, select one from the Account popup menu.

3. Select the type of server, either POP or IMAP, from the Protocol popup menu.

4. Enter your username and password in the fields provided (**Figure 9.19**).

5. Tap the Details button.

6. Enter your email address as others will see it when you send messages in the Email Address field.

7. Write the name or IP number of the servers in the Incoming Mail Server and Outgoing Mail Server fields (**Figure 9.20**).

8. Tap OK, then OK again on the Mail Servers screen to exit.

Figure 9.19 POP is the protocol that handles your incoming email. If you don't assign a password, you will be asked to enter it each time you connect.

Figure 9.20 If you don't already know it, get the server information from your system administrator or ISP.

Figure 9.21 The Palm OS's Network preferences panel controls dial-up Internet access.

Figure 9.22 If you're on a speedy connection, consider using Messages to download full messages; otherwise, Subjects Only quickly grabs the address and subject information.

Figure 9.23 These options can reduce the time it takes to receive mail.

Connecting to Your ISP

Dial-up email clients rely on the Network preferences screen to establish an initial connection with your ISP's servers. If you want to open a connection before working in your email program, tap the Connect button (**Figure 9.21**).

If you don't connect manually, the clients will automatically initiate a connection when you send or retrieve mail if you've properly specified the settings.

To retrieve mail headers and/or messages:

1. In VersaMail, tap the Get & Send button to initiate a connection, which displays the Get Mail Options dialog.

2. Tap the Subjects Only button to download only the incoming subject lines. This lets you preview the sender and subject of an email, then decide if it's something you want to download (**Figure 9.22**).

3. Tap the Messages button to download all pending emails without reviewing them first.

4. Tap OK to send and receive your email.

To filter incoming email:

1. Before tapping OK, above, tap the Details button.

2. Mark these options to determine which mail you receive (**Figure 9.23**).

3. Tap OK to return to the Get Mail Options dialog.

To attach files to outgoing emails:

1. After tapping the New button to create a new message, choose Add Attachment from the Options menu, or write /-A. The Attachments dialog appears.

2. Choose a file format from the Type popup menu (**Figure 9.24**). You can send text files from Memo Pad, applications, addresses, calendar items, or Palm databases.

3. Tap Done.

To send or save mail:

1. After composing your outgoing mail, tap the Send button to dispatch it immediately. If you have a connection established, that message will be sent; if not, VersaMail will dial your ISP.

2. Tap Outbox if you want to store it in the Outbox for sending later (switch to the Outbox and tap Send when you're ready).

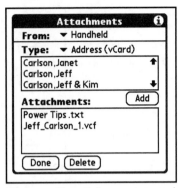

Figure 9.24 VersaMail supports several types of email attachments, ranging from Memo Pad records to addresses (both shown here).

Figure 9.25 Write quick notes that are sent immediately.

Figure 9.26 Messages can be sent immediately, or saved for editing later.

SMS Text Messaging

I don't mind a good long conversation now and then, but sometimes I need to keep things short. Using SMS (included in the Palm Mobile Internet Kit or on your installation CDs), you can send brief text messages to GSM-capable phones or to Internet email addresses.

To send an SMS text message:

1. Launch the SMS application. It acts much like the Palm VersaMail program, with mailboxes for new, sent, deleted, archived, and draft messages.

2. Tap the New button to create a new message. Enter the recipient's phone number in the To field, or tap the To button to perform an Address Book lookup.

3. Write your message in the lines provided (**Figure 9.25**).

4. Tap the Send button to dispatch the message immediately, or tap Outbox to store it for later (**Figure 9.26**).

✔ Tip

■ You can insert a signature to your messages. Choose Add Signature from the Options menu or write ╱-Z.

SMS TEXT MESSAGING

The Palm.Net Network

Even with its built-in transmitter, the Palm VII, VIIx, and i705 would be just regular organizers without the Palm.Net network that supports its access. Palm.Net piggybacks on Bell South's Mobitex Network, a nationwide (covering about 260 highly populated areas of the U.S.) wireless network used for shuttling data for pagers and similar devices. When you enable the built-in antenna, the transceiver finds the nearest broadcast tower and relays your data requests to the rest of the Palm.Net network.

Palm.Net service isn't necessarily the fastest option out there, but Palm's engineers have gone to great lengths to maximize every byte. You can always view the status of your account using the Palm.Net application, or by going to `wireless.palm.net`.

Diagnostics

To determine the current strength of the incoming Palm.Net signal, plus view the location of the nearest radio tower, launch the Diagnostics application. A display of five stair-stepped bars indicates how strong the wireless signal is.

✔ Tip

- The network identifies you online by your Palm's serial number and the location of the nearest relay tower. That means, however, that you can easily be pinpointed. If you're uncomfortable with broadcasting your location, go to the Preferences application and choose the Wireless screen from the popup menu in the upper-right corner. Mark the Warn when sending ID or location information checkbox to get the option of cancelling any transaction that would send this info.

10

WEB ACCESS

When someone first suggested that I could access the World Wide Web using my handheld, I thought he was out of his mind. What, take the graphics-rich Web and compress it onto that little screen? *Riiight.*

Shows how much I knew at the time. With an Internet-enabled handheld and the right software, getting onto the Web from your Palm device is now no big deal (and quite luxurious compared to most Web-enabled cellular phones). You can even use Palm Query Applications (PQAs), the miniscule Web-clipping programs first popularized on the wireless Palm VII handheld, on nearly any device.

If you don't have a handheld that connects directly to the Internet, you can still download Web content during the HotSync process using AvantGo. I find that I read articles from a handful of sites on my handheld that I normally wouldn't remember to look up when I'm at my computer—which is perfect for the times when I'm waiting in line, stuck in traffic, or otherwise stalled.

Browse the Web via AvantGo

Of all the cool things a handheld can do, the most fun to demonstrate to people is browsing the Web, which can often work faster over a 14.4 Kbps connection than their expensive multimedia-tricked PCs at home.

As with email, there are two approaches to getting Web content on your handheld: Hot-Sync and direct-connect. Using HotSync to connect is great for saving news stories and other longer documents to be viewed later; having a direct connection is helpful when you need to look up information on the spot.

Using AvantGo (www.avantgo.com), you download content from various channels when you perform a HotSync, then view it on your handheld (**Figure 10.1**).

To set up AvantGo:

1. Download the AvantGo client software from the company's Web site, and run the installer.

2. After the desktop software is installed, the AvantGo QuickStart process will open in your default Web browser. Follow the directions to choose the channels you wish to subscribe to; you'll have to perform a HotSync twice before you're finished.

✔ Tips

- The AvantGo installation software may have been included with your device. Check the CD-ROM that came with your handheld before downloading AvantGo from the Web.

- As of this writing, AvantGo has still not updated its software to work under Mac OS X, though versions for Mac OS 8 and 9 continue to function.

Figure 10.1 AvantGo offers news stories from several key content providers.

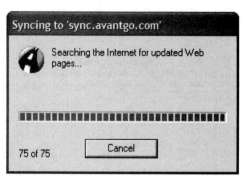

Figure 10.2 When you perform a HotSync, AvantGo downloads the most recent headlines and articles from the channels you specified during setup.

Figure 10.3 Tap a channel name to view the contents that were downloaded during the last HotSync.

Figure 10.4 AvantGo acts like the Web browser on your desktop, with back, forward, and home buttons in the upper-right corner of the screen.

To connect to the Web:

Once you've chosen your channels and installed the software, HotSync the handheld—that's it. When the AvantGo conduit springs into action, it will connect to the Web and download the most recent news and information (**Figure 10.2**).

To view AvantGo content on your handheld:

1. Tap the AvantGo program icon to launch AvantGo.

2. Tap a channel from the list on the home screen to view its content (**Figure 10.3**). The home icon (🏠) takes you back to the main list, while the arrows beside it move back and forward as in most Web browsers (**Figure 10.4**).

3. Tap an article title to read its full contents.

✔ Tip

■ AvantGo does its best to format a Web page's content to suit the small Palm device screen. For this reason, table cells aren't displayed by default. However, if you want to get a better feel for how a page is laid out (since designers often use tables as page structure), or just want to view tabular data coherently, choose Preferences under the Options menu (or write ╱-R), and mark the Show Tables checkbox. You'll find yourself scrolling horizontally as well as top to bottom, but the contents may be more readable.

BROWSE THE WEB VIA AVANTGO

To add new channels:

1. On your PC, connect to the AvantGo site (www.avantgo.com).

2. Browse the selection of available channels grouped into several categories (**Figure 10.5**). Click the Add Channel icon to add it to your list of channels.

3. HotSync your device.

To remove channels:

1. In the AvantGo application, choose Channel Manager from the Channels menu (**Figure 10.6**).

2. Check the channels you wish to delete, then tap the Clear button.

3. HotSync your device.

   You can also remove channels from your account at the AvantGo Web site.

✔ Tips

- You can add any Web site to your list of active channels. Click the Custom Channel link at AvantGo's Web site and enter the URL for a site.

- AvantGo supports active loading of Web sites if you have a modem connection. Use the Connect option in the Channels menu to initiate a connection (if you're not already online), then choose Modem Sync from the same menu.

- Try not to go crazy when adding AvantGo channels to your profile—having too many can substantially increase your download times, and in a worst-case scenario, cause the HotSync process to time out before completing.

Figure 10.5 Edit, add, or delete channels using the AvantGo Web site.

Figure 10.6 Mark the channels you no longer wish to read and they'll be deleted at the next HotSync operation.

Figure 10.7 I'm tired of typing these common characters on my desktop's Web browser, much less writing them in Graffiti, so it's nice to see shortcuts for them in Blazer's Open Page dialog.

Figure 10.8 Web Browser displays Web images and text. To scroll around the page, tap the stylus and drag.

Direct Web Browsing

Before I launch into the wonders of hand-held Web access, let me first say that if you're used to browsing the Web using a PC, you might be underwhelmed. We've grown accustomed to highly visual Web pages, with multiple graphics and scrolling Java whatsits. You're not going to get the same experience on a 320 by 320-pixel screen.

What you will get is extremely portable access to information anywhere in the world—not all of it just text-based, either. Using a browser such as Blazer (www.handspring.com/software/blazer_overview.jhtml) or Palm's own originally named Web Browser, you can access the Web as if you were on your PC. For this discussion, I'll be using Web Browser as the sample program.

To connect to a Web site:

1. Choose Open URL from the Page menu, write ╱-O, or tap the open icon (●). The Open URL dialog appears.

2. Write the destination address in the field provided. Choose an item from the buttons to insert commonly used URL text (**Figure 10.7**). If you previously visited a site, the address is inserted as you write it.

3. Tap the Go button to access the site.

Navigating Web Browser

◆ Web Browser's interface is wonderfully minimal. Tap the scrollbars at the right edge of the screen to scroll vertically. Better yet, tap anywhere on the screen (except on a link, of course) and drag— the contents move under your stylus (**Figure 10.8**).

◆ Links are marked with underlines in the text, just like desktop Web software; tap them to jump to their destination URLs.

DIRECT WEB BROWSING

To save a bookmark:

1. To keep a page location in memory for accessing later, choose Bookmark URL (/-A) from the Page menu. The Bookmark URL dialog appears.

2. Assign a category, or change the name or URL of the bookmark.

3. Tap OK.

To edit bookmarks:

1. Tap the Bookmark icon (♥), to access the Web Content dialog (**Figure 10.9**). You can edit a bookmark's name and URL by highlighting it and tapping the Edit button. Also available are buttons to create a new bookmark (Add), or jump to bookmarked URLs (Go).

2. Tap Done to exit.

To save pages:

1. You can store Web pages on your device for viewing later. Choose Save Page (/-A) from the Page menu (**Figure 10.10**).

2. To view the page later, tap the Bookmarks icon and switch to the Saved Pages screen.

3. Tap the name of the page you wish to view.

✔ Tip

■ Web Browser can display images in up to thousands of colors or shades of gray, depending on your device. That takes more processing power, though. To speed up image rendering, go to preferences (choose Preferences from the Options menu, or write /-R) and turn off the Load images option.

Figure 10.9 Bookmarks make it easy to access frequently viewed Web sites.

Figure 10.10 Save pages on your handheld to be viewed later offline.

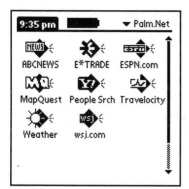

Figure 10.11 Palm Query Applications appear in a new Palm.Net category. PQAs are identified by three "energy burst" lines in their icons.

Palm Query Applications

If you have a Palm Tungsten W or similarly equipped wireless handheld, you can run Palm Query Applications (PQAs). Each of these small programs is, in effect, a customized Web form that interacts with servers on the Internet to deliver specific information (**Figure 10.11**).

Web clipping

In order to minimize the amount of data passing over the network (and thereby costing you money), PQAs employ a technique called "Web clipping."

Unlike Web browsing, which involves kilobytes of images and code designed to make a Web page appear on a regular computer screen, Web clipping delivers only the essentials. The images all reside within the PQA, so when you submit a query using an application, the only data going out are the few bytes required to process your request and the bytes to deliver the response. When you're searching for driving directions, for example, only the beginning and ending addresses are sent over the network, and only the text result returns.

The Web clipping interface

Web clipping essentially works as one application, with PQAs acting as individual components. For that reason, all PQAs share the same interface elements (**Figures 10.12** and **10.13**).

- ◆ **Status indicator.** When a query is in progress, the title bar changes to indicate what's happening (such as "Sending" or "Receiving").

- ◆ **Stop button.** Tapping the Stop button during a query aborts the action. The button also pulses as a visual indicator of an active network connection.

- ◆ **Back button.** Like in a Web browser, the Back button takes you to the last Web clipping screen.

- ◆ **Signal strength indicator.** The stair-stepped icon displays the current signal strength.

- ◆ **Network access indicator.** Three lines beside a link or within a button indicate that tapping it will initiate a network connection to retrieve the information.

- ◆ **Key icon.** Tapping a button with a key icon indicates that the data transfer will be securely encrypted.

Status indicator   Stop button   Back button

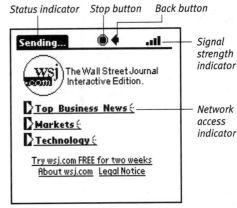

Signal strength indicator

Network access indicator

Figure 10.12 Web clipping applications share the same interface elements.

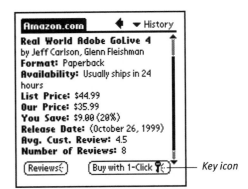

Key icon

Figure 10.13 Secure transactions are marked with a key icon and encrypted.

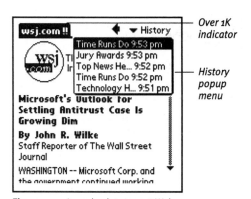

Over 1K indicator

History popup menu

Figure 10.14 Jump back to recent Web clipping pages with the History menu.

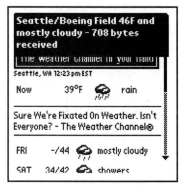

Figure 10.15 Tapping a PQA's title bar expands it to display the number of bytes transferred to access the page.

◆ **History popup menu.** Tap this menu to quickly go back several screens' worth of Web clippings (**Figure 10.14**).

◆ **Bytes received.** After a screen has loaded, tap the title bar to see how many bytes were received (**Figure 10.15**). If the number exceeds 1K (1,024 bytes), two exclamation points (!!) appear in the title.

✔ Tips

■ Since PQAs are all smaller components of the larger Web clipping feature, the Back button works between PQAs, and can even be used to get back to the Applications screen.

■ If you want to store lots of PQA applications, but only use a few on a regular basis, recategorize the lesser-used ones to a new category such as "Palm.Net2." That way, the most frequently used ones will appear when you lift the antenna, without the clutter of the rest.

Recommended PQAs

Like any other category of Palm software, developers are hot to create new PQAs. Here are a noteworthy few.

MapQuest

MapQuest (www.mapquest.com) is one of my favorites. If I misplace my directions, or just end up completely lost, I can enter starting and ending addresses and find my way (**Figure 10.16**). It also includes some U.S. traffic reports.

Moviefone

How many times have you wanted to see a movie but didn't have a newspaper or telephone at hand to look up show times? With Moviefone (www.moviefone.com), enter your zip code to find the closest theaters and schedules.

Weather.com

The Weather Channel (www.weather.com/services/) was one of the first to release a PQA, in this case a nifty application for checking the latest weather conditions.

Starbucks Coffee Store Locator

Okay, this doesn't qualify as an "essential" PQA (www.starbucks.com), but it's come in handy a few times when I'm staying at a hotel that serves particularly bad coffee (**Figure 10.17**).

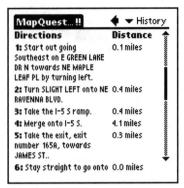

Figure 10.16 People will think that you finally know your way around town.

Figure 10.17 It's the sign of the apocalypse, but good to the last drop. They could have made this simpler by just displaying, "At the next corner."

Part 3
Your Handheld, Your Life

Getting Control of Your Information

I first bought a Palm OS-based device based on needs: I needed to improve my organizational skills, keep track of people's contact information, and maintain a list of to do items so I could stay focused on the work at hand. This section deals with many ways a handheld can not only record your information, but also help improve the way you use it.

Chapter 11, **Images & Multimedia**, displays how you can add images, movies, and digital audio files to the Palm OS's predominantly text-based environment.

Chapter 12, **Long Texts**, breaks the 4,000 character barrier of the Memo Pad. Read reports, memos, or even a classic novel on the train ride home.

Chapter 13, **Managing Your Time**, points out several techniques for tracking and making the most of your time.

Chapter 14, **Managing Your Data**, covers ways to control the ever-increasing load of information that comes from all directions.

Chapter 15, **Games and Entertainment**—I just couldn't leave this out. Here are a few favorites that can significantly aid your efforts to facilitate a stress-free paradigm amid the ever-changing global business zeitgeist.

IMAGES & MULTIMEDIA

For years, Palm handhelds stuck to the mantra of simplicity that Jeff Hawkins envisioned (i.e., a text-based information retrieval system). This meant that Palm was slow to add functionality for imagery and multimedia while third-party developers added such bells and whistles.

But as users clamored for more of these features, Palm slowly opened the floodgates to multimedia expansion possibilities. Now, with Palm OS 5-compatible devices, you can use your handheld to display a slide show of digital photos, play your favorite MP3s, and view QuickTime and MPEG videos.

There are also other options: Who would have guessed a few years ago you could turn your handheld into a digital camera? Not I, but the Zire 71 and several Sony CLIÉ models now incorporate this functionality.

And while the addition of Note Pad has been a boon to my yen for doodling, there are still other, more powerful outlets for sketching ideas, map directions, and funny cartoons.

Importing Photos into Your Handheld

Soon, having a set of photographs in your wallet will be *so* passé. Palm OS 5.2 includes the Photos app, which enables you to view your images as well as organize them into albums.

Palm Desktop 4.1 for Windows includes a built-in application called Palm Photos that makes transferring images from computer to handheld as easy as performing a HotSync. Palm Desktop 4.1 for Macintosh does not have built-in support for adding photos, but the solution via the Finder is easy enough.

To import photos in Windows:

1. In Palm Desktop, select the Palm Photos application from the toolbar.

2. Click the Add Photos button at the top of the Palm Photos application and locate .jpg or .bmp image files on your hard drive—sorry, .gif files aren't compatible (**Figure 11.1**). Alternatively, drag and drop image files from Windows Explorer into Palm Photos.

3. Perform a HotSync operation.

✔ Tips

- When you add image files to Palm Photos on either Windows or Macintosh, they're not just added to your handheld. First, they're copied into the Photos folder within your user directory. Then they're reprocessed into a .pdb file, which can be read by the Photos app on your handheld (**Figure 11.2**).

- If you add image files to the Quick Install application, they will be converted to a .pdb file automatically.

Figure 11.1 Adding Photos using Palm Desktop for Windows. You can also drag and drop files from Windows Explorer into the Palm Photos application.

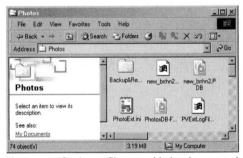

Figure 11.2 After image files are added and processed by Palm Desktop's Add Photos tool, a copy of the image file and a .pdb version of the file are added to the Photos folder within your user directory.

Figure 11.3 Drag and drop images onto the Send to Handheld droplet, located in the Palm folder within Applications in Mac OS X. For easier access, move it to your desktop.

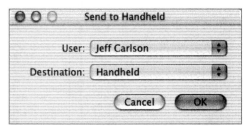

Figure 11.4 After dragging and dropping, you'll be asked to verify the files destination. If you have an expansion card, choose that option to save memory on your handheld.

To import photos in Macintosh:

1. Locate the Send to Handheld application (also referred to as a "droplet")—it is placed by default in the Palm folder within Applications.

2. Drag and drop image files from your hard drive onto the Send to Handheld droplet (**Figure 11.3**).

3. Confirm the destination of the file (either the handheld's memory or its expansion card) (**Figure 11.4**).

4. Perform a HotSync operation.

✔ Tip

■ In addition to storing images in the Photos folder within your user directory, Zire 71 users will also find these files copied to two folders entitled "HandHeld" and "Expansion Card," depending upon their destination in your handheld. In Mac OS X, these folders are located in a directory with your user name within Home > Pictures > Palm Photos. For Mac OS 9 users, images are stored in the directory with your user name, within Documents > Palm Photos.

Using Photos

Once you've imported images from your PC, you can show them off to friends, family, and hijacked party goers using the Photos application.

To view images:

1. Launch the Photos app to view thumbnails of imported images (the default view) (**Figure 11.5**). Alternatively, tap the List button at the bottom left of the screen to see the details of your image library (**Figure 11.6**).

2. Tap an image in either view to open it in full screen mode.

3. Tap the full screen again to return to either the list or thumbnails view.

4. Tap the Slide Show button to review all images in order.

To edit image details:

1. With a selected image (either in full screen mode or highlighted in either thumbnail or list view), choose Details from the Photo menu or write ╱-I (**Figure 11.7**).

2. Modify the image's file name. By default, the camera names files starting with "Set," then it adds the session number and the shot number within that session.

3. Assign the image to an album. To create a new album, tap Edit Albums in the pop-up menu, then tap the New button.

4. Add a descriptive message in the Notes section.

5. Tap the Done button. To discard the image, tap Delete or write ╱-D.

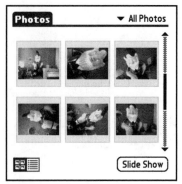

Figure 11.5 View your image library via the Thumbnails view...

Figure 11.6 ...or view details such as capture date and file name in the List view.

Figure 11.7 Give your image a more intelligible name, associate it with an album, and add notes in Photo Details.

USING PHOTOS

Figure 11.8 To add several images to an album, select that album, then tap the Organize button to display the Organize dialog.

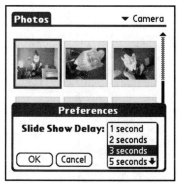

Figure 11.9 Speed up or slow down the delay between images in Slide Show via the Option menu's Preferences.

To move images to an expansion card:

The Zire 71 only has so much memory (OK, 16 MB to be exact), so it's wise to utilize expansion memory cards to store loads of snapped photos.

With an image selected, choose Copy to Card or write ∕-C. You can also beam images to other Palm OS handhelds (choose Beam Photo) or send via e-mail (choose Send Photo).

To add multiple photos to an album:

1. Select a photo album from the drop-down menu at the top right of the screen.

2. Tap the Organize button.

3. Tap selected images to add them to this album; a green plus sign will denote that it's ready to be added (**Figure 11.8**).

4. Tap Done.

✔ Tips

■ To change the delay between images in Slide Show, choose Preferences from the Options menu and adjust the timing (**Figure 11.9**).

■ There's only one on-board photo editing option: rotating an image. Choose Rotate Photo or write ∕-R. For a more robust application, PhotoBase (www.arcsoft.com/en/products/photobasepalm/) adds a bit more image management and editing features—you can even draw on images.

USING PHOTOS

217

Viewing Photos in Palm Desktop for Windows

While simple enough, the Palm Photos application within Palm Desktop also features some helpful editing and organization tools (**Figure 11.10**).

To edit photos:

Double-click an image to open it in Photo Editor, or select an image from the View pane and click the Editor button (**Figure 11.11**). Within Photo Editor:

◆ Click the Crop button in the toolbar to reduce the size. Drag over the area that you want to save, then click the Crop Photo button.

◆ Rotate the photo by clicking either the 90° Left or 90° Right buttons.

◆ Click the Enhance button to improve the brightness and contrast. If you don't like the enhancement, press Ctrl-Z to undo.

◆ To reduce "red-eye" effect from a flash, click the Red-eye button. Select the area you wish to fix, and a thin, barely visible gray line appears. Click the Red-eye button again to save the changes.

To organize albums:

◆ To create a new album, choose New Album from the Tools menu or after right-clicking within the Album bar. Alternatively, select Edit Album to create, delete, and rename albums.

◆ Drag single or multiple image selections from the View pane and drop onto a desired album in the Album bar. Photos can reside in multiple albums.

Figure 11.10 Main view of Palm Photos in Palm Desktop for Windows.

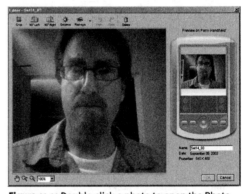

Figure 11.11 Double-click a photo to open the Photo Editor, which provides editing options in the toolbar and a rendering of how the photo will look in your handheld.

Figure 11.12 The Details view enables you to add a photo to an album as well as type a note about the image.

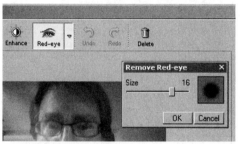

Figure 11.13 Click the arrow to the right of the Red-eye button to adjust the size of the selector brush.

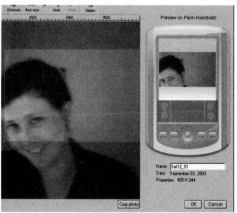

Figure 11.14 Use the crop tool to modify a photo's size or to highlight a specific area. Check to see how it renders using the Preview on Palm Handheld.

✔ Tips

■ You can change the views within Palm Photos by clicking the tabs at the bottom of the application: Thumbnail displays small images, List shows file information, and Details replicates the file information while also adding the ability to file the image into an album and add notes (**Figure 11.12**).

■ The resulting brush stroke from the Red-eye tool is hard to pick out. When making adjustments, bump up the viewing size of your image, then use the hand tool to maneuver to the spot that needs help. Then change the size of the Red-eye selector brush by clicking the arrow to the right of the Red-eye toolbar button and adjusting the slider on the dialog box (**Figure 11.13**).

■ After making a selection with the Crop tool, you can click and drag that selection rectangle to highlight another area of your image. You'll be able to see how the photo will render on your handheld in the Preview on Palm Handheld section to the right of the main window (**Figure 11.14**).

■ If you want to crop an image but save its original file, rename the opened file's name in the field below the Preview on Palm Handheld area before making any adjustments.

VIEWING PHOTOS IN PALM DESKTOP (WINDOWS)

Capturing Images

So, with technology producing ever-smaller components for devices, why not throw a digital camera into the handheld mix? Sony and Palm offer devices with built-in cameras; I'll continue to use the Zire 71 as an example.

To take a picture:

1. Hold the Zire 71 in one hand. With the thumb of your other hand, slide open the camera by pushing up from the ridged bottom of the blue front plate.

2. The lens will be revealed on the back of the Zire 71 and the screen will change to an active camera view. The bottom of the screen displays the Viewfinder button, the selected resolution, the number of shots you have left (depending on available memory), and remaining battery power (**Figure 11.15**).

3. Aim the lens at your subject, then press the camera shutter button at the bottom of the metal housing. Alternatively, you can press the directional rocker.

4. Slide the blue front plate back into its closed position to open the Photos app and review your shots.

✔ Tip

- If you've taken multiple shots during a camera session, tap the Thumbnail button. Within the Thumbnail section, you can delete unwanted photos without waiting to turn off the camera (**Figure 11.16**). To return to the active camera, tap the Viewfinder button.

Figure 11.15 The Viewfinder view in the Zire 71's camera (the default view).

Figure 11.16 Tap the Thumbnails view to see all images that have been captured since starting this camera session.

Figure 11.17 Tap the Options button to set preferences, including the ability to review and/or discard images after you shoot them.

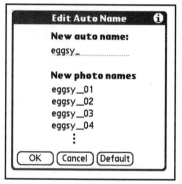

Figure 11.18 Change the default auto-naming convention to something more useful or personal.

Figure 11.19 Under Advanced Controls, modify settings for white and contrast.

To change image capture options:

1. With the camera active, tap the Options button.

2. Changing the resolution from the default 640 x 480 pixels (to either 320 x 240 or 160 x 120) will enable you to store more images on your handheld. But be advised, the resulting images will be grainier.

3. If you set the Review photo before saving option to On, you'll be given three seconds to choose to delete or keep an image (**Figure 11.17**).

4. Save photos the handheld's memory or an expansion card using the Save to popup menu.

5. Choosing to add a date stamp to your photo adds the current date to the upper-right corner of your image (much like a film camera's quartz date feature).

6. To change the default naming convention for image files, choose Custom from the Auto name format popup menu, then modify the naming prefix (**Figure 11.18**).

7. For stealthy snapping, keep the Shutter sound selected to Off.

8. For more control over your imagery, tap the Advanced button. Here you'll be able to choose from four white balance settings (Automatic, Fluorescent, Indoors, and Sunlight) plus adjust the contrast and brightness (uncheck Auto brightness to bring up a slider) (**Figure 11.19**). Tap the Default button to make these setting stick for all image capturing.

9. Tap Done to return to the main Options screen, then Done again to return to capturing images.

Importing Movies

Adding video to your handheld isn't quite as easy as HotSyncing a QuickTime file, but Kinoma makes it fairly painless to convert video clips from a variety of formats (AVI, DV, MPEG, and QuickTime .mov files).

In addition to the Kinoma Player for your handheld (compatible with Palm OS 3.1 and later), you'll need the Kinoma Producer software to convert source files.

To convert a video file:

1. On your PC or Mac, launch Kinoma Producer and add files either by browsing your hard drive or dragging and dropping into the Convert Files area.

2. To optimize for your handheld, choose it from the Device drop-down menu. You can also choose All Palm OS 5, All Color Palm OS, or All Gray Palm OS devices.

3. From the Export Location drop-down menu, select HotSync folder. The Choose Palm User dialog then appears, enabling you to choose its ultimate destination: your handheld's memory or an expansion card (**Figure 11.20**).

4. Click the Convert button to start the conversion process. When your file is ready, click Close (**Figure 11.21**).

✔ Tip

■   Choosing HotSync folder as the destination places the file in the Install folder within your Palm user folder and adds it to your handheld at your next HotSync, eliminating the need for you to add the file to the Quick Install application yourself.

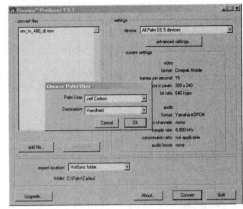

Figure 11.20 Choose between your handheld or an expansion card as the video's final destination.

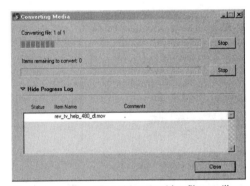

Figure 11.21 After converting your video file, you'll need to click the Close button—this dialog doesn't go away on its own.

IMPORTING MOVIES

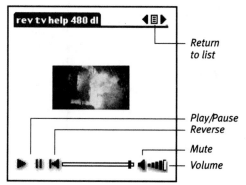

Return to list

Play/Pause
Reverse

Mute
Volume

Figure 11.22 The Kinoma Player play-back controls at the bottom, and list navigation controls at the top.

Figure 11.23 Tweak Kinoma Player's preferences to change sound output and whether the movie automatically replays.

Playing Movies

After jumping the hurdle of converting your video file and synchronizing, it's time to sit back with some popcorn.

To play a video:

1. On your handheld, launch Kinoma Player.

2. Tap a title from the list to start playing. Titles with a card icon are stored on an inserted expansion card (**Figure 11.22**).

3. The video starts playing automatically. To stop it, press the Pause button. Tap the slider to move forward or backward. Tap the speaker icon to mute, or adjust the 5-level volume bar.

4. To go to another video, tap either arrow in the top-right corner. To return to the title list, tap the icon between the arrows.

To delete a video:

While in video play-back mode, tap the menu icon on the silkscreen area, then choose Delete from the Media menu.

✔ Tips

- Tap within the main screen to hide the controls at the bottom of the screen and the icons and tab at the top.

- The Kinoma Player doesn't have a lot of bells and whistles, but it can provide good information about stored video files. Tapping the controls at the bottom of the list shows you a video's format, resolution, running time, and file size. When viewing a movie, choose Preferences from the Media menu to change the playback looping and adjust audio channels and maximum volume (**Figure 11.23**).

- On the Tungsten T3, you can view letter-boxed-sized movies in horizontal mode.

Painting Basics

You're holding a stylus and a touch-sensitive screen. Doesn't it just make you want to draw a squiggly line, or a caricature of your best friend? Art historians will have a field day in the future with our creations, but there's no doubt that, given the same circumstances, most people will doodle—even just a little bit.

There are several painting programs available, but the one I'll use as an example is TealPaint (www.tealpoint.com/softpnt.htm). In addition to basic painting tools, it offers the ability to zoom in on a picture, select elements by drawing a marquee around them, and insert text.

To sketch using TealPaint:

1. When you first launch the program, you're asked to name a new image database where your pictures will be stored. Several image databases can coexist on the same device (**Figure 11.24**).

2. Tap the New button to create a new image, appropriately named New Image.

3. Select a painting tool (such as pencil, line tool, or geometric shape) from the second button from the left at the bottom of the screen (**Figure 11.25**).

4. The third button from the left chooses the pattern. Tap it to determine what type of "ink" the painting tool will use. If you're using a color device, choose the foreground color from the color swatch next to the Undo button (**Figure 11.26**).

5. Specify the size and shape of the painting tool by tapping the fourth button from the left. Sketch away! You can undo the previous action by tapping the Un button. Tapping the Grid snap selector in the lower-left corner constrains some tools to an invisible 8 by 8-pixel grid.

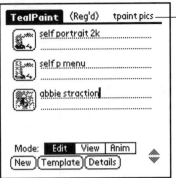

Tap the database name to open other image databases

Figure 11.24 You can store many images within multiple TealPaint databases. Tap a thumbnail to view and edit a drawing.

Figure 11.25 Using TealPaint's painting tools, you can add a few happy UFOs (or trees, or whatever) to your masterpiece.

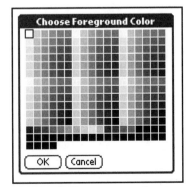

Figure 11.26 (Time to use your imagination again in my grayscale book.) Now you can paint in color if you own a color handheld.

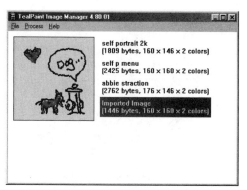

Figure 11.27 TealPaint Image Manager extracts your images from the TealPaint databases on the handheld.

Figure 11.28 Tapping Details displays the file size and image dimensions. Tap Done to go back to the drawing screen, or Delete to remove the image entirely.

Exporting and Importing TealPaint Images

TealPaint comes with a Windows desktop utility called TealPaint Image Manager, which extracts images from TealPaint databases and saves them as Windows bitmap (.bmp) image files (it lets you print images as well). A bare-bones Mac utility is also available from the TealPoint Web site.

To export TealPaint images:

1. Perform a HotSync to update the database files on your desktop.

2. Launch TealPaint Image Manager, and select Open database from the File menu.

3. Databases are stored in the Backups folder located within your Palm user folder. In the TealPaint Image Manager program, open the database file, then click OK (**Figure 11.27**).

4. Click on an image name at right, then select Export image from database to .BMP from the Process menu.

5. Name the file, choose a location on your hard drive, then click the Save button.

To import images into TealPaint:

1. Make sure the image you want to transfer to TealPaint is in Windows bitmap format.

2. In TealPaint Image Manager, choose Import .BMP image into database. Locate your image file and click the Open button.

✔ Tips

■ To remove the green coloring of a Palm image, click Yes in the dialog that asks if you want to force black and white colors when you export the file.

■ To view information about an image on your handheld, tap Details (**Figure 11.28**).

Playing Digital Music

Playing digital music from your handheld computer: the notion was probably less than a glimmer in most people's eyes at first, yet today the idea is becoming as natural as storing your addresses. As long as the information is digital, why not? With the rise of the MP3 music format, it's now possible to take a selection of your music collection with you, without the bulk of CDs or a separate music player.

The Sony CLIÉ PEG-N710C was the first Palm handheld to add digital music, and Sony CLIÉ handhelds continue to add built-in support for digital audio (**Figure 11.29**). For its Palm OS 5 handhelds, Palm has partnered with Real Networks to include the RealOne Player for Palm application.

You will need to install the RealOne Player software on your PC. Note, also, that a memory card is required to store digital audio.

Figure 11.29 Sony pioneered adding digital music to Palm OS handhelds, and most of their current handhelds (including the CLIÉ SJ33 shown here) offer built-in support for digital audio.

✔ Tips

- Since digital music files take up a lot of memory, plan on purchasing a 64 MB or 128 MB (or higher!) memory card.

- Sony CLIÉ handhelds also support ATRAC3-formatted files, a method of encrypting the files so that they can only be used on one device. If you use ATRAC3 files, you can only store them on special MagicGate Memory Stick media.

- If you use an older Sony CLIÉ and a Macintosh, install The Missing Sync by Mark/Space (www.markspace.com/missingsync.html) to transfer files to Memory Sticks.

PLAYING DIGITAL MUSIC

Figure 11.30 The list of MP3 files added to your Palm Handheld in RealOne's Device list. Make sure your handheld is connected and on, otherwise you'll get the Disconnected red light icon.

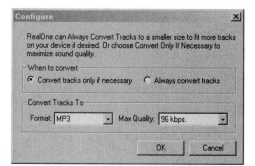

Figure 11.31 Automatically convert your MP3 files to a lower bit rate using the Configure button in RealOne.

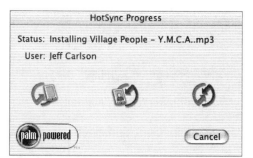

Figure 11.32 It takes a HotSync to transfer Village People MP3 files from your Mac to your handheld (unlike the Windows version, which uses RealOne to transfer files).

To transfer digital music files to your handheld (Windows):

1. Place your handheld with inserted memory card into your HotSync cradle (but do not press the HotSynch button).

2. In your PC's RealOne Player, click the Devices icon at the bottom of the screen.

3. Double-click Palm Handheld in the Devices list, select the Palm Handheld icon at the top of the list, or select it from the Devices drop-down menu (**Figure 11.30**).

4. Click the Add Clips icon and select from the list of audio files that are in your RealOne library. Alternatively, when in one of the My Library views, select an audio file, click the Copy To icon drop-down menu, and select Palm Handheld.

5. Click the Transfer button to send audio files to your handheld—you do not need to perform a HotSync.

✔ Tips

- Create a playlist in My Library, then add it to your handheld using the Copy To maneuver mentioned above. All associated MP3 files will be added to the Palm Handheld Device list, then to your handheld after a HotSync.

- With Palm Handheld selected in Devices, click the Configure button to have RealOne automatically convert files to a lower bit rate (**Figure 11.31**).

To transfer digital music files to your handheld (Macintosh):

1. Drag and drop MP3 files onto the Send to Handheld droplet.

2. Select your memory card as the destination for the file(s).

3. Perform a HotSync (**Figure 11.32**).

PLAYING DIGITAL MUSIC

227

To listen to digital music:

1. Launch RealOne Player (**Figure 11.33**).

2. Tap the Songs button to select from the audio files available on your memory card. Alternatively, tap the Playlists button to view song lists either created on your handheld or transferred from the Windows version of Real One. The audio file begins playing immediately after your selection.

3. Switch between songs by tapping the Forward or Backward buttons.

4. Tap the Information button to view deails about the current track (**Figure 11.34**).

5. Tap the Continuous Play button to move forward through the Songs list or a selected playlist. Tap the Random Play button to mix things up.

6. Tap the Volume button to adjust sound through your headphones or through the handheld's AM-radio-like speaker.

To create or edit a playlist:

1. Tap the Playlists button, then tap New. Or, select a playlist and tap Edit.

2. Add a title in the Name field.

3. Tap the Add button, and check the songs from your memory card that you want added. Tap Done.

4. Select a song and use the up and down arrows at the lower-right corner of the screen to adjust the position of songs within your list (**Figure 11.35**). Or, select a song and tap Remove to delete it from the list.

5. Tap Done to save the playlist and return to the Playlist library. Tap Done again to return to the Player.

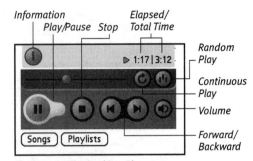

Figure 11.33 The RealOne Player includes controls familiar to anyone who has used a portable audio device or the PC version of RealOne.

Figure 11.34 Tap the Information button to see details about the song, including album title, MP3 file encoding, and file size.

Figure 11.35 Mix and match your own music collection. No more carrying around an entire CD just to listen to the one good song on it.

PLAYING DIGITAL MUSIC

LONG TEXTS

Like the concept of a truly paperless office, the notion of electronic books replacing traditional printed texts has been floating around for years. Instead of carrying around an armful of bound paper, you can store hundreds or thousands of books without felling a single tree or throwing out your back.

However, people haven't yet embraced a completely digital reading experience, though not for a lack of options. High profile devices such as the Gemstar eBook garnered a lot of press for their "revolutionary" approaches to distributing long texts, but ultimately flamed out for being too large and too expensive.

The funny thing is, Palm OS device owners have been enjoying the same capability for years. The Doc format has enabled readers to take any text file on the go, while third-party options use their own formats. You can read Adobe's Portable Document Format (PDF) on the Palm OS. Publishers also offer book-length works: Online Originals (www. onlineoriginals.com) and Palm Digital Media (www.palmdigitalmedia.com) are thriving.

Reading a lot of text on a small screen isn't an ideal task, but it's not as bad as I first thought. Plus, 400 pages of fiction are a lot lighter to carry when stored in a shirt pocket.

Reading Doc-Formatted Texts

A number of applications are available for reading documents that you install on your handheld. An early document format, Doc, is read by most reader applications. For the sake of example, I'll focus on TealDoc (www.tealpoint.com).

Doc files can contain bookmarks that jump down to main sections of the document. Bookmarks can be preformatted (see "Converting Texts to Doc Format" later in this chapter), or created by the reader.

To open Doc files:

1. After installing a Doc file into the handheld, open TealDoc. You'll see a list of available Doc files that are stored in the device's memory (**Figure 14.1**).

2. Tap the Open button at the bottom of the screen, then tap the title of the document you want to read.

To navigate a document:

◆ Tap anywhere in the lower half of the screen to scroll down; tap the upper half to scroll up. You can advance through the files without having to be precise about tapping a scroll bar or arrow.

◆ You can also move to the top or bottom of the document by choosing Go Up Page (✓-U), Go Down Page (✓-D), Go to Top (✓-T), or Go to Bottom (✓-B) from the View menu.

◆ Tap the percentage indicator to display the Scroll panel (**Figure 14.2**). Drag the horizontal scroll bar at the bottom of the screen to scroll through the document; the percentage will change depending on the slider's location.

Figure 14.1 Any Doc-formatted files that you install show up in the Doc reader's list view.

> The blood drained from Adrian's face. He wouldn't hear the end of this for some time. "Uh," he said.
>
> "Just listen to me, kid, don't say anything else. You're in enough trouble as it is. I've got your father conferenced in, and I can tell you he isn't looking like he's very happy.
>
> "Now, here's how it's going to be. I've set up an appointment with Bosco in one hour. I had to call in a lot of favors

Drag to scroll through the file

Figure 14.2 Move swiftly through your document by dragging the horizontal scroll bar in TealDoc.

READING DOC-FORMATTED TEXTS

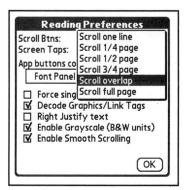

Figure 14.3 Control the scroll rate by choosing from the Scroll Btns and Screen Taps popup menus.

> The blood drained from Adrian's face. He wouldn't hear the end of this for some time. "Uh," he said.
>
> "Just listen to me, kid, don't say anything else. You're in enough trouble as it is. I've got your father conferenced in, and I can tell you he isn't looking like he's very happy.
>
> "Now, here's how i » Edit Bookmarks... set up an appointr » Add Bookmark... one hour. I had to « » Add Note...
>
> (X) ← (35%)

Figure 14.4 Bookmarks can be set up before the file is installed, or you can add them to access your favorite passages.

✔ Tips

■ You can specify that tapping advances the text by screen (the default), partial page (a full screen minus one overlapping line), or line. Choose Reading Prefs from the Special menu (✓-P) and choose the degree of advancement from the Screen Taps popup menu. You can also specify scroll options for the physical scroll buttons on the handheld's case (**Figure 14.3**).

■ If you have the Scroll one line option selected above, tapping and holding the stylus to the screen will scroll the text until you lift the stylus. Depending on where you tap, the scrolling speed will be slower (closer to the middle) or faster (closer to the lower or upper edges).

■ If you want to be able to select and copy text with your stylus, choose Select text from the Screen Taps popup menu in the Reading Prefs screen.

To use bookmarks:

1. Tap the icon in the lower-right corner of the screen to view the bookmarks popup menu (**Figure 14.4**).

2. Tap the section name you want to access.

To add bookmarks:

1. Scroll up or down to display the section you wish to bookmark.

2. Choose New Bookmark from the popup menu, or Add New Bookmark from the Marks menu (✓-1), and enter a descriptive title. Tap OK.

✔ Tip

■ To remove, rename, or scan the document for bookmarks, choose those options from the Marks menu.

To automatically scroll the document:

1. When AutoScroll is active, the screen advances automatically. Under the Special menu, choose AutoScroll Go (✓-G) to begin. AutoScroll Stop (✓-S) turns the feature off.

2. Tap the percentage indicator to display the Scroll panel, or choose Show Scroll Panel from the View menu.

3. The smaller horizontal bar at the bottom of the page indicates the scrolling speed; tap the plus (■) or minus (■) buttons to the right of the bar to adjust the speed (**Figure 14.5**).

4. Tap the go button (■) to start, or the stop button (■) to stop scrolling.

✔ Tip

■ You can also control the scrolling speed using the application buttons on the front of the handheld's case. Choose Reading Prefs (✓-P), then tap one or both buttons under the heading App buttons control autoscroll on.

To perform a search within the current document:

1. Choose Show Font Panel (which also displays the search controls) from the View menu, or tap the percentage indicator.

2. To search, tap the magnifying glass icon, or choose Find from the Doc menu (✓-F) (**Figure 14.6**). Enter the text you want to find, and mark any of the four search options.

3. To search again for the same term, tap either of the arrows surrounding the magnifying glass icon; or, choose Find Next (✓-N) or Find Last (✓-L) from the Doc menu.

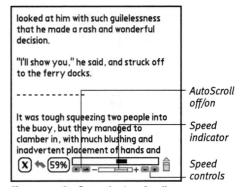

Figure 14.5 Configure the AutoScroll rate by tapping the controls at the bottom of the screen.

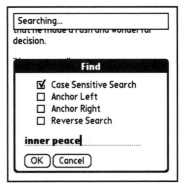

Figure 14.6 Tap the magnifying glass icon to perform searches.

READING DOC-FORMATTED TEXTS

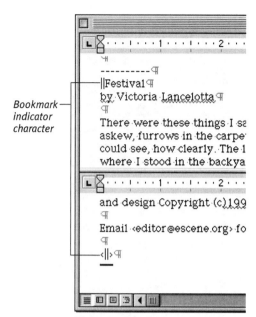

Bookmark indicator character

Figure 14.7 Specifying a unique character set at the end of the document (bottom) instructs Doc readers to add a bookmark where the characters are found within the text.

Converting Texts to Doc Format

You can create your own Doc files from existing text files using utilities such as MakeDocBatch (`www.freewarepalm.com/utilities/makedocbatch.shtml`), QEX2 (`www.qland.de/qex2/`) and Sync Buddy (`perso.wanadoo.fr/fpillet/`). (Some Doc utilities, such as TealDoc, include a conversion program as well.)

To prepare the text file:

1. Your text is going to be viewed on the small screen, so strip out any long breaking lines of repeated dashes (----), or reduce them to about 20 characters.

2. Make sure there's a carriage return after each paragraph, not each line. This gives you more flexibility when viewing at different font sizes.

3. Save your document as a text-only file.

To specify bookmarks:

1. Choose a character combination that isn't likely to show up in your text (such as ||).

2. At the end of your document, put it between brackets (<||>) to define the file's bookmark notation.

3. Add the character combination (without brackets) before each section you wish to bookmark (**Figure 14.7**). When the Doc reader encounters the characters, it creates a new bookmark, using the text that follows as a bookmark label.

To convert the file:

Drag and drop the text file onto the conversion utility, or open the utility and use the Browse button to locate the file.

✔ Tips

■ TealDoc offers the ability to embed pictures, links, and Web bookmarks into text files, similar to HTML markup. For this to be activated, though, the document needs to be converted to TealDoc format on the handheld. From the main list screen, select All to TealDoc format. To return the files to standard Doc state, select All to public format. See the documentation that comes with TealDoc for instructions on how to mark up your text to accommodate these features.

■ You can also edit Doc-formatted files directly on the handheld (**Figure 14.8**) using the editor/word processor QED (www.qland.de/qed/).

Figure 14.8 QED can edit Doc-formatted files, as well as open them.

CONVERTING TEXTS TO DOC FORMAT

Figure 14.9 Since Palm Digital Media books require the purchaser to unlock titles, mainstream authors and publishers are offering books in the Palm Reader electronic format.

Figure 14.10 Palm Reader's preferences enable you to find the best method of reading the books.

Reading Books with Palm Reader

Palm Digital Media (www.palmdigitalmedia.com/) (formerly Peanut Press, before being purchased by Palm) developed their own software for reading electronic books under the Palm OS. They also had another requirement: ensure that books purchased from their site could be opened only by the people who bought them. The result is Palm Reader, which includes features not found in the other electronic readers (**Figure 14.9**).

Features of Palm Reader

◆ Mark favorite sections by tapping the Bookmark icon (🔖).

◆ Add notes to the text by tapping the Annotations icon (▣).

◆ Invert the screen for better readability (especially with backlighting on) by tapping the Invert Screen icon (◪).

◆ For those times when you get engrossed in a book, be sure to check the time by tapping the Current Time icon (🕒).

◆ Change the screen orientation and the tapping control of the screen by choosing Screen Orientation from the Options menu (**Figure 14.10**).

✔ Tips

■ Palm Reader understands Doc files, so you can use it to swap between multiple text formats on your handheld.

■ If you own a device that has a rectangular screen, such as a few Sony Clié models, rotate the screen orientation to view more text while reading.

■ For more reading options, buy Palm Reader Pro ($15), which supports more fonts and includes a built-in dictionary.

Reading and Editing Microsoft Word Files

If you're like a lot of people, you may not want to read books or preformatted files on your handheld. Instead, wouldn't it be great to take some of your word processor documents with you and edit them on the road?

DataViz's Documents To Go (www.dataviz.com) and Cutting Edge Software's Quickoffice (www.cesinc.com) enable you to do just that. Drag files in Microsoft Word and other formats to Documents To Go (**Figure 14.11**) or Quickoffice (**Figure 14.12**) to convert them with styles and most formatting (including tables) intact (**Figure 14.13**). Both programs also include modules for viewing Microsoft Excel spreadsheets on the handheld.

✔ Tips

■ For a faster method of specifying files to be converted by Documents To Go, select the file in the Finder (Mac) or Explorer (Windows), then either Control-click (Mac) or right-click (Windows) to select Take File to Go from the popup menu that appears. Under Windows, you can optionally select Documents To Go from the Send to submenu of the contextual menu.

■ Although much of the document's original formatting is translated to the handheld, keep in mind that the file is being converted, not just sent directly between the PC and handheld. So, some formatting (such as style sheets) may not be retained when you open the file again on the PC after editing it on the handheld.

■ You can use Quickoffice or Documents To Go as standalone word processors too: create a new file on the Palm, then transfer it back to your PC at the next HotSync (a great use with an external keyboard).

Figure 14.11 Simply drag Word files to the Documents To Go window to prepare them for installation at the next HotSync operation.

Figure 14.12 Quickoffice retains the native Word file format when moving the file to the handheld.

Figure 14.13 Documents To Go retains formatting from the word processor that created the original file.

READING AND EDITING MICROSOFT WORD FILES

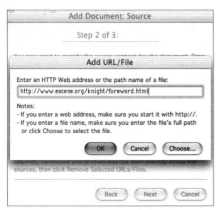

Figure 14.14 Use iSilo's desktop tool to grab Web pages for viewing on your handheld.

Figure 14.15 iSilo formats text defined by the underlying HTML, and includes links to other converted pages.

Figure 14.16 Control the page scroll rate by defining four screen regions.

Viewing HTML Documents

iSilo (www.isilo.com) and HandStory (www.handstory.com) take HTML pages and format them for viewing on a handheld. You can use them to read an individual HTML file, or point to a Web site and specify how many levels of links to follow. (I'm using iSilo as the example below.)

To convert a file for viewing with iSilo:

1. Using the separate iSiloX application, select an HTML file you wish to convert (**Figure 14.14**). You can also provide a Web address that iSilo will connect to.

2. After the file has been converted, HotSync your organizer.

3. On the handheld, launch iSilo and choose the page(s) you installed. If you converted several pages of a Web site, you can tap the dotted-underlined words to bring up linked pages (**Figure 14.15**).

✔ Tip

■ Most text readers for the Palm OS separate the screen into two areas, usually top and bottom, to control whether the text advances up or down when you tap it. iSilo wisely splits the screen into four equal areas, letting you control the amount of scrolling based on where you tap (**Figure 14.16**).

Viewing PDF Documents

Adobe's Portable Document Format (PDF) began as a method of displaying print materials onscreen in a format that would retain the layout, fonts, and appearance of the original file, without requiring that the recipient own QuarkXPress, InDesign, or other page-layout application. Over time, PDF has become a way to view nearly any document on any computer, so it's only natural that you can now view PDF files on a Palm OS handheld.

A number of programs enable you to convert PDF files for viewing on the handheld, such as Adobe Reader for Palm OS (www.adobe.com/products/acrobat/readerforpalm.html). Other document applications, such as Data-Viz's Documents To Go Premium, can also convert and read PDF files.

To convert a PDF file:

1. Simply drag a PDF file to the main window of Adobe Reader for Palm OS; alternately, click the Add button (**Figure 14.17**). The PDF is converted to a format optimized for the handheld.

2. HotSync your handheld to transfer the files.

3. Launch the reader application to view the PDF document (**Figure 14.18**).

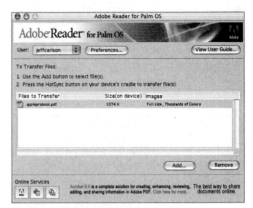

Figure 14.17 Adobe Reader for Palm OS prepares PDF files for your handheld.

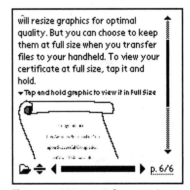

Figure 14.18 You won't forget you're viewing a device with a small screen, but the information (including images) from a PDF is available on the handheld.

MANAGING
YOUR TIME

Believe me, I'm not a slick-suited time management guru, a master of every minute and second. The truth is, I've never really been *great* at time management, which is what led me to buy a handheld in the first place.

What I am is a full-time freelancer/free agent/independent contractor (pick your favorite term) who has managed to get control of his schedule and tasks with the help of a remarkable pocket-sized gadget. When I started using a handheld, I was amazed to discover that it wasn't a tool people used only during business hours. Organizers soon became integrated into their owners' lives, instead of gathering dust on the corner of their desks.

We're all trying to manage our time, whether that means setting up an efficient workflow system at work, or keeping track of where to take the kids throughout the week. It's likely you carry your Palm device everywhere—so use it to help take control of your time.

Track Your Time

I always enjoy stories or movies where the hero has to track something through an impenetrable jungle or forest. In these scenes, the star is the Expert Guide who inspects every branch, leaf, and mismatched clump of dirt to divine the path of his or her prey. It's that attention to detail that I find fascinating, of looking at the same thing everyone else is viewing, but seeing something different.

If there ever was an impenetrable wilderness to be explored, it's the schedule that many of us live with every day. Your desire to tame it may have led you to buy a Palm organizer in the first place. Like the Expert Guide who notices all details, it's important that you do some tracking before you can reach your goal of personal organization.

Many people have a natural aversion to tracking their time, myself included. If I'm recording every minute, I sometimes feel I'm focused more on tracking than on whatever task I need to accomplish. However, it's important that you know where your time is going before you can redefine where you want it to go. Keep track of where (or when) you spend your time for a week or a month.

For a visual approach that's built in to your handheld, consider using Date Book to track your time (**Figure 13.1**). Instead of scheduling only upcoming events, mark things as you do them.

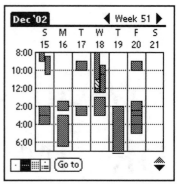

Figure 13.1 Your calendar will start to fill up, but by tracking everything you do plus your appointments, you can see how much time your tasks are taking.

Figure 13.2 To make it easier to differentiate between appointments and tracked items, use a special character (such as ~) to indicate your tracking.

To track your time using Date Book:

1. Launch the program by pressing the plastic Date Book button on the front of the case. This also displays today's events in the Day view.

2. Tap New, or tap the current time to create a new event. Write your activity on the event's title line.

3. If you know how long the activity will last, tap the Details button and enter an end time. If not, just stick with the default one-hour time span.

4. When you've finished, go back into the record and adjust the end time, then start a new record for your next activity.

✔ Tips

- To keep scheduled events and tracked events separate, mark the title with a unique character or word; you can set up a ShortCut (see Chapter 2) to quickly enter the notation (**Figure 13.2**).

- This can also be a good opportunity to also add notes about your activity for reference later. Tap the Note button in the Event Details screen, or select Attach Note (╱-A) from the Record menu.

- If you don't want your Date Book screens cluttered with appointments *and* tracking information, mark the tracking events Private (see Chapter 4). They won't be visible, but they will be stored.

- Don't purge the old records from your Date Book until you've finished your time-tracking period.

TRACK YOUR TIME

Use a Tracking Program

A few applications have been designed specifically to track time. One application I use is HourzPro (www.zoskware.com), which lets me record my billable hours as well as non-billable time that I want to keep tabs on. Other similar applications include Timesheet (www.seatechnology.com.au/timeSheet.html) and TEAK (www.eb7.com).

To track your time using HourzPro:

1. Launch HourzPro (**Figure 13.3**). Tap one of the view icons at the lower left to choose between the project view (▦) and the day view (⊡). Tap the New button to create a new record.

2. From the Project popup menu, choose Edit Projects to set up a new activity; if this is a business-related project, enter the client name and rate. Tap OK and then select the activity from the popup menu.

3. The timer begins when you create a new record, which will be shown on the HourzPro Entry screen (**Figure 13.4**). Tap Done to return to the main screen.

4. When finished with the activity, tap the stopwatch icon to the right of the description to stop the timer; the duration (and charge, if you entered a rate) is automatically calculated.

✔ Tip

- If you're interrupted by something that you don't necessarily need to record, open your record and enter the amount of interrupted time in the Break field.

Figure 13.3 HourzPro offers advanced options for tracking your time.

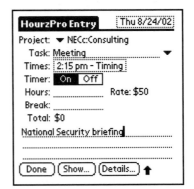

Figure 13.4 When you create a new record, the timer begins tracking. Specify a project and task for later reference.

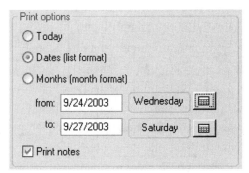

Figure 13.5 Specify Dates (list format) when printing your Date Book entries to see your events' details and save some paper.

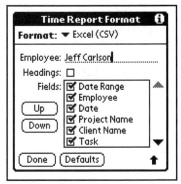

Figure 13.6 Set up the contents of your reports for when you export them.

Figure 13.7 Generate comma-delimited time reports that can be opened in Excel on your PC.

Review Your Tracks

When you're finished recording your moves, you will have a wealth of raw data. Seeing where your time actually goes isn't always heartening, but at least you'll have a basis to build upon and improve. The next step is to analyze that data.

If you used the Date Book method mentioned earlier, go back and review where you spent your time. One easy method of doing this is to make a printout of the time period you spent tracking. If you're using HourzPro, a companion application, Reportz, makes it easy to create reports.

To generate a Date Book report:

1. Perform a HotSync to update your Palm Desktop records.

2. Choose Print from the File menu, or press Control/Command-P. The Print Options dialog box appears.

3. Under Print Options, choose Dates (list format) (**Figure 13.5**). Only days with events on them will print. Click OK.

To generate an HourzPro report:

1. From the HourzPro screen, tap the Reportz icon (📃), or choose Go To Reports from the Options menu.

2. Tap the Time Report button to create a new report. You'll have to specify an employee (you) and default export format the first time you run Reportz (**Figure 13.6**). Tap Done when finished.

3. Name the report in the Title field, then select criteria from the Project, Period, Status, and Action popup menus.

4. Tap Create to generate the report. It will be added to the Reportz List (**Figure 13.7**). At your next HotSync, the reports will be transferred to your PC.

Fine-Tune Your Time Management

Now that you have your data, look it over carefully. Are you spending too much time preparing for meetings? Too little? Do phone calls routinely interrupt your workflow? Examining this type of schedule overview tends to make previously minor annoyances or hidden successes stand out.

Know your own schedule

Most people have an internal clock that seems to pay no attention when they need to crunch on a deadline or be awake for a poorly scheduled important meeting. Look at how you space your activities throughout the day, then restructure accordingly.

If you're a walking corpse at 3 p.m., don't plan meetings or appointments or important tasks; high doses of caffeine can sometimes overcome mid-afternoon sluggishness, but not always. Set up a repeating event ("Siesta" perhaps?) that spans 3:00–4:00 each business day (**Figure 13.8**).

Be alarming

Have you ever been so involved in a project that several hours can slip by without notice? Date Book's alarm features help keep me focused on when I need to shift gears.

I've set up my Date Book preferences so that every event is assigned a 10-minute alarm. Select Preferences from the Options menu (/-R) and mark the Alarm Preset checkbox (**Figure 13.9**). Make sure you're being realistic about the alarms—adjust each event's alarm preset to take into account things like travel time and preparation (yes, you should shave before dinner with the boss).

Another option is to use reminder software like BugMe! (www.electricpocket.net) (**Figure 13.10**).

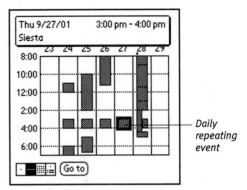

Daily repeating event

Figure 13.8 A scheduled break can help you get through the most unproductive time of the day.

Figure 13.9 I'd rather endure multiple alarms during the day than miss an appointment. Each new event is assigned an alarm when you activate the Alarm Preset option.

Figure 13.10 Think of BugMe! as a helpful Post-it note that's stuck to you.

Figure 13.11 Agenda lets you see which events and tasks are coming up when you tap the tabs at the top of the screen.

Prioritize events and tasks wisely

Is everything really a number-one priority on your To Do list? I find myself entering To Do items without paying attention to their priority settings—as long as they're on the list, that should be good enough, right?

Maybe that works for some people, but being smart about prioritizing items generally improves my ability to deal with them in a timely manner. If you have to manually scan through the list each time you finish a task, you may be wasting valuable time. If, on the other hand, you figured out each item's priority ahead of time, you can jump through the list quicker.

See the bigger picture

The Palm OS is great at taking lots of little scraps of information and organizing them in one place. The problem is that your information is then all "hidden" behind the current application—you can't see what's coming up if you don't look at your schedule or To Do list. The saying "out of sight, out of mind" can be apt, but not beneficial, for Palm owners. (I've seen people with handhelds in larger carrying cases that are festooned with sticky notes.) Use a "big picture" utility such as TealGlance (www.tealpoint.com) or Agenda (www.dovcom.com) to get an overview of what's lurking beneath the surface (**Figure 13.11**).

✔ Tip

- Give yourself some breathing room between appointments. A common scheduling mistake is to run meetings together, made all the easier because the Date Book defaults to hourly blocks of time. Use the alarm preset option to give you a breather before the next appointment.

Mark items for quick scanning

Don't start a memo with "Memo" or "Important Note," or list a To Do item as "business stuff." Assume that you're going to be quickly scanning through the items most of the time—you don't want to waste time with two or three taps just to decipher something you wrote two hours ago. Launch right into the meat of it, and explain later. You should be able to identify the memo, task, or event just by looking at its title in a list.

Use ShortCuts

The ShortCuts feature is one of the most underutilized aspects of the Palm OS (see Chapter 2). ShortCuts are great for saving several Graffiti strokes when writing long words, and they're also ideal for frequently used items.

Look back at your time report and mark which events or keywords are most often repeated. Then go to the Prefs application, choose ShortCuts from the popup menu in the upper-right corner, and create ShortCut strokes for those items (**Figure 13.12**).

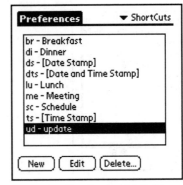

Figure 13.12 Figure out which tasks and events you write often, and create ShortCuts for them.

The Palm OS's Personal Touch

Another amazing thing about Palm devices is that they aren't just business devices. People schedule birthdays, anniversaries, reminders to watch favorite TV shows, etc. Your schedule is your life's schedule, which is why many more "non-business" people are buying handhelds.

However, some people think that if you enter a personal appointment (such as "dinner with Kim") into your impersonal gadget, then somehow that person has been "impersonalized." Not true—scheduling personal and family time is just as (or more) important than scheduling a meeting with the boss.

Build Your Time Management Skills

Now that you have a better idea of where your time has gone and how to get more of it in the present, you can begin taking steps to shape where it will go in the future.

Notes: your secret workhorses

They seem so inconsequential, making an appearance only when the little note icon shows up to the right of an item. However, notes can be one of the most useful features you'll find. I attach notes to everything: alternate addresses, driving directions, and miscellaneous data (such as spouse and children's names to Address Book items). Meeting notes, flight schedules, and even people notes get added to records in my handheld ("Andrea: wore cream-colored suit and cool glasses; quick responses, good ideas, but poked fun at my good-luck teddy bear"). In the Date Book, Address Book, and To Do applications, select Attach Note from the Record menu (✓-A).

Categorically speaking

One of the first things I did when I started using my organizer was to reassign the categories (see Chapter 2). "Business" and "Personal" are just too broad for practical use, and invite catch-all disorganization (it's similar to creating a folder called "Misc" on your desktop—everything ends up there).

Try to be as precise as you can: "Office Phone Calls," "Kids," etc. That way, you've started creating an organizational system before there's anything to organize (the pile of unfiled bills and receipts on my desk is a testament to the benefits of setting up categories prior to accumulating stuff).

The Power of Motion

One of the more important aspects of time management is being able to stick to the schedule you've created. Yet, there are times when an effectively plotted out day gets bogged down: phone calls, fatigue, a difficult project, whatever. These are the times that I need to get off my posterior and move around a little.

Take a break. If you're pressed for time, create a Date Book event that signals an alarm in 10 minutes. Better yet, if you find yourself working for long stretches of time without resting (a practice that looks good from management's viewpoint, but can quickly lead to health problems and burnout), set up several repeating events that signal alarms every two hours or so. If you're using DateBk5 (see later in this chapter), create a floating event that you can dismiss until later if you absolutely can't get away at that moment.

Or, set up a To Do item that reminds you to take a break, get some coffee, or step outside for two minutes of fresh air. Position its priority so that after you complete the first one or two items on your list, you feel compelled to take a break in order to mark it off your list.

Motion has power, so it's in your best interest to keep moving, even if you spend most of your day in front of a computer. Remember that this type of motion is not counterproductive to "real work."

Overcome the endless To Do List

This is my worst problem. Stuff that doesn't get done each day gets rolled over to the next day. It's hard sometimes to feel like anything is ever completed.

The solution? Mark long- and short-term tasks with their own categories. When you finish your pressing items, view your short-term list and reassign those tasks (**Figure 13.13**). If you don't want them to show up when you view All records, mark them hidden—just don't forget they're there! (And remember, categories don't have to be just "Business" or "Personal.")

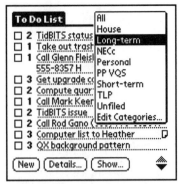

Figure 13.13 Set up long-term and short-term categories so you're not just thinking about your immediate tasks.

✔ Tip

■ Stay realistic. Including "World Peace" on your To Do list is admirable, but not practical for day-to-day use (unless you really want a constant reminder—set up a low-priority, dateless To Do item that will never go away).

Be generous with time estimates

Estimating accurately how long a project will take is a skill built upon experience. Until you've done something at least once (and it usually takes several times), it's hard to nail a realistic estimate. A seasoned contractor once advised me to estimate a project's time commitment, then double the result. It sounds like overkill, but at some point—usually on deadline—you'll realize that the higher estimate was probably closer to reality.

Prepare Ahead

Finally, some of the best advice I've received from others is to prepare for tomorrow today. I know, it sounds like a bad insurance commercial, but you'd be surprised at the results. Before you leave work or go to bed at night, take some time to go over the next day's appointments and tasks.

Set up tomorrow before you're in the thick of it: that much more time will be saved the next morning, when unexpected pressures and tasks are likely to begin appearing. For many people, knowing how tomorrow is going to work out makes them sleep easier the night before.

BUILD YOUR TIME MANAGEMENT SKILLS

Linking Records with DateBk5 and Actioneer

One of the most frequently voiced complaints about the built-in applications is that they aren't tied together well. Although you can perform phone lookups within other applications, you can't create a To Do item and have it show up on your schedule, for example. Two developers have come up with methods of bypassing this limitation.

DateBk5 (www.pimlicosoftware.com) builds upon the strengths of Date Book by adding "floating" appointments, which get copied to successive days until marked Done.

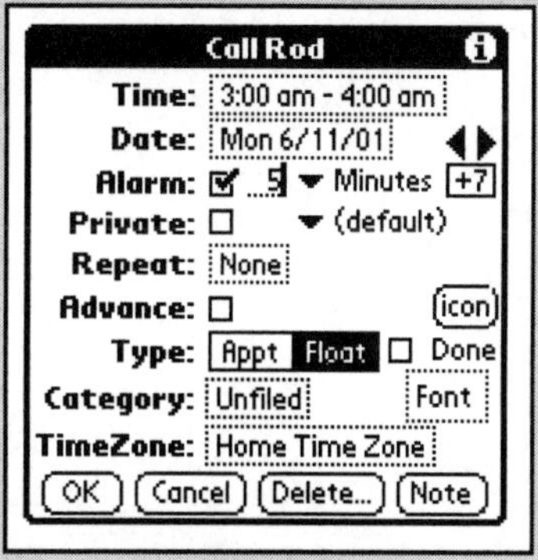

To create a floating appointment in DateBk5:

1. Create a new event at the time and date you want to work on it, then tap Details.

2. In the Type category, tap the Float button (**Figure 13.14**). In DateBk5 you can also set up categories for events using the Category popup menu.

3. Tap OK. When you return to the Day view, you'll notice a circle icon at the far right of the event's name. After completing the task, tap the circle to checkmark it, or go to the Event Details screen and select Done from the Type popup menu.

Actioneer (www.actioneer.com) works ahead of the built-in applications by scanning what you write for keywords (such as times, days of the week, names, and others that you can set up).

To create new events and tasks using Actioneer:

1. Launch Actioneer and write your event or task. As you write, the icons on the right will become highlighted if a matching keyword is found (**Figure 13.15**).

2. If you want to refine Actioneer's matches before exiting, tap the icons to view options that can be added to your event.

3. When you're satisfied, tap OK. The record will appear in each application that Actioneer highlighted.

Figure 13.14 DateBk5 adds categories and the concept of "floating" events to the normal Date Book features.

Figure 13.15 Actioneer looks for keywords in what you write, then creates new records in the built-in applications.

MANAGING
YOUR DATA

I've gone on and on about how simple the Palm OS platform is, how its design is based on the idea that an *extension* of one's PC is better than an attempt at a miniaturized PC, and how this "less is more" approach is one key to the Palm OS's lead in the market.

"Yes, okay, fine, we *get it* already."

And yet, after owning a handheld for only a few weeks, many of us find it crammed with information other than what the built-in applications support. With thousands of programs available for downloading, and up to 64 MB of memory available in off-the-shelf devices, we can't help but store and manipulate all sorts of data. My Palm is stuffed with outlines, ideas, sketches, spreadsheets, stories to read, groceries to buy, and important numbers—and that pales compared to some other people's organizers I've run across in the past.

A Palm OS-based organizer is ideal for storing all sorts of data, anything that you need to access or edit without opening a laptop computer or driving to the office late at night. Despite the volume of data, the resources for organizing it all are able to do more with less.

Outlining and Brainstorming

I never liked outlining in school, preferring instead to just begin writing and see what I ended up with. After a few less-than-encouraging grades on some of my reports, I realized that perhaps some advance planning and structure might help me after all. Now, I do quite a bit of outlining, not only for writing, but also to organize thoughts, plans, and even which videos to rent.

I use Ultrasoft's BrainForest (`www.ultrasoft.com/BrainForest/`), which is what I'll use as an example in this chapter; other good outliners include Hi-Note (`www.cyclos.com/hi-note.htm`), and ThoughtManager (`www.handshigh.com/html/thoughtmanager.html`). Of course, you can also achieve similar, though significantly limited, results with the built-in Memo Pad application.

To understand how BrainForest works, you have to think hierarchically in terms of trees and branches: an outline is the tree, the main entries are branches, and entries filed under the branches are leaves (**Figure 14.1**).

To create outlines with BrainForest:

1. Launch BrainForest, then tap the Create button, or choose Create Tree (✓-U) from the Tree menu. An empty tree is created.

2. To create a branch, tap the New button or choose New Branch from the Tree menu (✓-N). Write the branch's title in the popup text field that appears, then tap the checkmark to finish (**Figure 14.2**).

3. You can either create more branches, which exist at the same level of importance as the first, or add leaves (subsidiary information) to the branch. Select New Leaf from the Tree menu (✓-1).

Figure 14.1 BrainForest makes it easy to create and edit hierarchical outlines.

Figure 14.2 When creating a new branch or leaf, BrainForest uses a popup text field to enter information.

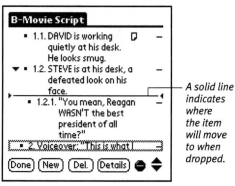

A solid line indicates where the item will move to when dropped.

Figure 14.3 Rearranging outline topics is as easy as tapping and dragging them to new locations.

Figure 14.4 Tabbed lines in Memo Pad are read as lower-level items when imported into BrainForest.

4. By default, trees are set up as actions (to-do items), with checkboxes running down the left side of the screen for each entry. To turn a tree, branch, or leaf into a standard item (identified by a black dot to the left), choose Toggle Action from the Edit menu (╱-T).

To edit outlines with BrainForest:

1. At the main screen, select the outline you want and tap the Open button, or choose Open Tree from the Tree menu (╱-L).

2. Tap and drag items to reposition them within the tree; a horizontal line appears to indicate where the item will end up when you lift your stylus (**Figure 14.3**).

To place an item under another item in the hierarchy (reducing its importance, as opposed to moving its position), drag and drop it onto the branch you wish to use as a parent item; the indicator line will disappear, and the parent will be highlighted before you drop the item.

3. To rename a branch or leaf, double-tap its title to display the popup text field.

✔ Tips

■ If you're brainstorming and don't want to tangle with BrainForest's trees and branches, go ahead and write your ideas in the Memo Pad. Later, when you have more time, choose Import from the Tree menu (make sure the plug-in "BF Text Plug.prc" has been installed) to bring your notes into BrainForest.

■ If you do write a note using the Memo Pad, add tab characters (·⌐) at the front of each line based on the level in the hierarchy the item will reside (**Figure 14.4**).

OUTLINING AND BRAINSTORMING

Making Lists

The first time I walked into the grocery store with a hastily scrawled list in one hand and my organizer in the other, I knew that one would have to go. Now, in addition to saving some paper, I have a shopping list that remembers everything I normally buy so I don't have to start from scratch every time.

Lists, of course, go beyond noting the things I need to pick up at the store. You can create reusable checklists of procedures, clothing to pack when you travel, music you want to buy...the list of lists is practically unending. For generating lists of all kinds, try List-Maker (www.synsolutions.com). JShopper (www.land-j.com) and HandyShopper (find it at www.palmgear.com) are advanced list tools tailored for shopping, with support for 15 different stores, item lookups, and even the ability to track coupons.

For Palm OS purists, the To Do List application can also expand its usefulness to include other types of lists.

To create lists using the To Do List:

1. Open the To Do List.

2. Tap the category popup menu in the upper-right corner of the screen and choose Edit Categories.

3. Each built-in application can support up to 15 categories, but there's no rule saying that they all have to be related (**Figure 14.5**). Tap the New button and name your category (such as "Grocery store").

4. When you want to access your list, simply launch the To Do List and select that category from the popup menu. You may want to mark the Show Completed Items checkbox in the To Do Preferences screen (✓-R), so you can uncheck items when you need them again (**Figure 14.6**).

Figure 14.5 The To Do list can be used for other purposes in a pinch. Set up a new category representing your topic.

Figure 14.6 Turning on the Show Completed Items option lets you go back and unmark the items you've completed to "reset" the list.

Figure 14.7 Priorities and due dates can be used to sort your lists.

✔ Tips

- Attach notes to items that require more explanation. In a grocery store list, you could include specific brand names in the note.

- If you already use several categories, things might get confusing if you choose to display them all at once; mark the non-task records Private to hide them during everyday use.

- To reorder items in your list, assign priorities or set varying due dates to the records (**Figure 14.7**).

A Spirited Use of Address Book

While visiting California, I ran into Doug Wilder, a wine expert for Dean & DeLuca. To easily keep track of the wines he tastes and sells, he stores the information in his Address Book under a Wine category. When a question comes up, he can check the Palm for details, and frequently beams the information to folks who also have Palm handhelds. (Email dougwilder@earthlink.com to subscribe to his electronic wine newsletter.)

Databases and Spreadsheets

It's always been the job of database and spreadsheet software to elevate computers above the "toy" stage into the realm of "serious business." The next time someone asks you if your Palm device is some sort of handheld gaming device, show them how you can crunch data with one of these programs (*then* you can get back to that game of YahtC—see Chapter 15).

JFile, MobileDB, HanDBase, and FileMaker Mobile

For actual database functionality, turn to JFile (www.land-j.com), MobileDB (www.mobilegeneration.com), or HanDBase (www.ddhsoftware.com). If you use FileMaker on your PC, FileMaker Mobile (www.filemaker.com) can read, edit, and create FileMaker databases. A number of existing databases are available to download, ranging from subway schedules to medical references.

To create a database:

1. Tap the New DB (JFile) or the New (MobileDB and HanDBase) button.

2. Write the name of the database, then enter the field names in the lines provided (**Figure 14.8**). Click Done.

3. Within your new database, tap the New button (MobileDB and HanDBase) or Add button (JFile) to create a new record.

4. Enter the field data for that record (**Figure 14.9**). Tapping New on this screen creates a new blank record.

5. Tap Done (or OK) to go back to the list of records, where you can sort the records, perform searches, or choose other options (**Figure 14.10**).

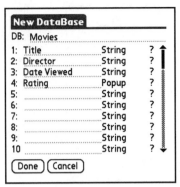

Figure 14.8 When creating a new database in JFile, enter the column headings in the New Database fields.

Figure 14.9 Once you're in a database (JFile shown here), you can enter your data next to the field titles you set up.

Figure 14.10 View, sort, and find the records from the database's main screen (HanDBase shown here).

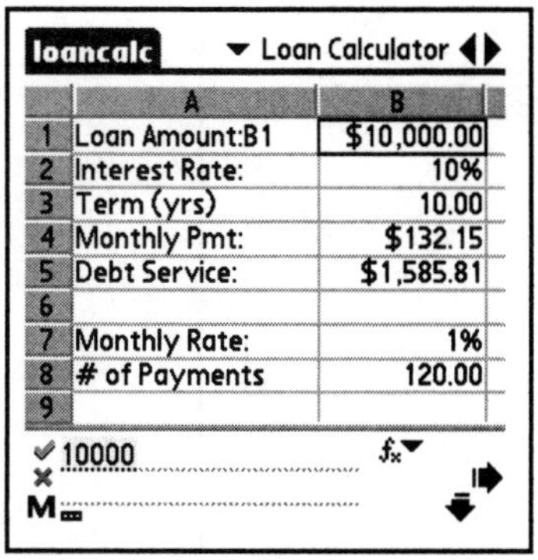

Figure 14.11 Quicksheet looks and acts like a desktop spreadsheet program.

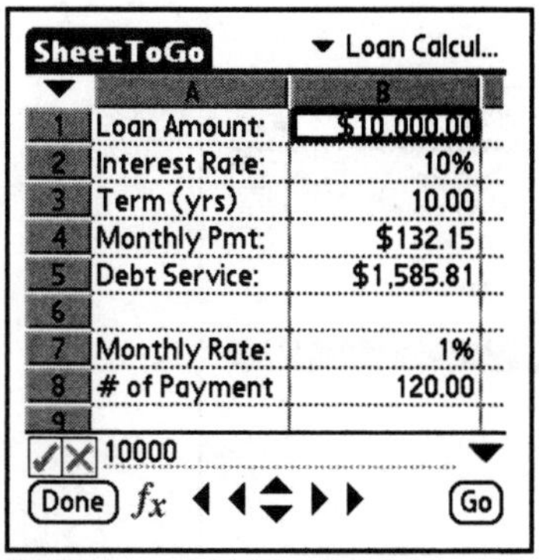

Figure 14.12 The SheetToGo component of Documents To Go displays and edits Excel spreadsheets.

Figure 14.13 Spreadsheets become more useful on devices with higher-resolution screens.

✔ Tip

■ You can also get a variety of programs that let you interface your handheld database with one on your PC. Check the Web sites of each database application for links.

Quicksheet, TinySheet, and Documents To Go

If you spend much of your time locked in Microsoft Excel's data cells, you'll be happy to know that Quicksheet (www.cesinc.com), TinySheet (www.iambic.com), and Documents To Go (www.dataviz.com) put a true spreadsheet onto your handheld's small screen, complete with built-in functions, linking of named spreadsheets within workbooks, and a surprisingly easy method of maneuvering lots of data within a small space (**Figures 14.11** and **14.12**).

All three spreadsheets include conduits that synchronize the data on your device with the data on your hard disk.

✔ Tip

■ If you're a regular spreadsheet user, you might seriously consider getting a high-resolution organizer such as a Palm Tungsten or Sony CLIÉ. The higher resolution screen can display more cells (**Figure 14.13**). Even better, get a Tungsten T3 or a CLIÉ such as the PEG-NZ90 with tall vertical screens: the Graffiti area can be hidden to make full use of the screen, and with some applications you can rotate the screen to view more columns.

DATABASES AND SPREADSHEETS

Printing from Your Palm

Remember all the hoopla about paperless offices? A Palm device would seem to be the perfect antidote to mass paper consumption, but every now and again it would be handy to print something from your handheld. A few utilities will do just that: TealPrint (www.tealpoint.com), PalmPrint (www.stevenscreek.com/palm/), and PrintBoy (www.bachmannsoftware.com/printboy.htm) enable you to connect to a variety of printers using a special cable or, better yet, via infrared.

To print from your Palm device:

1. Launch your printing utility (I'm using PrintBoy as an example), and select the type of document you wish to print, or choose which application to print from (**Figure 14.14**).

2. If the printer is equipped with an infrared port, aim your handheld at the printer and tap the Print button (**Figure 14.15**).

✔ Tips

- If your printer doesn't have a built-in infrared port, consider buying the InfraReady adapter, an IR adapter that plugs into a printer's serial port (www.bachmannsoftware.com).

- Sometimes it's just easier to print out a portion of your schedule and share it with someone. If you're not near your PC, use one of these printing programs to output your appointments over a span of time (**Figure 14.16**).

Figure 14.14 Don't wait to HotSync before printing something. Most document types can be printed directly from your handheld.

Figure 14.15 Printing from the Memo Pad is as simple as reading a memo.

Figure 14.16 If you want to share a week's schedule, it may be easier to simply print the week's appointments.

GAMES & ENTERTAINMENT

You're a working professional with a lot to accomplish in a limited time. Since purchasing your handheld, you've discovered new ways to squeeze your workload into the tight confines of your daily schedule, and finally carved out the quality time you've been dreaming about for months.

And yet, while on the bus or train, standing in line at the grocery store, or waiting at the airport—transitional time that would be ripe for reviewing the latest project outline—you just don't have it in you to *work*. These are the moments when a Palm device really shines, when you realize the full power of your investment.

These are the times to play games.

I couldn't hope to cover all the games that are available for the Palm OS platform, but my conscience wouldn't allow me to write a book about these splendid devices without including a chapter about games and entertainment. The following programs are games I've become addicted to at one time or another, or are beguiling diversions that just deserve notice.

Puzzles

Bejeweled!

Bejeweled! has a simple premise: move jewels into rows of three or more to get rid of them and bring on new gems (**Figure 15.1**). Like its spiritual ancestor Tetris, Bejeweled! (www.astraware.com) will make you put off work to play for just one more minute…

Vexed

There are games that try to squeeze the best 3D graphics performance out of their processors, but every once in a while a simple gem arrives and gets all of the attention. Vexed (vexed.sourceforge.net) asks you to clear the screen of patterned tiles by making two or more touch and disappear. The 59 levels vary from easy to fiendishly obscure, and will occupy your thoughts as well as your time (**Figure 15.2**).

Bookworm

I find myself playing games like Bookworm (www.astraware.com) most often on my Palm, because I can pick them up at any time, and play for a few minutes or longer. In Bookworm, tap letter tiles to create words and earn points; the longer the word, the more points (**Figure 15.3**). Watch out for burning tiles: if they get to the bottom of the screen, the library burns down.

Tetris Classic

Cultural anthropologists of the future will stumble upon Tetris one day, and either wonder at how backward our society was or marvel at how fast the human mind could move shapes into place in order to get rid of horizontal rows (www.handmark.com). I'd ponder this some more, but I really must clear a few more rows…just one or two…really, I can stop when I want to… (**Figure 15.4**).

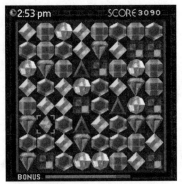

Figure 15.1 Bejeweled! is yet another classic battery-draining obsession.

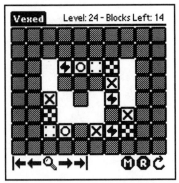

Figure 15.2 Vexed seems easy enough, though you might not think that when you've run your batteries down trying to get past its 59 levels.

Figure 15.3 Find words by connecting letters before the library burns down.

Figure 15.4 Spinning, shifting, rotating, interlocking...the obsession known as Tetris will keep you entertained on even the longest plane trips.

Figure 15.5 It's not Deep Blue, but PocketChess Deluxe sometimes makes me realize that I'm no Kasparov.

Figure 15.6 Blast away at your opponent's fleet in Battleship.

Classics

YahtChallenge

"Hmm," I thought, "a Yahtzee game...this should be entertaining for a few minutes." If I had only known then that YahtChallenge would occupy all of my spare time (home1. pacific.net.sg/~kokmun/palmpilot.htm). Roll dice and come up with combinations to score the most points against a friend or the Palm.

PocketChess Deluxe

This excellent chess program provides all the functions an average chess player needs (**Figure 15.5**). Chess geeks (a term I use affectionately) will appreciate a game synchronization tool under Windows, as well as databases of famous games by the masters. PocketChess (www.handmark.com) sometimes kills me—I mean, um, friends of mine—on level one!

Klondike and FreeCell

No consumer electronic device should exist without a solitaire game installed. These two variations, the traditional Klondike and the more nefarious FreeCell (both at www.electronhut.com), can occupy your hours without the need for table space to set up real cards.

Battleship

"You just sunk my battleship!" Reproduced down to the look of the plastic ship pieces, Battleship (www.handmark.com) improves on the original board game (**Figure 15.6**). For more fun, find a buddy and play head-to-head over infrared, Bluetooth, or the Internet (if your Palm has Net access).

Notable Diversions

Zap!2000 and Zap!2016

Zoom through space blasting everything in sight in Zap!2000 (www.astraware.com). The game play is fast, the graphics are crisp, and the color version, Zap!2016, takes advantage of the thousands of colors available on some devices' screens (**Figure 15.7**).

DopeWars

Are you a budding entrepreneuer, looking for the high life? Does the thrill of making deals pump through your veins? Then perhaps you need to try your hand at DopeWars (www.pdaguy.com/dopewars/), a game geared toward making as much money as possible within a given timeframe. If you're uncomfortable with the DopeWars theme, install Taipan (find it at www.palmgear.com) instead and trade across the high seas of the Orient.

Tricorder II

More than a few people have noticed that the Palm is about the same size and shape as a Star Trek tricorder, an all-in-one device with the power to scan and analyze nearly anything. Jeff Jetton (www.jeffjetton.com) took that one step further by developing the software for this fictional device (**Figure 15.8**). When you're finished scanning the household pets for baryon particle build-up, be sure to peruse the program's Read Me file, certainly one of the best I've read in years.

Figure 15.7 One of the best uses of color, Zap!2016 is beautiful and action-packed.

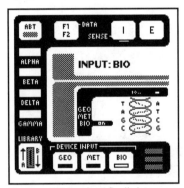

Figure 15.8 Tricorder II finally lets you scan for your television's tachyon emissions. Now you're ready for that away mission, Ensign...sorry, what was your name?

BASIC
TROUBLESHOOTING

A

My handheld is one of the most trustworthy electronic devices I've ever owned, but that doesn't mean it doesn't act up on occasion. Often the cause of problems and error messages is a conflict among the installed applications (sometimes applications or system extensions can be picky neighbors with other programs' code). Occasionally the problem is hardware-related, ranging from the components of the device itself, to batteries, to third-party accessories. Knowing how to deal with possible problems goes a long way toward reducing that first moment of panic when something isn't working.

If the problem requires you to send it back to the manufacturer, the situation is actually rather good. Although I've only needed to send back one device (knock on wood), when my original PalmPilot Personal developed a black smudge on the screen, Palm sent a padded shipping container marked with the correct postage. After doing a complete backup of my data, I sent it off, then was amazed when it returned three days later—including the shipping time (and that's the only device I've owned that required returning). Your mileage may vary, as they say, but in general the companies understand the value of keeping their customers happy.

BASIC TROUBLESHOOTING

263

Back Up Your Data

When you perform a HotSync, the data
on your handheld gets copied to your user
directory on your PC or Macintosh—or
rather, *most* of it gets copied. The data from
third-party applications may get backed up
at HotSync, but the applications themselves
sometimes don't, depending on which version of the Palm OS you're running (versions
prior to Palm OS 3.3 can be problematic in
this respect). In the event of a hard reset,
where all data on the device is lost (see
next section), it's great to be able to restore
everything to the state it was in before the
reset. To ensure that you're getting a full
backup, I recommend two essential utilities: BackupBuddy (`www.bluenomad.com`)
and, for Macintosh users only, Palm Buddy
(`perso.wanadoo.fr/fpillet/`).

Both programs allow you to back up
and restore your full data, as well as perform incremental backups. If you have to
do a complete restoration of your data,
BackupBuddy users simply do a HotSync.
BackupBuddy VFS can back up your data
to a memory expansion card in the device.
Palm Buddy owners drag the data from their
backup folder in the Finder to the active
Palm Buddy window.

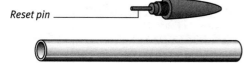

Reset pin

Figure A.1 Most Palm handhelds include a reset pin in the tip of the stylus. A straightened paperclip also works in a pinch.

Resetting Your Handheld

Like turning your desktop computer off and on, a Palm organizer occasionally needs to be reset (though infrequently). Three methods of resetting the device are available.

A *soft reset* is like rebooting a computer, initializing its internal system files and libraries. All of your data remains intact.

If something is giving you errors as your device starts up from a soft reset (such as a system update patch, for example), try doing a *warm reset*. This is analogous to booting Windows in Safe Mode or starting a Mac with extensions turned off.

A *hard reset* is the action of last resort, erasing all of your data and taking the handheld back to its original state. Be sure you have a recent backup of your information!

To perform a soft reset:

Insert the straight end of the stylus's reset pin into the reset hole on the back of the device (**Figure A.1**).

To perform a warm reset:

1. Hold down the plastic Scroll Up button on the front of the device case.

2. Insert the reset pin into the reset hole on the back of the device, then release the button. The screen should flash, then restart normally.

To perform a hard reset:

1. Hold down the power button.

2. With the power button still held down, insert the reset pin into the reset hole on the back of the device, then release the power button.

3. A confirmation message appears on the screen. Press the Scroll Up button to erase the memory, then restore your data.

Restoring applications after a hard reset

For the most part, performing a HotSync operation after a hard reset should reinstall your data files and any applications that were loaded on your handheld. However, a glitch in system versions prior to Palm OS 3.3 would sometimes cause applications you had deleted from the handheld to be reinstalled. This was because deleted programs still hang out in your User folder, but the handheld knew they should be ignored. Palm OS 3.3 improved the way it treats backed-up files, so now doing a HotSync operation resets the device to the state of the last HotSync.

To determine which version of Palm OS you are running, go to the Applications screen and choose Info from the App menu or write ╱-I. Tap the Version button at the bottom of the screen (**Figure A.2**).

Rechargeable device refuses to turn on

Most likely, the battery has drained to the point where it's passed all of the low battery warnings. Put the device into its charging cradle to feed it a little power. Perform a soft reset, then let it charge for at least three hours.

Some applications run poorly under Palm OS 5

Palm OS 5 is a dramatic rewrite of the operating system; one consequence is that some programs written for earlier models don't work properly on new devices. To see which ones are compatible, download AppCheck from Palm's Web site (www.palmone.com/ support/), and also check Palm's support pages for other compatibility information (updated frequently).

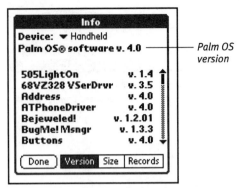

Figure A.2 The Info screen displays the version numbers of your applications as well as the Palm OS.

Contacting Handheld Technical Support

PalmOne, Inc. support*

♦ Web site:
http://www.palmone.com/support/

♦ Technical Support (847-262-7256) can answer your software questions.

Sony CLIÉ support

♦ Web site:
http://www.ita.sel.sony.com/ support/clie/

♦ Technical Support: 877-760-SONY

Kyocera Smartphone support

♦ Web site:
http://www.kyocera-wireless.com/ kysmart/kysmart_support.htm

♦ Technical Support: 800-349-4478 or phone-help@kyocera-wireless.com

* At the time of publication, PalmOne was in the process of acquiring Handspring, Inc. By the time you read this, support *should* be available from PalmOne.

HotSync Troubleshooting

If you have any troubles at all, they're likely to be related to HotSync. Although in practice HotSync is a simple process, it relies on several factors that control the communication with your computer.

Common HotSync fixes

◆ In Palm Desktop, check that your settings in the HotSync Setup screen are correct.

◆ Under Windows, exit HotSync Manager, then launch it again. On a Macintosh, make sure Local HotSync is enabled; if it is already on, disable it manually, wait a few seconds, then re-enable it.

◆ Verify that the HotSync cable or cradle is plugged into the correct port on your computer.

◆ Reduce the port speed in the Setup screen.

◆ Disable any software that might be sharing the communication ports. Fax software is often the culprit, because it's always monitoring for incoming faxes.

◆ Under Mac OS 9, turn off AppleTalk by opening the Chooser and clicking the AppleTalk Inactive button.

◆ If you're using a USB hub, try plugging the HotSync cradle or cable directly into the USB connection on the computer.

To set Mac OS 9 memory allocation:

1. Try increasing the memory allocated to the Conduit Manager application. On your hard disk, open the Palm folder and click on the Conduit Manager.

2. Choose Memory from the Get Info submenu under the File menu.

3. Increase the number in the Preferred Size field, then close the Get Info window.

Windows COM port conflicts

If the previous suggestions don't produce a successful HotSync, your COM ports may be misconfigured or confused. COM ports are the physical ports used to hook up devices such as modems and mice to the back of your computer. Some machines also use COM ports for internal devices.

To work together, these ports communicate with the computer's processor over Interrupt Request (IRQ) channels. Often, one IRQ channel is shared by two COM ports, which means they can both be vying for attention (COM 1 and COM 3 usually share an IRQ, while COM 2 and COM 4 share another IRQ). If you have the option of doing so, move your HotSync cable to a different COM port. If not, and if you're skilled in complex computer configuration, try reassigning the port settings.

Keep in mind that tinkering with IRQ settings has the potential to cause conflicts where none existed before. Make changes one at a time; if they don't fix the problem, undo the change and reboot your computer before making any more changes.

To modify Windows COM settings:

1. Double-click the System icon from the Windows Control Panels.

2. Click the Device Manager tab, then click the plus sign next to Ports (COM & LPT).

3. Double-click the Communications Port you want to change.

4. Click the Resources tab. If the Use automatic settings checkbox is on, click to unmark it.

5. Choose an alternate configuration from the Settings based on popup menu.

6. When finished, click OK, then restart your computer.

INDEX

INDEX

INDEX

INDEX

INDEX

INDEX

INDEX

INDEX

WWW.PEACHPIT.COM

Quality How-to Computer Books

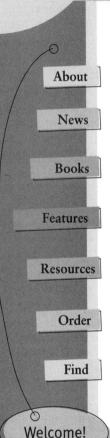

About

News

Books

Features

Resources

Order

Find

Welcome!

Visit Peachpit Press on the Web at www.peachpit.com

- Check out new feature articles each Monday: excerpts, interviews, tips, and plenty of how-tos

- Find any Peachpit book by title, series, author, or topic on the Books page

- See what our authors are up to on the News page: signings, chats, appearances, and more

- Meet the Peachpit staff and authors in the About section: bios, profiles, and candid shots

- Use Resources to reach our academic, sales, customer service, and tech support areas and find out how to become a Peachpit author

Peachpit.com is also the place to:

- Chat with our authors online
- Take advantage of special Web-only offers
- Get the latest info on new books